Figures of the Past From the Leaves of Old Journals

Figures of the Past

From the Leaves of Old Journals.

BY

JOSIAH QUINCY,
(CLASS OF 1821, HARVARD COLLEGE).

BOSTON
LITTLE, BROWN, AND COMPANY
1910

Copyright, 1883,
By J. P. Quincy.

261575

Printers
S. J. PARKHILL & Co., BOSTON, U. S. A.

INTRODUCTION.

NOT long ago I received an application from a New York editor to furnish a series of papers upon former men and things. For nearly sixty-four years it has been my habit to keep journals; and it was suggested that extracts from these records, or the reminiscences they awakened, would be acceptable to the public. My impulse was promptly to decline the proposition. My authorship had been limited to railroad reports, occasional speeches, and pamphlets upon public measures; and, weighted with nearly four-score years, I could not think of entering the lists of general letters. I was about to succumb to this embarrassment when a friend, who had read my journals with interest, offered me his most valuable aid in what may be called the literary responsibilities of the undertaking. My narratives have gained in grace of expression as they passed beneath the correcting pen of my obliging critic, and I am confident that a stern exercise of his right of curtailing reflections and omitting incidents has been no less for the reader's advantage. The first paper, as originally published, contained an explicit avowal of this indebtedness; and it is right that I should repeat it still more emphatically in allowing the series to be put in a permanent form.

It may be mentioned that William O. McDowell, the proprietor of "Thoughts and Events," was the only begetter of these narratives, and that upon the discontinuance of his journal they were fortunate enough to receive the hospitality of the "Independent."

It has been my purpose that the papers should convey the contemporary impressions made by events and persons they describe, and that all imperfect memories or unauthenticated anecdotes should be distinctly so designated.

THE preceding Introduction was written by Mr. Quincy a few months before his death, and was left with the direction that it should be prefixed to the collection of these papers which Messrs. Roberts Brothers had desired to issue. A few omissions, made for the sake of brevity, have been restored in the present publication. The college class of the author is given on the titlepage to distinguish him from others of his family who have borne the same name.

CONTENTS.

	PAGE
A PURITAN ACADEMY	1
HARVARD SIXTY YEARS AGO	16
COMMENCEMENT DAY IN 1821	49
REMINISCENCES OF THE SECOND PRESIDENT	58
VISITS TO JOHN ADAMS	66
TALKS WITH JOHN ADAMS	76
THE OLD PRESIDENT IN PUBLIC	86
"ECLIPSE" AGAINST THE WORLD	96
LAFAYETTE IN BOSTON	101
LAFAYETTE AND COLONEL HUGER	110
HOW COLONEL HUGER TOLD THE STORY	119
LAFAYETTE ON BUNKER HILL	127
DANIEL WEBSTER AT HOME	138
LAFAYETTE LEAVES MASSACHUSETTS	147
THE DUKE OF SAXE-WEIMAR AND CAPTAIN RYK	157
THE GOVERNOR AT NANTUCKET	174
A JOURNEY WITH JUDGE STORY	188
FROM NEW YORK TO WASHINGTON	199
VISITS TO JOHN RANDOLPH	209
RANDOLPH IN THE SENATE	219
COMMODORE STOCKTON	230
THE SUPREME COURT AND THE "MARIANNA FLORA"	242

CONTENTS.

	PAGE
WASHINGTON SOCIETY IN 1826	254
THE HOUSE OF REPRESENTATIVES	280
THROUGH BALTIMORE TO BOSTON	291
THE REVEREND CLERGY	302
SOME PILLARS OF THE STATE	316
TWO NOTABLE WOMEN	328
SOME RAILROAD INCIDENTS	338
JACKSON IN MASSACHUSETTS	352
JOSEPH SMITH AT NAUVOO	376

FIGURES OF THE PAST.

A PURITAN ACADEMY.

I HAVE been asked to furnish for publication sketches of events with which I have been connected, and of distinguished men whom I have had the privilege to know. It has been urged upon me that the journals I have kept these many years contain matter of historical interest. But these records were never intended for the printer, and the pictures their pages present to me would appear most imperfectly to others. My memory of the remoter past is singularly vivid, and for me these old journals contain far fuller narratives than any other reader could find written in them. As they begin with my second year in college, I must rely on my unaided recollection for notices of life at Phillips Academy. Fortunately the impressions of youth are cut so deeply upon the brain that written memoranda are unnecessary to revive them.

The Academy at Andover was the first school incorporated in New England; the act bearing the date of October 4, 1780. It was founded by Judge Phillips, an eminent patriot and honored citizen. Like most of the best men of his day, he was a firm believer in the Westminster Catechism; and he meant that posterity should believe it too, so far as the liberal endowments of himself and his family might conduce to that result. The town of Andover, when I arrived there, nearly seventy years ago, seemed a good way from home. Travelling in those days was slow and expensive. Postage upon a letter was twenty-five cents for every sheet it contained. Newspapers amounted to very little, and were not generally read. The remotest settlement of Kansas or Nebraska knows far more of the thought and feeling of the great world than Andover then knew of Boston, which was only twenty miles off. In the Academy were two classes of scholars,— those whose expenses were paid by their parents, and "charity boys," as they were called, who were supported by certain funds controlled by a society for supplying the ministry with pious young candidates. These were persons who, having reached manhood, had determined to enter the sacred profession. They had served out an apprenticeship at some trade or in farming, and were generally uncouth in their manners and behavior. We, who were the real boys, never liked their sanctimonious demeanor. We claimed that they were spies, and shrank from them with all the disgust which their imaginary calling could not fail to excite. There were, however, two marked exceptions. One of them was William

Person. I remember once asking him how he got his name. He replied with some cynicism, "Why, I found myself in a tanyard, and nobody could tell who I was. All that seemed to be certain was that I was a *person*, — and so, from lack of any other, I took that name." This big boy was very popular, and we were proud of him as the finest writer in the school. The pet name, Pelly, by which he was universally known, was a contraction of Pelliparius, a signature which he always affixed to his compositions, whether in prose or verse. The word in English would be written "Tanner," it being compounded of *pellus*, a hide, and *pario*, to finish. The history of this interesting young man was sad and romantic. He had been deserted by his parents, who were known to be persons of social importance, who desired to avoid the stigma of his illegitimate birth. For the first years of his life he had been permitted to attend a private school in Andover, where he showed remarkable aptitude for study. But in 1801, when he was eight years old, he was suddenly taken from school and apprenticed to a tanner in Providence. A cruel reason was given him for this step. He was told that he was altogether too promising, and that if he was allowed to grow up an educated man, he might take measures which would lead to the discovery of his birth. For thirteen years he was compelled to serve in this trade, and deprived of the education he so ardently desired. At the end of this time, finding himself his own master, he entered the Academy at Andover, — supporting himself by manual labor, with some trifling assistance from charitable funds. Person entered Harvard College in 1816, and was immediately distinguished for high scholarship. At one time he reached the highest rank in his class, — his close competitor for that honor being William G. Reed from South Carolina. But the brilliant scholar was always struggling with poverty, though constantly working with brain and hands to provide the means for study. A man with whom he had business relations deceived him; college bills were presented for which there was no money to pay; and Person suddenly found himself compelled to leave Harvard. With despairing heart he took up his Livy to prepare for the last recitation that he could hope to attend; but on opening the book a letter dropped from its leaves. It contained a hundred dollars, — a sum that was much larger at that time than at present; and this had been collected by the efforts of his generous rival. It may be mentioned that Person ascertained beyond reasonable doubt the facts of his parentage, though he was never acknowledged by either father or mother. But the world had found him out, and a career of honor and usefulness seemed to be opening before him. Yet the sad and too familiar sequel to a youth of privation and effort was not to be avoided; the seeds of consumption were suddenly developed, and Person died before completing his college course. No man could be more beloved than our gentle Pelly. His classmates erected a stone to his memory, which is still to be seen in the Cambridge churchyard. It bears a long epitaph in Latin from the pen of Reed. The concluding words, "Plorat amissum præmature Scientia; plorat Religio; plorat Amicitia," the old commonplaces of commemoration, simply expressed the feelings of those who were privileged to know this excellent man.

The other big boy who was popular among us was the late Rev. Dr. E. M. P. Wells, — a clergyman of the Episcopal Church, well known in Boston, who has left a cherished memory as a devoted friend of the poor. Wells, who was always good whether as man or boy, did not choose to adopt a certain cant of piety which was supposed to be acceptable to the authorities of the school. He was the leader of our Demosthenian Society, which maintained a vigorous opposition to the Social Fraternity, an association which represented the bluest type of New England orthodoxy. Indeed, Wells was so little of a puritan that he once took part in a theatrical performance which, to the great scandal of the saints, was gotten up among the boys. The fact that the principal of the school, Mr. Adams, was confined to his room by a six weeks' fit of sickness, had encouraged us to attempt this profane exhibition. I remember that Wells, who personated a king who took advanced views of the responsibilities of the royal office, was at much pains to prepare a crown which was worthy to surmount the head of so exemplary a monarch. An affair of pasteboard, painted yellow and cut into high peaks, was no doubt striking, but yet seemed hardly worthy of the character. Finally, however, the player-king bethought himself of a certain neck-

unerring certainty. An exception to this rule was found in the doctrine of election as not inconsistent with individual freedom. This was a craggy theme with which the Andover divines were accustomed to grapple with great spirit. They certainly showed, or appeared to show, that we were perfectly free to choose a destiny which, nevertheless, had been absolutely decreed beforehand; but the reasoning which dissolved this formidable paradox was altogether too subtle for the youthful brain to follow.

A report of an occasional sermon may give some idea of the gallant style in which the Andover ministers faced sin — or what seemed to them sin — under difficulties. It happened that a proposition to teach dancing in the town had been made by some rash professor of that accomplishment. Under this visitation there was clearly but one subject for the next Sunday's discourse. The good minister rose in the pulpit fully armed for the encounter; but he was not the man to take unfair advantages. The adversary should be allowed every point which seemed to make in his favor. In pursuance of this generous design, a text was given out which certainly did seem a little awkward in view of the deductions which must be drawn from it. It was taken from the Book of Ecclesiastes, and was announced with unflinching emphasis, "There is a time to dance." The preacher began by boldly facing the performance of King David,

"When before the Ark
His grand *pas seul* excited some remark!"

But, notwithstanding the record, we were assured that David did not dance. A reference to the original Hebrew made it plain that "he took no steps." All he did was to jump up and down in a very innocent manner, and it was evident that this required no professional instruction. And now, having disposed of the example of the father, the way was clear to take up the assertion of Solomon that there was a time to dance. Were this the case, it were pertinent to consider what that time might be. Could a man find time to dance before he was converted? To ask such a question as that was to answer it. The terrible risks to which the unregenerate were exposed, and the necessity that was upon them to take summary measures for their avoidance, clearly left no time for dancing. And how was it with a man while he was being converted? Overwhelmed with the sense of sin, and diligently seeking the remedy, it was simply preposterous to imagine that *he* could find time for dancing. And how was it with the saints who had been converted? Surely such time as they had must be spent in religious exercises for the conversion of others; obviously *they* had no time to dance. And so the whole of human life had been covered, and the conclusion was driven home with resistless force. What time for dancing Solomon might have had in mind it was unnecessary to inquire, for it was simply demonstrable that he could not have referred to any moment of the time allotted to man on this earth. After this discourse it is needless to say that no dancing-master showed his face in Andover during my acquaintance with the town.

But if it shall happen that I speak freely of forms which have no longer the spiritual meaning that once filled them, I must also emphasize the fact that a stern pressure towards morality was characteristic of the school. Emulation was abandoned because it appealed to lower motives than Christians should entertain, and the phrase "unhallowed ambition" was applied to the pursuit of excellence for any selfish end. A society for the cultivation of the moral virtues, composed of candidates for the Divinity Department and some of the smaller boys, existed in the school, and a pledge to abstain from intoxicating liquors was exacted from its members.

During the six years I spent in Andover there were several revivals of religion. The master believed in their utility and did everything in his power to encourage them. We had prayer-meetings before school, after school, and in recess, and a strong influence was exerted to make us attend them. I am tempted to give a little circumstance in this connection because it shows the absolute sincerity with which our teachers held their religious views. One summer's day, after a session of four hours, the master dismissed the school in the usual form. No sooner had he done so than he added, "There will now be a prayer-meeting: those who wish to lie down in everlasting burning may go; the rest will stay." It is probable that a good many boys wanted to get out of doors. Two of them only had the audacity to rise and leave the room. One of those youngsters has since been known as an eminent

Doctor of Divinity; the other was he who now relates the incident. But no sooner was the prayer-meeting over than Mr. ADAMS sought me out, asked pardon for the dreadful alternative he had presented, and burst into a flood of tears. He said with deep emotion that he feared that I had committed the unpardonable sin and that he had been the cause. His sincerity and faith were most touching; and his manliness in confessing his error and asking pardon from his pupil makes the record of the occurrence an honor to his memory.

The War of 1812 put a stop to navigation and compelled all transfers of property to be made by wagons. It was said to cost six thousand dollars to transport a piece of ordnance from New York to Buffalo. A great number of teams bearing produce from Vermont and New Hampshire, and smuggled goods from Canada, passed through Andover. In the absence of mercantile news, the arrival of these wagons was announced under the head of "Horse-marine news." One of the humors of the war was an amusing parody upon the "Mariners of England" entitled the "Wagoners of Freedom," a ditty of which I can still repeat several verses. These teamsters had, however, adopted one article of the sailors' faith that was by no means acceptable to the people of Andover. They held that "there was no Sunday off soundings," and continued their progress on that day greatly to the scandal of the righteous town. It was plain that the law must be enforced, and accordingly tithingmen lay in wait on Sunday at the tavern, and at the corners of the public roads. They succeeded in stopping the heavy teams, but horsemen and light carriages slipped through their fingers. But a way was soon devised to meet this difficulty. A deacon was joined to the tithing-men the very next Sunday, and the party were put in command of the toll-gate, about a mile out of the town on the road leading to Boston. It was known about the school that a trap had been set which no Sunday traveller could hope to escape, and great was the interest in waiting for a victim. At length a gentleman driving a fine horse passed along the street, and, all unconscious of his fate, proceeded towards the toll-gate. The excitement was now intense, for we expected to see him brought back by the deacon in ignominious captivity. But the spectators were disappointed, for this part of the programme was not carried out. In what wonderful way the traveller had managed to elude the deacon and his guard we could not divine. The return of the party at sunset brought the explanation, and a doleful tale of depravity passed from mouth to mouth. It appeared that the gentleman had been duly stopped at the toll-gate and informed that he could go no farther. But instead of showing the indignation which his captors had expected, he expressed himself as delighted to find that Andover was bent on enforcing the admirable Sunday laws, and had selected agents so prompt and capable as to preclude all chance of their evasion. "But the law, gentlemen," he went on to say, "as you well know, excepts those who travel upon errands of necessity or mercy; and I assure you that my mother is lying dead in Boston." Upon this statement the gate was reluctantly opened, and the traveller allowed to proceed. But no sooner was he fairly out of danger than he reined in his horse and delivered himself of these heartless words: "Good-by, Deacon; tell the busybodies of Andover that my mother is lying dead in Boston, — and you may add, if you like, that she has been lying dead there *for the last twenty years!*"

It need not be said that this occurrence was improved, as the text of a lecture to the boys on the sin of prevarication, which is, perhaps, the reason why I remember it so vividly. A short time after this, another attempt to enforce the Sunday law was much talked of in the town. One Sabbath morning, a hack containing four gentlemen drove through the place and took the road to Salem. The deacon and a tithing-man, who were again on the alert, stopped the carriage, and ordered the passengers to return to the tavern. As there was no toll-gate in the way this time, the travellers irreverently consigned the ecclesiastical functionaries to hot quarters, and commanded their driver to whip up and go on. This greatly exasperated the deacon and his companion, who, considering that the arrest of such hardened offenders was undoubtedly a work of necessity and mercy, hired a light carriage and gave pursuit. But a stern chase, as the sailors say, is apt to be a long chase, and the hack kept on till it reached Salem, where the pursuers felt certain of making a capture. And this might have been effected had the parties stopped at any tavern or house, as it was reasonable to suppose that they would. But, unhappily, on went the hack till it reached the end of the wharf. Here the passengers jumped out, sprang into a boat that was in waiting, and were instantly rowed to a frigate which was lying in the harbor, — their would-be captors gazing after them in mute consternation. As it did not seem quite prudent for an Andover deacon to attempt the arrest of officers on board a man-of-war, there was nothing to be done but to retrace a tedious journey, and to submit to such chaff as a heartless world bestows upon unsuccessful attempts to make it better.

It was provided that every pupil at the Academy should be taught to sing, and a special master was kept to train us in an accomplishment which was held to be of the first importance in the next world, if not in this. English literature was presented in the sober guise of "Vincent's Explanations of the Westminster Catechism," and "Mason on Self-Knowledge," and from each of these books we were required to recite once a week. The sole work of imagination tolerated by the authorities was the "Pilgrim's Progress." There was, nevertheless, an awful rumor, only to be mentioned under one's breath, that Dr. Porter, professor of rhetoric in the divinity schools, had upon his shelves the writings of a person called William Shakespeare, a play-actor, whose literary productions were far from edifying. I mention this scandal, not as asserting its truth; it may be one more specimen of those reckless stories boys will get up about their betters.

But I must pause in my recollections of Andover, or there will be no end to them. What has been said has been given from a pupil's point of view. They are simply the salient points which happen to stick in a boy's memory. They are not to be mistaken for an estimate of the worth of the institution, or of the work done by the good and honorable men who conducted it.

HARVARD SIXTY YEARS AGO.

I.

IN the summer of 1871 a few old men who had entered Harvard College together in 1817 met to commemorate the fiftieth anniversary of their graduation. Some of them had met annually in Cambridge for half a century, and this was to be their last class-meeting. The memories of early times were revived, pleasant passages of college life were recounted, and the hearts of the survivors were lighted up in gratitude for being permitted to come together to take a solemn farewell. More than half of those who were present at that last class-meeting have since gone. The few that remain are daily awaiting the summons to follow, and any moment it may be too late to hear from living lips an account of life at Harvard sixty years ago.

Two only of my classmates can be fairly said to have got into history, although one of them, Charles W. Upham, has written history very acceptably. Ralph Waldo Emerson and Robert W. Barnwell, for widely different reasons, have caused their names to be known to well-informed Americans. Of Emerson, I regret to say, there are few notices in my journals. Here is the sort of way in which I speak of the man who was to make so profound an impression upon the thought of his time: "I went to the chapel to hear Emerson's dissertation: a very good one, but rather too long to give much pleasure to the hearers." The fault, I suspect, was in the hearers; and another fact which I have mentioned goes to confirm this belief. It seems that Emerson accepted the duty of delivering the poem on Class Day, after seven others had been asked who positively refused. So it appears that, in the opinion of this critical class, the author of the "Wood Notes" and the "Humble Bee" ranked about eighth in poetical ability. It can only be because the works of the other seven have been "heroically unwritten," that a different impression has come to prevail in the outside world. But if, according to the measurement of undergraduates, Emerson's ability as a poet was not conspicuous, it must also be admitted that, in the judgment of persons old enough to know better, he was not credited with that mastery of weighty prose which the world has since accorded him. In our senior year the higher classes competed for the Boylston prizes for English composition. Emerson and I sent in our essays with the rest, and were fortunate enough to take the two prizes; but — alas for the infallibility of academic decisions! — Emerson received the second prize. I was of course much pleased with the award of this intelligent committee; and should have been still more gratified had they mentioned that the man who was to be the most original and influential writer born in America was my unsuccessful competitor. But Emerson, incubating over deeper matter than was dreamt of in the established philosophy of elegant letters, seems to have given no sign of the power that was fashioning itself for leadership in a new time. He was quiet, unobtrusive, and only a fair scholar according to the standard of the college authorities. And this is really all I have to say about my most distinguished classmate. Let us be merciful to the companions of the deer-stealer of Stratford, that it never occurred to them to take notes of his early sayings for the benefit of posterity.

The first scholar of the class was Barnwell, of South Carolina, a noble specimen of the Southerner, high-spirited, interesting, and a leader of men. It was said that, when he left college, he told Upham, who was his most intimate friend among Northerners, that he would undergo perpetual imprisonment to free his State from the curse of slavery. I cannot vouch for the authenticity of this story; I know only that it was current at the time. Language scarcely less strong had been used by Jefferson and other representative Southern men. But the set of the tide was the other way, and Barnwell became a leader in the great rebellion which resulted in emancipation. He was a Senator of the United States before the war and of the Confederate States during the whole of their existence. He takes a firm grasp upon history as chairman of that extraordinary committee that came to Washington to agree upon a division of the property which had once belonged to the United States! The letter to the President, which Buchanan had the spirit to return, was probably of his draughting. At all events his name leads the others, and will always stand there to awaken the interest of future students of our American annals.

One other of my classmates attained distinguished political office. This was Edward Kent, who was our Minister to Brazil, and Governor of the State of Maine. Certainly these are offices which it must have required a good deal of activity to obtain if not to hold. Yet in college the future Governor had so little of the quick movements of the politician, that he was known as the "President of the Lazy Club." This was said to be the highest distinction in an imaginary association whose members were pledged to spare themselves all unnecessary exertion. The story ran that Kent was one day seen running across the college yard, and that a meeting of the club had been called to consider this outrageous conduct on the part of their President, and to learn what defence he might find to offer. The report continued that Kent acknowledged the truth of the accusation, but drew himself up with an air of offended innocence and put in this pathetic defence: "Brethren of the Lazy Club, do not condemn me unheard. I was standing in perfect quietness on the steps of Holworthy, when some villain came behind me and gave me a push. That was the way I got started; and I kept going on and on, because the fact was that *I was too lazy to stop*." The speech was probably as fictitious as those which the Roman historians were in the habit of composing for their heroes. Its currency as a college story illustrates the general feeling as to what Governor Kent ought to have said under the given circumstances.

One day early in November, 1818, I find a dry twig pasted upon the leaf of my journal and underneath this inscription: "Resistance to tyrants is obedience to God. This twig was my badge; all the class tore them from the Rebellion Tree, and agreed to wear them in their bosoms." The rough and unmannerly proceedings which characterized this memorable outbreak have long since ceased to be possible in first-class colleges. Boarding in Commons was at that time compulsory, and the freshmen and sophomores were fed in two large halls which were separated by folding doors. These portals were generally kept carefully locked and bolted; but, one Sunday evening, they had unhappily been left open. Taking advantage of this circumstance, some sophomore threw a plate into the quarters of the freshmen. It was promptly returned; every one started up from the tables; and a hot and furious battle commenced. Cups, saucers, and dishes were used as missiles, and the total destruction of the crockery belonging to the college was the result. Of course it was necessary for the government to take notice of such an outrage as this; and it was soon announced that five of my classmates were suspended and must leave the town. Two of these victims were from New York, two from South Carolina, and one from Massachusetts. The students selected happened to be very popular, and it seemed to us unjust that they alone should be punished for an offence of which so many others were equally guilty. Accordingly we followed them out of Cambridge with shouts and cheers, and, on returning, assembled about the Rebellion Tree and awaited results. After a little time the President's freshman came upon the scene, and summoned Adams, Otis, and myself to appear at once in his study. Dr. Kirkland told us that he was a good friend of our fathers, and wished to get us out of mischief; he must accordingly advise us to leave town for the present, and should command us at our peril not to return to the tree. Under the excitement which ruled the hour, we promptly went back to the rendezvous; and Adams, who was appointed our spokesman, addressed the assembly in a vigorous speech. I happen to remember the climax of his remarks: "Gentlemen, we have been commanded, at our peril, not to return to the Rebellion Tree: *at our peril we do return!*" This morsel of defiance seemed to us to have as fine a ring as the famous, "Sink or swim, live or die, survive or perish," which Daniel Webster subsequently attributed to the grandfather of the speaker. The applause was immense, and we voted to remain in session all day, and to absent ourselves from all college exercises. Even the rain which soon began to descend was powerless to disperse us; for we adjourned in force to the great porch which then stood in front of University Hall. The end of it was that there was a new crop of rustications and suspensions; and this burlesque of patriots struggling with tyrants gradually played itself out, and came to an end. But the events of that fervid time impressed themselves so deeply upon us, that, when "the great rebellion" is spoken of, my first thought is that the allusion must be, not to Charles I. and the Puritans, nor yet to the American colonists and England, but to that magnificent protest against oppression that was made at Harvard College sixty-three years ago.

Perhaps the reader will like to see how two men who afterwards achieved the highest distinction in letters appeared to a college student before whom they lectured. Here is what I find recorded of the eminent historian of Spanish literature. "In the evening I attended Ticknor's lecture, which was most beautiful and delightful, and on a subject as dry as possible. He explained to us on the map how languages progressed, and what was their origin. There is something very pleasing in his style and delivery, and he introduced figures very appropriately. But independently of this, there is a melody in his voice truly delightful. When describing the softness and beauty of the Provençal, it seemed as if he spoke in that delicious language. When he said of St. Louis, 'whether he desired his canonization or not, he certainly was one of the truest patriots, one of the bravest knights, and one of the noblest gentlemen who ever lived,' it seemed as though his eulogy was complete. Those words seemed to express all that was virtuous, lovely, and honorable, so that no addition could be made to his character."

A far greater orator than Professor Ticknor — one to whose matchless eloquence I shall hereafter find occasion to refer — is disposed of with all the confidence of a critic in his teens: "Attended Everett's first lecture, and was not so much pleased as I expected to be. He is not eloquent or interesting, and is rather given to egotism; however, by his prolixity we gained a miss from Farrar for the fourth time this term. This was much to the gratification of the class, who in general hate his branch though they like him." Professor Farrar's unpopular branch was the mathematics, which then as now was attractive to only a small minority of the students. There were no electives in those days, and our tastes were not consulted in the selection of studies.

II.

HARVARD COLLEGE, at the time of which I am writing, was very different from the noble university which at present bears the old name. Some students entered at twelve years of age, though fifteen was nearer the average among those whose parents were well off. We were treated as boys, and not without reason. The law declared that we must not go to Boston without permission, or pass a night away from Cambridge without a special license from the authorities. Moreover, in the early part of 1819, the President, in behalf of the corporation, promulgated a statute to the effect that a fine of ten dollars would be exacted from every student who was caught at the theatre, while five dollars must be paid by any one who attended a party in Boston. But it is probable that the corporation made no attempt to carry out the system of espionage which their savage edict seemed to necessitate. We certainly used to go to the theatre and to parties with some freedom, and seldom got into difficulty from doing so.

But there were natural impediments to leaving Cambridge, which would have astonished the pampered young gentlemen who are now complaining that a horse-car every three minutes does not furnish suitable communication with the metropolis, and demand an elevated railroad to give them their full rights in this particular. We knew but a morning and evening stage. At nine and at two o'clock, Morse, the stage-driver, drew up in the college yard, and performed upon a tin horn to notify us of his arrival. He was a great hero among the students, for coachmen have some mysterious charm about them which wins the regard of young gentlemen in their teens. Those who went to Boston in the evening were generally forced to walk. It was possible, to be sure, to hire a chaise of Jemmy Reed (who held the same place that Hobson did in the Cambridge of Milton), yet his horses were expensive animals, and he was very particular in satisfying himself of the undoubted credit of those to whom he let them. And it was probably well for us that we were so often compelled to resort to the primitive means of locomotion; for the necessity of regular exercise for students was unrecognized at the time, and such as we obtained was taken very irregularly and with some end in view. There was a favorite summer walk to Sweet Auburn, which was then as Nature made it; and when the skies were perfectly favorable we consented to avail ourselves of its attractions. This beautiful piece of country was afterwards christened Mount Auburn, and became the first garden-cemetery in the country.

There were some half-a-dozen houses on the avenue leading from the colleges to Sweet Auburn; they had been built before the Revolution, and were abandoned by their tory proprietors. The largest and most conspicuous was the fine mansion which had been the headquarters of Washington, and which has since gained additional interest as the residence of the poet Longfellow. It was then occupied by Mrs. Craigie, the widow of a gentleman very notable in his day. He had made a large fortune by buying up government promises, and by other speculations during the Revolution. He kept a princely bachelor's establishment at the old house, and was in the habit of exercising a generous hospitality. A curious story relating to his marriage was current among his contemporaries, and there can be now no harm in giving it as I have heard it from their lips.

A great garden party had been given by Mr. Craigie, and all the fashion and beauty of Boston were assembled in his spacious grounds. The day was perfect, the entertainment was lavish, and the company were bent on enjoying themselves. Smiles and deference met the host upon every side, and newcomers were constantly arriving to pay that homage to wealth and sumptuous liberality which from imperfect mortals they have always elicited. "Craigie!" exclaimed an intimate friend to the host during one of the pauses of compliment, "what can man desire that you have not got? Here are riches, friends, a scene of enchantment like this, and you the master of them all!" "I am the most miserable of men!" was the startling reply. "If you doubt it, you shall know my secret: do you see those two young ladies just turning down the walk? Well, they are both engaged, and with one of them I am desperately in love." There was no time for more, for the crowd again surged round the host, and the friend was left to meditate upon the revelation which had been made. One of the ladies who had been pointed out was a great beauty of the time, and it so happened that Mr. Craigie's confidant was on very intimate terms with her family. It was well known that the match she was about to make did not gratify the ambitious views of her relations. Now whether Mr. Craigie's friend betrayed his secret to the father of this young person cannot certainly be known; but the current report was that he did so. At all events, shortly after the garden party, he broke in upon the Crœsus of Cambridge with an exultant air, exclaiming, "Craigie, I have come to tell you glorious news; the coast is clear; Miss —— has broken off her engagement!" "Why, what the deuce is that to me?" was the disappointing reply. "Good heavens, man, don't you remember telling me that you were desperately in love with one of the young ladies you pointed out at the garden party?" "To be sure I did," sighed Mr. Craigie, "but unfortunately I referred *to the other young lady.*"

Now there is a fallacy of which logicians warn us, and which they designate as the fallacy of *post hoc, ergo propter hoc.* Bearing this in mind, it seems quite clear that the disclosure that was made respecting the supposed state of Mr. Craigie's affections had nothing whatever to do with the dissolution of the young lady's engagement. It was undoubtedly only one of those queer coincidences which seem to connect events that have really no connection with one another. And this is the more probable because another of these strange freaks of chance is found in the sequel of the story. For it happened — or was said to have happened — that "the other young lady" subsequently found good reason to break off *her* engagement, and, as Mrs. Craigie, came to preside over all future garden parties. But this climax to the tale was perhaps added by some unscrupulous narrator. Indeed it seems to bear on its face an improbability which gives evidence of fabrication. It only shows that gossip was busy with this fine old mansion long before it was known as the residence of Mr. Longfellow, and that we, old college boys, found something to talk about as we strode past it on our way to Sweet Auburn.

I have said that the decrees of the corporation did not prevent us from going to the theatre; but if I am to tell the whole truth, I fear it must be acknowledged that they actually added a zest to that forbidden enjoyment. For there is a good deal of human nature in the familiar story of the gentleman who, being very fond of pork, protested that fate had been cruel to him in not so arranging matters as to have caused him to be born a Jew,— "for then," said he, "I should have had the pleasure of eating pork and of sinning at the same time." The latter delight, whatever it may have amounted to, the authorities of Andover and of Harvard College had taken good care that we should have in connection with all scenic representations. There was but one theatre in Boston, and performances were held three days in the week. The box office was opened only on the day of the play, and a battle often occurred in the efforts of the crowd to reach the window from which tickets were dispensed. Morse, the stage-driver, was our champion upon these occasions, and we waited his return with eagerness to know how the fight had gone, and what spoils he had brought us from the box office.

My freshman year was marked by the appearance of Incledon, in what were then called operas, that is to say, plays of which two thirds were dialogue and the rest song. In one of these performances he introduced his famous song, "The Bay of Biscay," and I well remember the storm of enthusiasm which testified to the wonderful pathos he threw into the earlier stanzas, and to the triumphant vigor of its conclusion. In those days demands for repetition and summons before the curtain had not degenerated into the unmeaning and annoying conventionalities they have since become. They were seldom given, and when bestowed carried a real compliment to the performer. Incledon, appeared in answer to the call; but, instead of the impassioned instrument of the superb vocalization to which we had listened, he stood before us as the exhausted old man he really was. "Ladies and gentlemen," said he, "it is impossible for any man to repeat that song without intermission." The wearied tone and fatigued attitude of the veteran were very touching; it was a striking change from the pathos of art to the pathos of nature. Yet it is humiliating to confess that my vivid remembrance of the circumstance is probably in part owing to the advantage that was taken of it by Bray, the comic actor of the day. For in the farce which succeeded the main performance he introduced one of those audacious "gags" which Shakespeare's good advice to his clowns, "to speak no more than is set down for them," has not succeeded in banishing from the stage. A popular song of the day, called "The Old Jackdaw and the Young Jackdaw," had been sung by Bray, who interrupted the applause with which it was greeted by suddenly assuming the manner of Incledon, and declaring to the audience with the utmost gravity that it was beyond the power of any mortal to repeat the song to which they had just listened. The peals of laughter which this sally occasioned ring in my ears yet. The incident serves to show how the nonsense of a buffoon may linger in the memory, after so many of the words of wisdom which the Harvard professors uttered are wholly effaced.

I will conclude my college experiences of the theatre by copying my impressions of Edmund Kean, as they are recorded in the journal of my senior year. "My father came for me and took me to the theatre to see Kean as *Richard Third*, and never until then had I any idea of acting. He is small, ugly, and voiceless; and yet his talents covered all defects. The parts with which I was most pleased were the courtship of *Lady Anne*, the tent scene, and the death. His long pauses have great effect. Sometimes he paused two minutes by the stop-watch; but his countenance spoke all the time. A dropped pin might have been heard all over the house. I sat in the same box with Miss S———, who talked in a most unprecedented manner, for she asked me more questions and said more in two minutes than she ever did before in two days. My hearing Kean will always be remembered by me to my last day, and hereafter when other actors fill the station he now occupies, I shall remark on their inferiority to him, and may also, with the garrulity of age, describe the superior beauty of the ladies of the present day when their granddaughters shall be belles in their stead. Nothing reminds us of the flight of time so much as taking the present moment, and anticipating what will be our emotions when we look back upon it from a distance."

As there is little to add to this sage proposition, I

will conclude by mentioning one annoying sequel of our visits to the city, which readers of the present day will find it hard to understand. The difficulty of getting a light with numb fingers, on a cold night, was a petty misery of life which has long been unknown. In vain were the flint and steel clashed together; too often it happened that no available spark was the result. The tinder, which we made from old shirts, would absorb dampness in spite of all precautions to keep it dry. Sometimes after shivering for half an hour, during our efforts to kindle it, we were forced to go to bed in the dark in a condition of great discomfort, and feeling that we had purchased our amusement at an extravagant cost.

III.

I MAKE the following extract from my journal of July 7, 1820: —

"After breakfast the College Company went to town accompanied by the full band. We marched through a great number of the dustiest and dirtiest streets. At last we arrived at Chestnut Street, where we partook of a most splendid collation at the house of General Sumner. We were received in a room in which there were all kinds of refreshments, and ladies among other things. This gave it a very genteel effect, though none were remarkably handsome except Misses S—— and B——. After parading before the house, we went to the Common, and then to Mr. Gray's, where we got good drink. From there we went to State Street, and after performing a variety of evolutions, we dined at the Washington Garden, where toasts, songs, etc., abounded. This being finished, we returned to Cambridge, where, wonderful to relate, the President gave us a treat, and we were dismissed. The day was exceptionally hot, and we all perspired in glory. I drank an enormous quantity, to say nothing of what I eat, and finished my exploits with hasty pudding and molasses at the club."

After this, the next day's entry is not surprising: "Stayed at home to recruit after our labors."

The Harvard Washington Corps, one of whose excursions is chronicled above, was composed of students of the two higher classes, but was officered exclusively by seniors. It was very popular among the undergraduates, though by no means approved by the older friends of the college. To hold a command in the company was considered a great distinction, and there was much rivalry among candidates. There was one condition necessary to promotion: the aspirant must have a good leg; for the uniform required the officers to appear in tights, and any crural deficiency was an obstacle which could not be surmounted. And so it came to pass that the first question asked concerning any candidate was this, "How is the man off for a leg?"

Now it happened that there was exhibited daily

before the students what may be called an ideal leg, by which all others might be measured, and their shortcomings noted. This shapely limb was the property of Dr. Popkin, the Greek professor; and the owner seemed fully conscious of the beauty of its proportions, for he was in the habit of nursing and smoothing it, while hearing recitations, to the great delight of his classes. And so, when inquiries were made touching the calves of any would-be officer, there was but this one answer that was really satisfactory, "Why, sir, his leg is as good as Dr. Pop's!"

The Greek professor, I may say in passing, possessed an individuality that, if somewhat odd, was clearly cut and impressive. He was once asked by a lady who admired a system of theology then much discussed, whether he was a Hopkinsian. "Not a bit of it, madam; I am always a Popkinsian," was the prompt reply. And it was even so, for never was man more vigorously himself. His antique simplicity, dry humor, and hatred of all shams were just the qualities to win the regard of young men; and it was more affection than offensive familiarity which led to the universal abbreviation of his name. It is said he once turned suddenly upon a stranger whom he had overheard designating him by the familiar college title, "What right have you to call me Dr. Pop, sir? you were never one of my boys at Harvard." Years after this, I happened to meet the Doctor wearing the baggy pantaloon which reduced all legs to that democratic equality which Jefferson's manifesto declares to be the birthright of the people who go about on them. I could not help remarking that he, of all men, had reason to lament the departure of breeches and the accompanying stocking. The old gentleman seemed much gratified with the allusion, and declared that the fashion was detestable which caused Apollo and a Satyr to be equally presentable.

There was a theory current among us college boys that Dr. Pop was, so to speak, a born bachelor. His queer habits, we thought, must have dried upon him in infancy, and to break through their crust was as far beyond his power as it was averse to his inclination. I might have held this opinion till the present day, had it not been for a few words that the Doctor once let fall at my father's table. The conversation was running upon the pronunciation of Greek names, and one of the family asked where the accent should be placed in *Iphigenia*. "Why, in my class-room," said Dr. Popkin, "I should certainly say *Iphigenīa*, but in common talk it is so often called *Iphigēnīa* that I have never attempted to change it." "Then you have never tried to change a lady's name outside your class-room!" said my father pleasantly. An expression never seen before darkened the face of the good gentleman, and there was a soft dewy quality in his voice as he sighed forth the words, "*Sir, I have never succeeded.*" It was plain that to this man, as to so many of his fellow mortals, a hope had arisen only to be crushed, and that his life had been thrust aside from a path which once seemed to open. Another Dr. Pop, whose existence we had never suspected, was for a moment revealed; there was a sacredness added to the bachelor professor after that little speech.

In striking contrast to Dr. Popkin was Professor Frisbie, a gentleman of whom I find several notices in my journals. He had lost the use of his eyes for purposes of study, but the clearness and condensation of his thought, as well as the exquisite finish of the language in which it was conveyed, showed that his mind had not suffered from the deprivation. Mr. Frisbie had entered the service of the college as teacher of Latin, but was promoted to the chair of moral philosophy. He died in the prime of life, soon after my class graduated. His friend, Professor Norton, in a touching address made at his funeral, mentioned, as a marked trait of his character, that he could never bear to hear treated with levity those vices which a lax public opinion has considered venial. There was a passage of Tacitus which he was in the habit of quoting with expressions of strong approval. The historian, speaking of the manners of the Germans, says, "Nemo illic vitia videt, nec corrumpere et corrumpi Sæculum vocatur;" or, as the substance may be rendered in very free English, "Vicious indulgence is never made the subject of a jest, nor are the customs of society admitted as palliating a departure from moral rectitude." The doctrine implied in the quotation is the rule of life for all good men, and Frisbie probably felt that its importance was too little realized by the impulsive youths who surrounded him. Let me add that this professor of moral philosophy was very human in some of his tastes. He was very fond of novels, and saw no harm in them if they were well selected. Where sound morality was deftly mixed with fiction, he held that it would tend only to good, — an opinion which seemed much stranger sixty years ago than it does to-day.

But I did not mean to get among the professors, — indeed, were these papers put together upon any literary plan, they would be all lumped together in some biographical department. But the reader will have already discovered that no symmetry of arrangement is to be expected in the compositions before him. They simply follow the drift of conversation, and are based upon such questions as my journals suggest to my friend who is turning over their yellow leaves. Sometimes it happens that I can throw no light whatever upon their records. For instance, I have just been asked to explain this allusion, "Capital story of the President and Dr. Pop!" What was that story that was once so enjoyable? Alas, I have fumbled through my memory in vain, — I cannot find a trace of it. No doubt it would light up this paper, could it only be recovered; but it lies somewhere in the past, as speechless as the lips of the old college boys who laughed together over the fun they found in it. Time silences not only *Yorick* the jester, but is apt to cover up with him his gibes and flashes of merriment, his songs and his good stories. We can no longer use his keen eyes in looking after the ludicrous. And yet no generation need despair of finding enough of it to cast a pleasant glow upon life. The foibles of human nature will always furnish abundant matter for wholesome mirth, and they will always be benefactors who provide it for their weary brethren who are trudging over the dusty highway of the world.

I have said that there were grave doubts in the minds of conservative citizens respecting the propriety of the College Company; but it is safe to say that there was no doubt whatever concerning the College Fire Department. From an outside point of view it was an unmitigated nuisance, — a circumstance which did not render it less dear to the hearts of the students. Like most vested interests, the college engine struck its roots into the good old times of our ancestors, and was very difficult to abolish. The corporation had long owned a little tub of a machine, which would be thought scarcely fit to water a flower-bed at the present day, and the undergraduates had always enjoyed the privilege of tearing off with this instrument whenever there was an alarm of fire. The captain of the engine was appointed by the President of the college, but as all the minor offices were filled by the suffrages of the students, the organization was democratic enough to be interesting. No sooner did the fire-bell ring than we got into all sorts of horrible and grotesque garments. Hats in the last stages of dilapidation and strange ancestral coats were carefully kept for these occasions. Feeling that we were pretty well disguised, there seemed nothing to hinder that lawless abandonment to a frolic which is so delightful to unregenerate man when youthful blood bubbles in his veins. I cannot remember that we ever rendered the slightest assistance in extinguishing a fire; indeed, there were so many good reasons for stopping on the way that we commonly arrived after it was out. And then, if we were tired, we had an impudent way of leaving the tub upon the ground, well knowing that the government would send for their property the next day.

Among the memorable fires that were attended by the college engine, the burning of the Exchange Coffee-House was the most impressive. This building was said to be the finest in the Union, and was certainly the pride and boast of Boston. It had noble halls, and over two hundred lesser apartments. It was quite a little town in itself, giving shelter to brokers, insurance companies, foreign consuls, and masonic lodges. It had cost about $600,000, which was then thought to be an immense sum to be put in bricks and mortar. The light was so great as to be seen over a large area of country, and far out to sea; and when, at nine o'clock in the evening, the dome came crashing down, a shudder ran through thousands of excited spectators. Strange to say, no life was lost through all the tumult and confusion of the night. It was not until the next day that an accident occurred which called to mind the end of Clarence in his butt of Malmsey. An immense caldron of beer lay open among the ruins, and into this a poor boy managed to fall with consequences quite as fatal as the wine brought to the royal duke.

On our return from this fire, exhausted with excitement and fatigue, we repaired to the engine-house, as was our custom, and were there regaled upon "black strap," a composition of which the secret, as I fervently hope, now reposes with the lost arts. Its principal ingredients were rum and molasses, though it is probable there were other simples combined with these conspicuous factors. Of all the detestable American drinks, upon which the inventive genius of our countrymen has exercised itself, this "black strap" was surely the most outrageous. It finally broke up the engine company, and this was perhaps the only good thing which ever came of it. For matters at last reached a crisis; the government came to their senses, sold the engine, and broke up the association. But to take the edge off the cruelty of this necessary act, it was decided that the company should be allowed a final meeting. And so we celebrated the obsequies of the old machine with an oration and a poem, following up these exercises with other proceedings of which a detailed account is unnecessary.

The present students of Harvard have more civilized modes of recreation. I hear of art clubs, and of societies which take pleasure in essays upon political economy and scientific research. I find, too, that some things are allowed which would have been thought scandalous by the wise men of the past. What would our college authorities have said about permitting students to give theatrical exhibitions in a public hall? What deductions of degeneracy would they not have drawn, had they been told that such a stigma as this would ever be attached to their cherished institution? Well, every age is apt to arrange the virtues on a scale of its own, and to be becomingly shocked when they get joggled out of place. The students of to-day have undoubtedly pleasures which a moral philosopher would pronounce superior to the rude sports of their grandfathers. But for rough, tumultuous fun, for a glorious abandonment *en masse* of the irksome restraints of social life, they are (fortunately, of course) more than sixty years too late. They know not what it was to run to a fire with the old Harvard tub.

IV.

FEW realize that college life sixty years ago was just a year longer than it is now. Cambridge was not deserted during the vacation; while at present from July to October everybody is off and all the rooms are vacant. The students' apartments of my day were not so attractive that one would wish to linger in them. I cannot remember a single room which had carpet, curtain, or any pretence of ornament. In a few of them were hung some very poor prints, representing the four seasons, emblematical representations of the countries of Europe, and imaginative devices of a similar nature. Our light came from dipped candles, with very broad bases and gradually narrowing to the top. These required the constant use of snuffers, — a circumstance which hindered application to an extent that in these days of kerosene and gas can scarcely be appreciated. Indeed, the dual brain with which mankind are furnished seemed to us to show intelligent design, not less than the famous illustrations presented by Paley. One brain was clearly required to do the studying, while it was the business of the other to watch the candles and look after the snuffers.

Our fuel was wood, which was furnished by the college; it being cut from some lands in Maine which were among its possessions, and brought to the wharf in the college sloop, the "Harvard." This arrangement was supposed to cause a great saving, and the authorities naturally prided themselves upon the sagacity which made this Eastern property so productive. It was not until Dr. Bowditch, the great mathematician, was given a place in the government that this arrangement was quietly abandoned. This eminent gentleman — perhaps from his natural aptitude for figures — succeeded in demonstrating to his associates that it would be much cheaper for the college to buy wood from the dearest dealer than to cut it on its own lands and transport it in its own sloop. It is strange how long-established methods of obtaining the necessaries of life will continue, when a little thought will show that better ones may be substituted.

When speaking just now of the decoration (or absence of decoration) of college rooms, I ought to have noticed one significant exception. My classmate, Otis, had ornamented his mantelpiece with two curious black stones, which excited great interest in his visitors. He had made a journey to Washington, to see his father, who was a Senator; and had brought these rarities home, as precious memorials of his travels. He had a strange tale to tell concerning them. It seemed that the people in Baltimore actually burned just such stones as these; and, wonderful to relate, there was no smoke in their chimneys. I believe that these singular minerals have become so popular in Harvard College that they are now brought there in considerable quantities. The only change is that they are no longer displayed on the mantelpiece, but just below it — in the grate. They will be recognized under the name of anthracite coal.

There were two college clubs, to which admission depended on scholarship. These were the Hasty Pudding and the Phi Beta Kappa. In the former there were nominally an essay and a discussion at every meeting. In reality there was nothing of the sort. There were pudding and molasses, and nothing more. The latter, with the exception of its annual dinner, had no meetings whatever, except those necessary to receive new members; but it possessed the attraction of being a secret society, and we were solemnly sworn never to reveal the mighty mysteries that were confided to us at the ceremony of initiation. During the great anti-Masonic excitement John Quincy Adams brought it to pass that all pledges of secrecy were removed, by a formal vote of the society; so that I am perfectly free to expose all its mysteries, could I only remember what they were. The secret of the brilliant annual dinners of the Phi Beta, under the presidencies of Edward Everett, Judge Story, Judge Warren, and others, lies near the surface. It was very difficult for outsiders to gain admission, so that the company was one in which distinguished men were willing to unbend. Add to this — as the secret within the secret — that we were absolutely secured against reporters.

There were other associations, known as "blowing clubs," in connection with which drunkenness was exhibited with a publicity that would not now be tolerated. One of these societies — which is yet in existence, though it is to be hoped that the habits of its members have improved — was wont to have a dinner on exhibition days. After the exercises in the chapel, the brethren would march to Porter's tavern, preceded by a full band; and the attempt was made to return in the same way. First would come the band, the only steady part of the show, whose music attracted a crowd of lookers-on. Then came, reeling and swaying from side to side, a mass of bacchanals, in all stages of intoxication. That this disgraceful sight should have been tolerated by the college authorities will seem surprising to those who fail to realize the radical and beneficent change in public sentiment which has taken place. To abstain entirely from alcoholic liquors — the only safe course for the young, and probably for the old also — was then considered a priggish and ridiculous asceticism. "When you get where you can't stop, Pat, be sure you hold up!" said an Irishman to his friend, who was running down a hill, with a precipice at the bottom of it. Some such advice as this may have been given to the young fellows who were hastening to their doom. But the customs of the time were all in favor of indulgence in strong drink. Liquor was openly sold from booths upon public days, and it was even supposed that an occasional debauch was beneficial to the health. Some of the victims were men of most generous character and of brilliant intelligence. All honor to the temperance party which has brought authority — physiological, religious, and social — to the rebuke of this monstrous evil.

But, among college clubs, the place of honor must be reserved for the Med. Fac. (so abbreviated from Medical Faculty), a roaring burlesque upon learned bodies in general and the college government in particular. In this association was to be found some of the most excellent fooling that I have ever met. We had regular meetings, conducted with mock decorum, at each of which a pseudo professor delivered a lecture on some topic of medical interest. I remember a capital discourse pronounced by my chum, Stetson, on the science of osteology. He began with the famous *De mortuis nil nisi bonum*, which he asserted to be a medical aphorism, meaning "You can get nothing from dead men but their bones." From this text he went on, with professorial gravity of manner, piling absurdities upon one another in a way that was simply irresistible. Those who knew this excellent man as the Rev. Caleb Stetson will remember how difficult it was for him to keep his rich sense of humor under due professional restraint. But as orator of the Med. Fac. there was no conventional fence to girdle in his honest love of fun, and it shone out brightly, before suffering partial eclipse behind the sacred desk.

The Medical Faculty were accustomed to issue diplomas and honorary degrees, in imitation of those dispensed by college officers. All sorts of queer people were made the recipients of these distinctions, and their names were at one time published in a catalogue, each being loaded with cabalistic letters, after the manner of those honored by academic bodies. Among these diplomas one was sent to the Emperor of Russia, informing that potentate that he had been elected a member of the Medical Faculty of Harvard College. The affair was engrossed upon parchment and got up in splendid style. It, moreover, gave a full list of the honorary distinctions which had been graciously bestowed upon the monarch on the occasion of his admission. Just what came of this piece of audacity I cannot say with any certainty; but the report was circulated and believed that in due time a fine surgical library arrived, consigned to the care of the authorities of the college. This they were requested to make over to their Medical Faculty, with the grateful acknowledgments of their good brother, the Emperor. Whether such an incident ever occurred is perhaps doubtful. If it did, the authorities may have thought that, under the circumstances, the best thing to be done was to keep dark and to keep the books. But, if there is any question whether our library was confiscated, there is no doubt whatever that the Medical Faculty was summarily broken up about the time that despatches were due from their august member in St. Petersburg. From some cause or other, the government suddenly acted with immense energy, and asserted that monopoly in the matter of conferring degrees which has since been maintained.

Under the date of April 26, 1821, I find recorded in my journal the impressions made upon me by the oratory of Daniel Webster. He was at that time thirty-nine years old, and had scarcely touched the maturity of his remarkable powers. The occasion was one of surpassing interest. James Prescott, judge of the probate of wills, was impeached before the Senate of Massachusetts, sitting as a high court of judicature. The trial was conducted under forms similar to those used in the famous prosecution of Warren Hastings. Indeed, the whole proceeding seemed like a provincial copy of that absorbing case; with this difference, however, that the great orators were retained for the defence, instead of the prosecution. Daniel Webster, Samuel Hoar, William Prescott, Samuel Hubbard, — the flower of the Boston bar, — appeared in behalf of Prescott. Articles of impeachment had been found by the House of Representatives, which adjourned to be present at the case. This popular body was represented by managers, as were the Commons of England in the prosecution of Hastings. When Webster was to make his final plea, the galleries were crowded with ladies, the floor was packed by such fragment of the crowd as could gain admission, and it might almost be said that the pulse of the community stopped, from the excitement of the moment.

By some extraordinary good fortune, or perhaps favoritism, I found myself in one of the best seats in that thronged assembly. On either side of me were personages of no less importance than President Kirkland and Harrison Gray Otis. This was much as if a student of Columbia College should find himself sitting between Secretary Evarts and Cardinal McCloskey on an occasion of great public interest. No, it would not be the same thing, after all; for none of the conspicuous men of to-day tower so majestically above the rest of the world as their predecessors seemed to rise above the smaller communities which were subject unto them. But how can the triumphs of the orator be represented upon paper? It can be said only that Webster spoke for nearly four hours, and held the great assembly breathless under his spell. I have noted in my journal the singular pathos of his conclusion. After exclaiming that no man had dared to come into that court to accuse his client of giving a wrong judgment, he turned suddenly upon one of the managers, and demanded whether, should God summon him to his account that very night, he would not leave the world in perfect confidence that the interest of his children would be safe in the hands of the upright judge against whom his impeachment had been brought. The words in themselves are no more than the libretto of an opera; but, with Webster behind them, they seemed to sweep away all adverse testimony, and to render an acquittal by acclamation a simple necessity. It is, undoubtedly, to the credit of the independence of the court that Judge Prescott was not acquitted on all the counts of the indictment; but to have heard the noble effort made in his behalf by Daniel Webster marked an epoch in the lives of those present. It gave me my first idea of the electric force that might be wielded by a master of human speech.

COMMENCEMENT DAY IN 1821.

SIXTY years ago Commencement Day was a State holiday. The banks were closed, business was pretty generally suspended, and numbers of sightseers repaired to Cambridge, as their ancestors had been accustomed to do a hundred years before. The college exercises were held, as they had been for a century, in the old Congregational meeting-house; and the building was by no means ill-adapted to this purpose. The galleries, which sloped at an angle of about forty-five degrees, displayed to great advantage the beautiful and fashionably dressed ladies with which they were crowded. At the end of each of the four aisles a wooden desk was erected, and from these forensics had formerly been read. The speakers, of course, delivered their parts from the platform. The students belonging to Boston families of wealth gave elaborate parties in honor of the occasion. These were frequented by all the strangers who happened to be in town, and advertised the college in a way that was thought useful. Indeed, the government were accused of giving parts to inferior scholars, whose sumptuous entertainments would be likely to lend dignity to the day.

The account of the conclusion of my college life shall be copied just as it stands written in my diary. I need not apologize for any crudities or egotism which may be found in the wholly private records of a youth who was legally a minor.

"*July* 16, 1821. — Attended a dissertation of Emerson's in the morning on the subject of Ethical Philosophy. I found it long and dry. In the afternoon we went to our last lecture on exhilarating gas. Gorham fought, Dinsmore danced, Curtis laughed, and Bunker swore, according as the ruling passion swayed their breasts. In the evening I paid my last visit to the Miss Hills. In the afternoon, went to the President and got my dissertation, which he had mislaid. He was quite facetious, for I had painted my coat against the wall. This is the last evening we spend in college. May I never look back upon it with regret! It strikes eleven, and I must go to bed.

"*July* 17*th*. — At nine in the morning I read my dissertation, and it had the good fortune to please our college critics. At half past ten we assembled at Keating's room, and marched from there to the President's, and escorted him, with the rest of the government, to the chapel, where Barnwell and Emerson performed our valedictory exercises before all the scholars and a number of ladies. They were rather poor and did but little honor to the class. We returned with the President to his house immediately after the exercises. At one o'clock all those who were fortunate enough to obtain *deturs* went to the

President to receive them. There were but eighteen who got them. I had Westall's edition of 'Young's Night Thoughts,' one of the best books that was given out. At two we marched down to Porter's, where we had a fine dinner. After the cloth was removed, Mr. Cushing [afterward well known as Hon. Caleb Cushing] came in, and gave for a toast: 'The bands of friendship, which always tighten when they are wet.' After he had gone, Wood delivered an oration, which was very witty and appropriate; and then Alden rehearsed the woes and pleasures of college life in his usual style. There were a number of original songs sung: Alden sung one much to the amusement of us all. When we had all drunk our skins full, we marched round to all the professors' houses, danced round the Rebellion and Liberty Trees, and then returned to the hall. A great many of the class were half-seas-over, and I had the pleasure of supporting one of them. This was as hard work as I ever desire to do. Many ladies came to witness our dancing, and were much scandalized by the elevation of spirit which some exhibited. We parted with more grief than any class I ever saw, every one of us being drowned in tears. Had I been told that I should have felt so much, I should have laughed at the idea. When it came to the point, however, I cried like the rest of them. In the evening Frank Lowell and I went over to Mr. John Lowell's, where we had a very pleasant time. Miss Eliza S—— looked prettier and talked better than I ever knew her to before.

"*August* 29, 1821, *Commencement Day.* — In the morning I went to prayers, to hear Mr. Cushing pray; for it is always customary for the particular tutor of the graduating class to perform that duty on Commencement morning. He read us an account of the fall of Babylon and of the emancipation of the oppressed Jews. This seemed very applicable to our escape from the government, though I do not believe he ever thought of it. His prayer was short and not impressive. About eight o'clock the ladies came over; and I got them into the meeting-house by opening the door while the sexton was away, for which I had a good scolding on his return. That, however, was but a small matter. I then went to Mr. Higginson's, and returned to wait on the ladies. The house was full of very beautiful women, and every one who spoke paid them some compliment or other; but most of them were rather lame ones. Hill Second, Sampson Reed in the master's oration, Burton, and Leverett were very pathetic toward them. A Miss ———, from Salem, attracted much attention on account of the beauty of her neck; and she, to oblige admirers, wore no ruffles. All the Amorys, Sullivans, Crowninshields, with long *et ceteras*, filled the house. After the exercises, which were very short, I went over to Porter's, where all the relations of our family were assembled. They appeared gratified with my performance. We had a very handsome dinner; and after it was over the Governor, Council, and all the great and learned men, both friends and strangers, came in and took wine with us. They all complimented me on my success, — in part payment, I suppose, for the wine which they drank. Among my relations was Mrs. Storer, who is eighty-six years old, and who attended the Commencements of my father and grandfather. She seemed to enjoy the day as highly as anybody. We visited Mrs. Farrar, after our company had gone, and found there many young ladies, in addition to all the gentlemen who had visited us. In the evening my sisters and myself went to Mr. Otis's great ball (given in honor of the graduation of his son), and there we enjoyed ourselves highly. It was nearly twelve o'clock before we returned. Thus ends my college life. I must now begin the world."

I will conclude this account of my connection with Harvard College by alluding briefly to my final appearance as a pupil of that institution. This was on the occasion of my taking a master's degree. Now this same degree was at that time given in regular course to every one who had been three years out of college and who chose to pay for it. A man might have forgotten the little he had learned, and have failed to acquire any new knowledge to take its place, he was still entitled to be proclaimed master of arts on the simple condition above specified. The change of policy, which now requires a serious examination to be passed before this degree can be conferred, is one of the many beneficial reforms which later times have instituted.

It was formerly the custom for at least two of the candidates for the master's degree to be assigned parts at Commencement. An oration in English and a Latin valedictory were commonly spoken by three-year graduates. A few days before the Commencement of 1824 I received a letter from President Kirkland, in which he said that the person to whom the valedictory had been assigned had not put in an appearance, and nobody knew where he was to be found. This was William Withington, a classmate of mine and an excellent scholar, but somewhat awkward in his manner and with small gifts as a speaker. As my rank in the class entitled me to succeed the missing Withington, the President begged me to prepare a Latin discourse without more ado; for it was to be a great day for the college, as General Lafayette was to be present. It may be that the graduates of our colleges to-day are capable of breaking into the dead languages at a moment's notice; but certain it is that the instruction that was to be had sixty years ago did not communicate this desirable facility. To comply with the President's request would have been simply impossible, had it not been for an important package which accompanied his letter. This contained a number of Latin compositions adapted to academic festivals. They had evidently been used with some freedom by past orators; but, as they had never been reported and as the bulk of the audiences did not understand a word of them, they were as bright and fresh as ever. It was evidently the intention of Dr. Kirkland that this useful literature should be largely drawn upon in preparing the valedictory. The conventional compliments to governors, magistrates, and others in authority were as good as ever. The only thing to be done was to add some original sentences applicable to the nation's guest, and then to recast, as well as my limited time allowed me to do, the matter which had been so thoughtfully furnished.

My reminiscences of Lafayette, whom I afterward had the privilege of seeing intimately, do not belong in this paper. My present concern is with Commencement Day at Harvard. The galleries of the venerable meeting-house had been thronged with ladies from an early hour in the morning. But the General, who had to be received at almost every cross-road, was waylaid at Cambridgeport, where a triumphal arch had been erected in his honor. Here addresses and replies must be exchanged, so that he was some hours behind time on reaching the colleges. Notwithstanding the expectant and wearied audience which was waiting in the meeting-house, the President did not see fit to omit his address of welcome, which was delivered from the porch which then stood in front of University Hall. The General's reply was brief, and concluded with a Latin quotation, which, being given with the European pronunciation of that language, was not understood. At length the procession was formed and proceeded to the meeting-house, and the most memorable Commencement exercises which those old walls had ever witnessed were begun, about two o'clock in the afternoon.

To describe the enthusiasm that greeted the guest of the day is simply impossible. Those who felt it

— those who were lifted up by it — knew that it was a unique experience of which nothing adequate could be said. Lafayette was seated in a conspicuous place upon the platform. Most of the speakers alluded in some way to his presence, and so permitted the repressed rapture to burst forth. Never was homage so unbounded, so heartfelt, so spontaneous. It was as if one of the great heroes of history had been permitted to return to earth. The exercises were all good; but the oration by Edward B. Emerson, the first scholar of the year, and the master's oration by my classmate, Upham, were probably as fine performances as have ever been given at a Harvard Commencement. Both these young men reached the level of the occasion; and what more can be said? The valedictory, of course, came last, and I felt rather awkward in rising to declaim my stilted Latin phrases before an audience which had been stirred by such vigorous English. The first part of my performance consisted of mere phrases of rhetorical compliment thrown out at creation in general. I rolled them out as well as I could; but they seemed neither stimulating nor, in fact, comprehensible to the audience. But the inevitable allusion came at last. I had drifted among the heroes of the Revolution, and suddenly turned to the General with my *In te quoque, Lafayette!* — and then what an uproar drowned the rest of the sentence! "Why, sir, do you know, the pit rose at me!" said Edmund Kean, after his first performance of *Shylock* at Drury Lane. The expression of the player is perhaps as good as anything I can borrow to indicate the scene before me. The entire audience upon the floor had sprung to their feet; the ladies in the galleries were standing also, and were waving their handkerchiefs with impassioned ardor. It was the last opportunity which the day was to offer to pay homage to the guest of America, and, as if by one consent, it was improved to the utmost. I could not but share the excitement provoked by the magic name I had uttered, and was scarcely responsible for the concluding sentences.

And thus my connection with Harvard College came to an end, — a satisfactory conclusion, truly, were it not for the awkward confession that I was not the man to whom that most memorable of valedictories rightfully belonged. It was by reason of the generosity or misfortune of my classmate, William Withington, that I took leave of Cambridge in a manner so agreeable.

REMINISCENCES OF THE SECOND PRESIDENT.

MY earliest recollections of the second President go back to the time when, as a child, hardly more than five years old, I used to gaze upon him in the Quincy meeting-house. I have a perfect remembrance of his being pointed out to me by my father, who told me that I must be sure to remember him, as he was an old man and could not be with us long. It was, of course, not supposed that he would attain the great and exceptional age which he reached, and that I should have the privilege of frequent association with him for so many years. I remember gazing at him with the wondering eyes of a child, and marvelling why he was called "President," and why he was considered better worth seeing than Captain Bass and the other old men of the village. The meeting-house in Quincy, so associated with John Adams, may be worth a brief description. I have no distinct remembrance of the building previous to its enlargement, in 1806, but have heard its appearance previous to that date often described by Mr. Adams and by members of my own family. It was built in 1731, and, according to our present ideas, was queer and comfortless. The body of the house was occupied by long seats, the men being placed on one side of the broad aisle and the women on the other. The oldest inhabitants were always seated in front. "I never shall forget," Mr. Adams once said to me, "the rows of venerable heads ranged along those front benches which, as a young fellow, I used to gaze upon. They were as old and gray as mine is now." The deacons were accommodated just under the pulpit, while the sexton had a bench in the rear, perhaps to keep a watch over the young people on the back seats. One of the oddest things about the church was a little hole high up in the wall, through which the bell-ringer might be seen in the exercise of his vocation. It was the duty of this functionary to keep his eye upon the congregation, and to mark by the customary tolling the arrival of the minister. As time wore on, some wall-pews began to appear in the old meeting-house. These were built by individuals, at their own expense, permission having been first gained by a vote of the town. And there are curious votes upon this subject in the early records. On one occasion it was voted that a prominent personage might "build him a pew over the pulpit, provided he so builds as not to darken the pulpit." And a friend of mine here suggests that, as a figure of speech, pews may now be said to be built over the pulpit with some frequency, and regrets that the good divines of the town, whose life-long sway was arbitrary and unquestioned, did not have the wit to prevent that perilous permission. For, notwithstanding the wholesome caution of the old record, it has been found impossible "not to darken the pulpit" when the pews are placed above it.

An ancestor of mine was permitted to fence off the first pew, and his example was quickly followed by others. This was a recognition of caste in the one place where men should meet on terms of perfect equality. I cannot but think that this innovation upon the good custom of our forefathers has had its effect in alienating from religious services a large portion of our population. A notable addition to the Sunday exercises in the Quincy meeting-house followed the introduction of the pews; for the seats in these aristocratic pens were upon hinges, and were always raised during the long prayer, for the purpose of allowing those who stood to rest themselves by leaning against the railing. At the conclusion of the devotion, the sudden descent of all the seats sounded like a volley of musketry, and was a source of considerable terror to those who heard it for the first time. When the increase of population rendered desirable an enlargement of the meeting-house, it was sawed through the middle; and, the two halves being separated, an addition was built to reunite them. The President's pew was conspicuous in the reconstructed edifice, and there the old man was to be seen at every service. An air of respectful deference to John Adams seemed to pervade the building. The ministers brought their best sermons when they came to exchange, and had a certain consciousness in their manner as if officiating before royalty. The medley of stringed and wind instruments in the gallery — a survival of the sacred trumpets and shawms mentioned by King David — seemed to the imagination of a child to be making discord together in honor of the venerable chief who was the centre of interest.

When I was about six years old, I was put to school to the Rev. Peter Whitney; and, spending the winter in his family, was often asked to dine on Sunday with Mr. and Mrs. Adams. This was at first somewhat of an ordeal for a boy; but the genuine kindness of the President, who had not the smallest chip of an iceberg in his composition, soon made me perfectly at ease in his society. With Mrs. Adams there was a shade more formality. A consciousness of age and dignity, which was often somewhat oppressive, was customary with old people of that day in the presence of the young. Something of this Mrs. Adams certainly had, though it wore off or came to be disregarded by me, for in the end I was strongly attached to her. She always dressed handsomely, and her rich silks and laces seemed appropriate to a lady of her dignified position in the town. If there was a little savor of patronage in the generous hospitality she exercised among her simple neighbors, it was never regarded as more than a natural emphasis of her undoubted claims to precedence. The aristocratic colonial families were still recognized, for the tide of democracy had not risen high enough to cover these distinctions. The parentage and descent of Mrs. Adams were undoubtedly of weight in establishing her position; although, as we now look at things, the strong personal claims of herself and husband would seem to have been all sufficient.

I well remember the modest dinners at the President's, to which I brought a school-boy's appetite. The pudding, generally composed of boiled corn-meal, always constituted the first course. This was the custom of the time, — it being thought desirable to take the edge off of one's hunger before reaching the joint. Indeed, it was considered wise to stimulate the young to fill themselves with pudding, by the assurance that the boy who managed to eat the most of it should be helped most abundantly to the meat, which was to follow. It need not be said that neither the winner nor his competitors found much room for meat at the close of their contest; and so the domestic economy of the arrangement was very apparent. Miss Smith, a niece of Mrs. Adams, was an inmate of the President's family, and one of these ladies always carved. Mr. Adams made his contribution to the service of the table in the form of that good-humored, easy banter, which makes a dinner of herbs more digestible than is a stalled ox without it. At a later period of our acquaintance, I find preserved in my journals frequent though too meagre reports of his conversation. But of the time of which I am writing there is not a word recoverable. I can distinctly picture to myself a certain iron spoon which the old gentleman once fished up from the depths of a pudding in which it had been unwittingly cooked; but of the pleasant things he said in those easy dinner-talks no trace remains.

I have mentioned the meeting-house as associated with President Adams, and as giving character to his native town. But there was another locality in Quincy which was a still more interesting resort for its inhabitants; at least, during the earlier portions of their lives. Among my boyish recollections there is distinctly visible a very pretty hill, which rose from the banks of the river, or what passed for one, and was covered with trees of the original forest growth. This was known as Cupid's Grove; and it had been known under that title for at least three generations, and perhaps from the settlement of the town. The name suggests the purposes to which this sylvan spot was dedicated. It was the resort of the lovers of the vicinage, or of those who, if circumstances favored, might become so. The trunks of the trees were cut and scarred all over with the initials of ladies who were fair and beloved, or who once had been so; for it was then the fashion to pay modest maidens a compliment which would be now thought in very doubtful taste. But, as Shakespeare makes his *Orlando* — a fine, spirited fellow and very much of a gentleman — cut the name of *Rosalind* upon every available bit of timber in the forest of Arden, it will not be necessary to apologize for the habits of my contemporaries in this respect. It is sad to mention that poor Cupid has long been driven from his sanctuary, which has suffered violence at the hands of his brother god of heathendom, who has so often gotten the better of him. Plutus strode by that humble hillock, and straightway the grove was cut down and sold for firewood; and not only this, but the little eminence itself was purchased for its gravel, and under that form, as I believe, has been dumped upon the vulgar highway. The fate of Cupid's Grove is typical of that of the romance which was associated with places of this nature in our older New England towns. In the days when there were no public libraries, no travelling operas, no theatre trains, — when, in fact, the one distraction of the week was going to meeting, — who can wonder that the flowery paths leading to the domestic circle were more frequented than at present?

In those old times it happened that a certain young lawyer, named John Adams, was wont to visit a good deal at the house of a great-grandfather of mine, who had a large landed estate and several daughters; and the family tradition is that one of these ladies was not wholly uninteresting to the young fellow, who had just begun his struggle with the world. Just what it all amounted to it is impossible to say, at this distance of time; neither would it be well to say it, even if it were possible. The historical facts are that my great-aunt married Ebenezer Storer — a gentleman of some pretension, who was for forty years treasurer of Harvard College — and that young Adams married Miss Abigail Smith. Eventful years rolled by, and I, a young man, just entering life, was deputed to attend my venerable relative on a visit to the equally venerable ex-President. Both parties were verging upon their ninetieth year. They had met very infrequently, if at all, since the days of their early intimacy. When Mrs. Storer entered the room, the old gentleman's face lighted up, as he exclaimed, with ardor, "What! Madam, shall we not go walk in Cupid's Grove together?" To say the truth, the lady seemed somewhat embarrassed by this utterly unlooked-for salutation. It seemed to hurry her back through the past with such rapidity as fairly to take away her breath. But self-possession came at last, and with it a suspicion of girlish archness, as she replied, "Ah, sir, it would not be the first time that we have walked there!"

Perhaps the incident is not worth recording, as there is really no way of getting upon paper the suggestiveness that it had to a witness. For a moment the burden of years seemed to be thrown aside, and the vivacity of youth reasserted itself. The flash of old sentiment was startling from its utter unexpectedness. I shall hereafter have occasion to copy from my journals fragments of the conversation of this distinguished man; but I can give nothing which made more impression upon me than this little speech. It is the sort of thing which sets a young fellow to thinking. It is a surprise to find a great personage so simple, so perfectly natural, so thoroughly human; and it needs but a little reflection to discover that he *is* great because — among more obvious reasons — he can always draw upon a good balance of these homely, commonplace qualities.

VISITS TO JOHN ADAMS.

DURING the last five years of the life of John Adams I enjoyed the privilege of constant intercourse with him during the summer months. Several times a week I went to his house, where I frequently read aloud to him or acted as his amanuensis. I shall give some gleanings from his conversations, as I find them recorded in my journals.

"*September* 6, 1820. — Judge Winston and Major Sommerville, gentlemen from the South, drove out this morning and stayed with us some time. Then we all went up to call upon President Adams. His visitors asked him his opinion of Patrick Henry, and whether he was not the greatest orator he had ever heard. His reply was: 'No, gentlemen. Much of Wirt's life of him is a romance. Why, I have heard that gentleman's father [pointing to one who was present] speak in a strain of eloquence to which Patrick Henry could never pretend.' He paused, and then added, 'You know Virginian geese are always swans.' Notwithstanding these remarks, the gentlemen seemed very much pleased with their visit."

In a letter addressed to Mr. Wirt himself, and bearing date January 5, 1818, I find that Mr. Adams's testimony is the same. The passage is characteristic enough for quotation. He writes: "James Otis electrified the town of Boston, the Province of Massachusetts Bay, and the whole continent more than Patrick Henry ever did in the whole course of his life. If we must have panegyrics and hyperboles, I must say that if Mr. Henry was Demosthenes and Mr. Richard Henry Lee was Cicero, James Otis was Isaiah and Ezekiel united."

"*November* 2, 1821. — To-day President Adams walked down to see us (the distance was about a mile), and arrived a little before noon. He gave us an account of his early law life. His father hoped he would be a clergyman; but the nature of the doctrines which were then taught repelled him. On leaving college, he went to Worcester, where he kept school and studied law at the same time."

From the journal of another member of the family I quote a fuller account of what passed at this visit.

"Mr. Adams talked freely, and said: 'After I left college, I came home to Braintree, to see my friends; and then went to Worcester, to keep school to support myself, while at the same time I studied law with Judge Putnam. I advise every young man to keep school. I acquired more knowledge of human nature while I kept that school than while I was at the bar, than while I was in the world of politics or at the Courts of Europe. It is the best method of acquiring patience, self-command, and a knowledge of character. After I had finished my studies, I opened an office in Braintree, and lived here some years, the town being then in Suffolk County. The bar was then crowded with eminent lawyers. I removed to Boston for two or three years, but was so overwhelmed with business that I was forced to return to Braintree, for my health.' Mr. Adams spoke of the advantages of keeping a regular journal, and said that he had kept one during the four years of his college life, which he had foolishly destroyed. He would now give anything in the world to have it again."

To go back a little, I will copy my entries made on September 27th, in the same year. "Mrs. Head and Miss Tyng called in the afternoon. They were full of complaints of the love which ladies in this town have for scandal. In the evening we all went up to President Adams's, where the fair ones of Milton and Quincy met in harmony. We had quite a pleasant time, dancing to the piano — not in the most graceful style imaginable. Miss Helen looked beautifully, played angelically, and talked wisely. President Adams gave the girls a fine account of the ancient belles and beaux of this place. And as future ages will, undoubtedly, inquire who were *our* divinities, I subjoin a catalogue. To posterity, you degenerate race that will be, — you who never saw Miss Lyman, nor Miss Brooks, nor the 'Panorama of Athens,'— know that in the town of Quincy, at the residence of President Adams, on the night of September 27th, 1821, assembled the following ladies: Miss Duncan and two Misses Codman, sojourners at Mrs. Black's; three Misses Marstons; Miss Whitney;

Miss Apthorp and three Greenleafs; Miss Baxter and Mrs. Barney Smith, in all the trappings of — I wonder how people will dress seventy years from now. I will leave a blank here for any gentle reader of that period to write down the mode. Now for all these ladies there were but six gentlemen, — the three Adamses, George Whitney, Mr. Smith, and myself."

"*August* 26, 1822. — George Otis dined with me, and in the afternoon Sam. Phillips, of Andover, arrived to spend the night. In the evening I accompanied him to the President's, and found the old gentleman well and lively. Speaking of the controversy between Dr. Stewart, of Andover, and Mr. Miller, of New York, concerning the eternal generation of the Son, he became quite eloquent, censuring the idea as inconceivable and impious. The conversation passed to his son, John Quincy Adams, of whom his father said, 'He has a very hard, laborious, and unhappy life; though he is envied by half the people in the United States for his talents and situation.' Speaking of the navy, he said that if we had thirty ships of the line no European nation would dare to attack us, as not even England could spare that number at such a distance from her own coasts."

"*September* 1, 1822. — Visited the President, as usual. He was quite amusing, and gave us many anecdotes of his life. He was particularly funny in an account of an interview he had with the Turkish ambassador in England, whom he astonished by his power of smoking. Also he spoke of the Emperor of Morocco, who made an easy treaty with us because we were Unitarians. (The meaning, of course, is because the nation put forward no dogmatic statement of Christian belief.) He spoke concerning the Jesuits, African religions, Belzoni, and total depravity. On this last topic he told us an anecdote of Governor Tichenor, of Vermont. After he had been in Congress, he sent for an old friend of his, with whom he had often disputed the question, and confessed to him that he was entirely converted, for his political life had established his belief in the total depravity of mankind. The President spoke of the Treaty of Ghent, and said that the shore fisheries on the coast of Labrador were much superior to those on the banks of Newfoundland. He said that the word 'liberty' was used in the first treaty, at the request of the English commissioners, as a sugar-plum to the common people. It was, however, expressly admitted that a right and a liberty were synonymous."

"*November* 6, 1821. — Went to take a farewell of the old President, and read to him for the last time this season. He thanked me repeatedly, quoting the words of the Apostle, and saying that he sorrowed most of all that he should see my face no more. He appears very well; but life at his age is precarious. He gave me an account of his forming one of a party of young men to be inoculated with the small-pox, and going with them to be confined for several weeks in a pest-house, as was the custom before vaccination was introduced. Before going, he called on

Dr. Byles (a personage much noted as a humorist). When they parted, Byles said: 'I give you my blessing, like a Romish priest,— *Pax tecum.* I mean, of course, *Pox take 'em.*' He asked me what I had been reading. I told him the life of Sir William Jones, and I remarked on the excellence of his mother. 'Young man,' said the President, 'did you ever hear of a great and good man who had not a good mother?' He mentioned a family which had long been influential, and said that the reason was because they gave good mothers to their children."

"*August* 18, 1822. — Visited the President this evening, and heard a number of his pleasant stories. He complained of the intolerance of Christians, and thought that the old Roman system of permitting every man to worship how and what he pleased was the true one. He liked the opinion of Justin Martyr that every honest, well-disposed, moral man, even if he were an atheist, should be accounted a Christian. He said that for nearly eighty years most of his leisure moments had been spent in examining the various religions of the world, and that this was the conclusion he had come to. Some one observed that in Kentucky everybody was either a bigot or an atheist. He replied that it was pretty much the same all the world over."

It is scarcely necessary to say that random conversational utterances, given without their context, and copied without even sequence of dates, are not to be taken as the measure of a great man's thought on the most solemn of all subjects. Mr.

Adams always professed himself a Christian, and was a constant attendant at church. His son, John Quincy Adams, when asked about his father's religious belief, used to tell this anecdote. John Adams was once visiting a town in Spain, where the archbishop, wishing to do him all honor, took him through the cathedral. During their inspection they came upon a shrine where some relics were being exhibited by the priest in attendance. At the sight of these holy remains, the archbishop and those about him bowed their heads and made the sign of the cross upon their foreheads. Mr. Adams, however, did not think it necessary to imitate this act of devotion. *"Comment!"* exclaimed the shocked custodian, in French, to his superior. *"Est-ce que Monsieur n'est pas Chrétien?"* Such a question relating to a guest to whom the archbishop was doing the honors was a little awkward. But the prelate was not disconcerted. He replied promptly and with a smile, *"Oui, à sa manière,"* — "Yes, in his own way." And, in the judgment of his son, this happy hit of the ecclesiastic was the best possible answer that could be made to the question. Mr. Adams was in the habit of speaking his mind with freedom upon the narrow views and bitter temper which were then too common among sects. He would tell a story which he has written out in a letter to Dr. Bancroft. A gentleman, being called upon to give to some missionary fund, confronted the man with the subscription book with this expression of his views: "There are in and about the town of —— ministers of nine congregations. Not one of them lives on terms of civility with any other, will admit none other into his pulpit, nor be permitted to go into the pulpit of any other. Now, if you will raise a fund to convert these nine clergymen to Christianity, I will contribute as much as any man." To conclude this subject, I will give a remark of John Adams, which made a great impression upon the lady to whom it was addressed, and which has lately been recalled to my remembrance. In 1820 Judge Cranch, a near relative of the President, lost two lovely daughters. The lady I refer to visited Mr. Adams, to express her sympathy, and said, among other things, that she feared the father would hardly be able to support such a loss. The old gentleman looked her in the face, and replied slowly, in a tone of rebuke and with great vigor of emphasis, "*Madam, I suppose Judge Cranch is a Christian!*"

"*October* 30, 1824. — After an early dinner, rode to Quincy, to see President Adams and keep his eighty-ninth birthday with him. I scarcely ever saw him look better or converse with more spirit. He spoke of Monday's election, and was especially rejoiced that all parties looked with such affection and confidence to our present form of government. What might be the state of things hereafter, when our territory and population increased, he said he could not tell; but he evidently had apprehensions. Finally, he said he would console himself with the reflection of an old woman he mentioned. This was that God was always above the devil."

"*February* 14, 1825. — Rode to Quincy with my

mother, to visit the President and to congratulate him on the election of his son. He appeared in good spirits, but was considerably affected by the fulfilment of his highest wishes. In the course of conversation, my mother compared him to that old man who was pronounced by Solon to be the happiest of mortals when he expired on hearing of his son's success at the Olympic Games. The similarity of their situations visibly moved the old gentleman, and tears of joy rolled down his cheek. Notwithstanding this he afterward said: 'No man who ever held the office of President would congratulate a friend on obtaining it. He will make one man ungrateful and a hundred men his enemies for every office he can bestow.'"

I now turn back to 1822, and make my concluding extract from the diary of October 30. "Visited the President in the morning; and, after writing a letter to Mathew Carey from his dictation, conversed with him on several literary subjects. Speaking of Cicero's treatise 'De Senectute,' he said that he read it every year. He declared Cato was quite a Christian in feeling when he says, 'Si quis deus mihi largiatur, ut ex hac ætate repuerascam et in cunis vagiam, valde recusem : nec verò velim, quasi decurso spatio, ad carceres a calce revocari.' The President recommended Cicero and Pliny as models of literary style, and a letter written to Lord Mansfield by — the name I cannot recall. He thought Lord Bolingbroke's 'Patriot King' was serviceable to public speakers. I do not admire Bolingbroke as much as he does; probably from want of taste. I read to him the last part of the 'Senectute,' where the orator combats the idea that the near approach of death is an evil. When I reached the passage where Cicero anticipates his reunion with those he had known and his meeting with those of whom he had read, the old gentleman became much excited and exclaimed: 'That is just as I feel. Nothing would tempt me to go back. I agree with my old friend, Dr. Franklin, who used to say on this subject, "We are all invited to a great entertainment. Your carriage comes first to the door; but we shall all meet there."' Who would think such an old age a burden, honored in this world and hoping soon to depart for a better, where he believes he shall meet not only the friends he has lost, but all the great and good who have gone before him?"

This last extract fairly represents the prevailing mood of mind of John Adams during his closing years.

TALKS WITH JOHN ADAMS.

I WILL make a few more extracts from my journal which report the conversation of the second President.

"*Sunday, September* 16, 1821.—Dr. Porter preached all day; in the morning from Job vii. 1, and in the afternoon from Ezekiel xxxiii. 13. He is quite a good preacher and seemingly alive to the doctrines he inculcates. He called to see us after church. In the evening my father and myself went, as usual, to President Adams's. There we found J. Q. Adams, and my father had a long discussion with the President and his son upon the hopes and benefits of peace. J. Q. Adams opposed the idea that war in the abstract was wicked, for in every war one side must be right. He said: 'I consider an unjust war as the greatest of all human atrocities; but I esteem a just one as the highest of all human virtues. War calls into exercise the highest feelings and powers of man. Alexander, Cæsar, and the Crusades were the great causes of civilization. If an army could march into the heart of Africa and wage war there for twenty years, we might hope that civilization and religion would be the consequences.' The old President said that he considered wars and battles as he did storms and hurricanes. They were the necessary evils of nature, which in the end worked for good. He thought that human society, like the ocean, needed commotion to keep it from putrefying. 'For my own part,' he exclaimed, 'I should not like to live in the Millennium. It would be the most sickish life imaginable.' Both the gentlemen were of the opinion that wars increased population. In this connection the old gentleman told a story of the great Condé. After a battle, in which he had lost twenty thousand and the enemy thirty thousand men, he was walking over the field, with his staff, and observed several of his officers weeping. Upon asking them the cause, they replied that they could not help feeling sadly for the thousands of their fellow-creatures lying dead around. 'Oh! is that all?' said the general. 'Depend upon it that Paris will restore the balance again in a single night.' My father defended his Peace Society, on the ground of the amelioration in the condition of mankind that peace would bring to pass. Finally, he got the two gentlemen into a dispute over the merits of Alexander the Great. He then rose and left them at loggerheads; saying, as he went out, much to their amusement, 'You see I have conquered by dividing the enemies of peace.'"

The social life in Quincy in those simple days did not necessitate late hours, as will be seen from my entry two days after this conversation. "We came home from Mrs. Black's at the orthodox hour of nine. This is such a standing time for breaking up in

Quincy that the very horses know the impropriety of staying a moment later. Mrs. Black's horse, for instance, the moment the nine o'clock bell rings, always sets off and goes home, whether anybody is in the carriage or not; but he never pretends to stir without that warning."

"*October* 10, 1822. — Spent a couple of hours this forenoon in writing for the President. He keeps copies of all the letters he writes, and told me that he had done so for most of his life. On returning from the debates in Congress, he frequently had to sit up till after midnight to copy letters. 'Nothing but the independence of my country,' he said, 'would have tempted me to labor as I have done.' He talked very freely of some of his contemporaries, and may have been prejudiced in his views. He accused Judge ——— of duplicity and of glorying in it, and gave an anecdote, by way of example. He thought, with Dr. Johnson, that Voltaire was the most correct and interesting of historians. Speaking of himself, he said: 'They say I am vain. Thank God I am so. Vanity is the cordial drop which makes the bitter cup of life go down. I agree with Mrs. Elizabeth Montague, who wrote to her uncle, the Bishop, to inquire whether the text "All is vanity and vexation of spirit" was not badly translated. She thought it ought to be "All is vanity *or* vexation of spirit." She implied that what was not vanity was sure to be vexation, and there I am with her.'"

And here my own reports of the conversation of Mr. Adams come to an end. I am, however, permitted to continue the subject by copying a few extracts from the diary of my sister, who was in the habit of keeping a daily record of events.

"*May* 22, 1821. — President Adams paid us a morning visit of two hours. Said he had been reading the history of the Fronde. He talked of Queen Elizabeth, and said he thought she was obliged to put Mary to death. She had three questions to ask herself: Shall I sacrifice my own life, the Protestant religion, and the laws of England? Self-preservation, religion, and law required the death of the Scottish Queen. Mary's family and education were bad and corrupted her character, and she transmitted them to her descendants. He advised the reading of Rapin's History of England, saying that Hume and Smollett were to be read only for their style, as you would read a poem like the 'Iliad.' Rapin is an impartial historian. If you cannot read his whole history, at least read the reign of Elizabeth. Hume and Smollett are party historians. Of Dr. Johnson's 'Rasselas,' he said that he did not like its tendency. It gave a false estimate of human life. He mentioned that Bishop Butler's sermons were always upon his table, and said of Pascal's 'Provincial Letters' that it was one of the most perfect books ever written."

"*June* 17, 1822. — Mr. Adams called to see us, and read a letter he had just received from Jefferson. He was asked to explain why he was now on such good terms with Jefferson and received such affectionate letters from him, after the abuse with which he had been loaded by that gentleman. He replied:

'I do not believe that Mr. Jefferson ever hated me. On the contrary, I believed he always liked *me;* but he detested Hamilton and my whole administration. Then he wished to be President of the United States, and I stood in his way. So he did everything that he could to pull me down. But if I should quarrel with him for that, I might quarrel with every man I have had anything to do with in life. This is human nature. Did you never hear the lines

"I love my friend as well as you,
But why should he obstruct my view?"

I forgive all my enemies and hope they may find mercy in heaven. Mr. Jefferson and I have grown old and retired from public life. So we are upon our ancient terms of good-will.'"

"*June* 9, 1823. — Old Mr. Adams and his son visited us, and the former talked a great deal. He was asked why we heard so little of Mr. Dickinson, the author of the 'Farmer's Letters' and one of the signers of the Declaration. 'He became discouraged,' replied Mr. Adams, 'and for some time was one of the most violent opposers of the Declaration of Independence. He had a wife and a mother who were both Quakers, and they tormented him exceedingly, telling him that he was ruining himself and his country by the course he was pursuing. If I had had such a mother and such a wife, I believe I should have shot myself. If they had opposed me, it would have made me so very unhappy. I could not have lived had I not pursued the course I did. One day in Congress, Mifflin, a relative of Dickinson, had a dispute with him. Dickinson had said, in the course of a speech, that, in driving a team of horses, it was necessary to rein in the most forward and to encourage the slow and lagging. Mifflin got up and said, "Not so, Mr. President. You had better knock the dull and lazy horses on the head and put them out of the team. It will go on much better without them." The circumstances of his family and his own timidity made Dickinson take the course he did. He was a man of immense property and founded a college in Pennsylvania.' Speaking of Washington, Mr. Adams said that his character stood upon a firm basis of integrity and must always remain unassailable. He doubted, however, whether he was so great a statesman as was popularly supposed. He said: 'Washington died very rich, but gained his property in a fair way, — by inheritance from his father, who was a man of large fortune; by the legacy of Mount Vernon from his brother; by his wife, who was the widow of a man of fortune. Then he made a good deal of money in his youth, when he was surveying in the woods. The Farewell Address to the people of the United States was, I think, written by himself, and then given to Hamilton and Jay. Hamilton read it, no doubt; but I think that Jay finally drew it up and finished it. I know that it has been attributed to Hamilton; but it is not in his style. It is in Jay's style.' Mr. Adams talked on for two hours. He told us how Judge Edmund Quincy knocked down a robber whom he met while travelling from Braintree to Boston. In lifting up his cane to illustrate the deed, the old gentleman nearly demolished a picture which hung just behind him. When he rose to go, he said, 'If I was to come here once a day, I should live half a year longer.' The reply was made: 'You had much better come twice a day, and live a year longer.' He said the suggestion was a good one, and that he would return again in the afternoon."

"*June* 12, 1823. — Mr. Adams called, and appeared rather feeble, saying that he had never known so cold a spring. He spoke of Mr. Quincy's popularity in Boston. I said, 'It is not to be depended upon.' 'No,' said Mr. Adams, 'it is not. In 1769, when Colonel Quincy, his grandfather, was a member from Braintree of a Convention of the Province, he made several speeches, and in one of them he said, "When I was a young man I courted Popularity. I found her but a coy mistress, and I soon deserted her." Now I am quite of his opinion. Madame Popularity is as whimsical as a girl in her teens.' He talked of the 'Pioneers,' by Cooper, and said it had merit as a description of the country, but had the usual tendency of all the Middle and Southern States to depreciate New England. 'Our ancestors, the Puritans,' continued Mr. Adams, 'were a most unpopular set of men; yet the world owes all the liberty it possesses to them. Mr. Hume acknowledges that this is so. The world owes more to the Puritans than to any other sect.'"

During 1825 Gilbert Stuart, the famous artist, came to Quincy to paint the portrait of John Adams, then in his eighty-ninth year. And this portrait is a remarkable work; for a faithful representation of the extreme age of the subject would have been painful in inferior hands. But Stuart caught a glimpse of the living spirit shining through the feeble and decrepit body. He saw the old man at one of those happy moments when the intelligence lights up its wasted envelope, and what he saw he fixed upon his canvas. And the secret of the artist's success was revealed in a remark which Mr. Adams made to me, while the sittings were in progress. "Speaking generally," said he, "no penance is like having one's picture done. You must sit in a constrained and unnatural position, which is a trial to the temper. But I should like to sit to Stuart from the first of January to the last of December, for he lets me do just what I please and keeps me constantly amused by his conversation." The method of Stuart is given in these few words. It was his habit to throw his subject off his guard, and then, by his wonderful powers of conversation, he would call up different emotions in the face he was studying. He chose the best or that which he thought most characteristic, and with the skill of genius used it to animate the picture.

It may be worth while to mention that I myself have sat to the artist to whom we are indebted for the likeness of Washington, and that, as I believe, I am the only person living who has had that privilege. The way it happened was rather peculiar, for I did not sit for my own portrait. Stuart was engaged in painting the likeness of a person deceased, who was connected with the Revolution and to whom it was said that I bore some resemblance; and it was owing to this circumstance that the sittings came about. He used certain of my features as parts of the material from which a likeness was to be evolved. The artist took snuff constantly, and talked with as much spirit as if he had some important personage to entertain. He gave me a very interesting account of his early struggles in London, and of his being suddenly lifted into fame by the exhibition of a single picture. I well remember the dramatic force he threw into his anecdotes. One of them, I remember, related to an Irishman who had acquired a castle by a fortunate speculation, and thereupon sent for Stuart to paint the portraits of his ancestors. The painter naturally supposed that there were miniatures or drawings, whose authority he was to follow; but, on arriving at the castle, he was told, to his great surprise, that nothing of the kind existed. "Then how the deuce am I going to paint your ancestors, if you have no ancestors?" asked Stuart with some temper. "Nothing easier," rejoined the proprietor. "Go to work and paint such ancestors as I *ought* to have had." The artist relished the joke, and, setting to work, produced a goodly company of knights in armor, judges in bushy wigs, and high-born ladies with nosegays and lambs. "And the man was so delighted with 'his ancestors who came after him,'" remarked Stuart, aptly quoting the saying of Shakespeare's *Slender*, "that he paid me twice what he agreed to." Notwithstanding this stroke of fortune, Stuart complained bitterly of the meagre compensation received by artists. "I get fair prices for my pictures," said he; "but the man who works with his hands can never become rich. A grocer will make more by buying a cargo of molasses in a day than my labor can bring me in a year."

Stuart, it may be said, was naturally improvident, as so many artists of genius have been. His pictures now command enormous prices. A few copies of his Washington, for which he received one hundred dollars, are now said to be worth three thousand dollars each.

THE OLD PRESIDENT IN PUBLIC.

I FIND in my journals notices of the appearance of John Adams in public upon two occasions. The first of these was the Massachusetts Convention of 1820. The District of Maine, which had long been part of Massachusetts, wished to set up an independent government; and this assembly was convened to make the necessary changes in an instrument which President Adams had drafted some forty years before. It was felt to be the last time that the venerable statesman would appear in public. He had been sent as a delegate by his native town, and the interest excited by his entrance was very great. He had declined the presidency of the convention, which, as a matter of compliment, was unanimously offered him. He was then eighty-six years old, and too infirm to discharge the duties of this office. Representative bodies at that time wore their hats during session, after the manner of the British Parliament; but every head was uncovered when the delegate from Quincy was conducted to a seat reserved for him on the right of Chief Justice Parker, who, on the refusal of Mr. Adams, had been chosen to preside. I note in my journal that the scene recalled a print of the Roman Senate, with the two consuls presiding in august dignity. And the assembly was as remarkable as any convened in the best days of the ancient republics. It was composed of men of the very first eminence, the flower of the State at a time when Massachusetts possessed more men of distinguished ability than at any other period in her history.

I heard Mr. Adams speak on one of the few occasions when he ventured to do so. The subject had to do with universal suffrage, as opposed to a property qualification; and upon this question he took what would now be thought the wrong side. But the old gentleman had then, as always, the courage of his opinions. He gave us a graphic sketch of the horrors of the French Revolution, which frightened so many of the best Americans of his generation, and finished by declaring that when our ancestors made a pecuniary qualification necessary for office and necessary for electors, they were supported by the opinion of all the wise men the world had produced. This interesting subject was fully debated in the convention; and it must be confessed that the arguments in favor of retaining the restriction, which limited suffrage to those possessing property to the amount of two hundred dollars, have not been weakened by subsequent history. It is worth while to do justice to the champions of this lost cause by saying that they never for a moment admitted that a small property qualification gave the rich an undue weight in legislation. They asserted, on the contrary, that, were rich men to act selfishly and as a class, they would remove all restrictions. It was the poor man, who had laboriously earned the two hundred dollars, who lost his political all when those who had no stake whatever in the community were admitted to vote him down. The rich man, by the influence resulting from his property over those who had nothing to lose and everything to gain from his favor, would make himself master of the situation. Has not our later political history in a measure justified these prophecies? Of course, there was much said (and it was well said) in the convention in favor of unlimited suffrage; and there is no use in reopening a question which has been forever decided. But it is simply just to John Adams, and to those who stood with him, that the chief reason of their opposition should be understood. It was to secure a genuine representation of the poor against the usurpations of the rich that they wished to impose a small pecuniary qualification upon voters. It is perhaps better that they should have failed, if we, now realizing the danger that they pointed out, shall hasten to remove all obstacles which prevent a man of reasonable industry from acquiring an independent home. Who can doubt that if those statesmen were with us to-day, they would tell us that this was the way to mitigate and finally abolish the evils which they foresaw?

The other occasion when I heard President Adams speak in public was during the visit of the West Point Cadets. This was an event of considerable magnitude at the time. The noble corps, numbering more than two hundred students, had marched all the way to Boston. Indeed, at that time this was the only way to come if they came at all. A fine band accompanied them, and they were treated with marked hospitality in every town through which they passed. We cannot wonder at the interest they excited. Here was a military corps, splendidly equipped and composed of the most promising young men in the country. The training at West Point was then far superior to any given at the colleges, and these young gentlemen were known to be subjected to an intellectual discipline which was quite as severe as their physical drill. The selectmen of Boston, attended by a cavalcade of citizens, went to meet their visitors at the boundary of the town. Salutes of artillery were fired as the Cadets crossed the line, and they were conducted to their camp on the Common with due ceremony. These young Hannibals were said to have found their Capua in the staid Puritan town. It may now be admitted that the infatuation about them was carried to an extreme. A stand of colors, bearing the motto *A scientia ad gloriam*, was solemnly voted them in town meeting, and presented by the selectmen with much *éclat*. Never was heard such martial music as was produced by their band; never were the capabilities of the bugle understood until the leading musician of the company performed upon that instrument. Governor Brooks, a capital judge of tactual merit, declared that their drill was perfect. Major Worth, their commander, was a very handsome man, and seemed to the ladies an ideal soldier, as there can be little doubt that he was. In short, the Cadets captivated us; and dinners, public collations, and entertainments of all sorts only did justice to our feelings. One day the corps marched to Cambridge, where the authorities of the college provided them with a banquet in Commons Hall. On another occasion they went to Bunker Hill, and Major Worth's marquee was pitched on the angle of the redoubt thrown up during the night previous to the famous battle. A visit to the venerated statesman of Quincy was, of course, included in the programme. The occasion was one of great interest, and I find an account of it in my journal; but the reader will thank me for suppressing my own narrative, and supplying its place with an extract from the diary of my sister, who was present at the scene, and which I am allowed the privilege of copying.

"*August* 14, 1821. — To-day the Cadets visited President Adams, and we passed them on the road to his residence. Major Worth, who rode a fine horse, recognized and saluted us. Our coachman, seeing the little fifer of the band running along the road, told him to get up behind the carriage, which he did; and our military footman excited some attention. Mr. Adams received us with his accustomed kindness. The Cadets halted at the foot of the hill to refresh themselves at the brook, after their seven-miles walk from Boston. They then formed in order and marched past the house, with their colors flying and the band playing. They went through their exercises in the field opposite, and then stacked their arms and marched into the courtyard. Mr. Adams stood on the piazza, with the Cadets before him and Major Worth at his side. The contrast between the venerable old man and the handsome young officer, in the prime of life, was very striking. His voice trembled as he began to speak, but as he proceeded it grew stronger. He began by saying that, although palsied by age, he would not deny himself the pleasure of addressing them. He spoke of real glory, and held up the character of Washington to the admiration and imitation of the young men before him. He assured them that their advantages of education should give them knowledge of much more than military tactics. He made a very excellent speech. When it was finished, the Cadets went to a collation arranged under an awning, at the side of the courtyard. After this, they threw themselves on the grass under the shade of the horse-chestnuts, and many of them were so fatigued that, notwithstanding the loud talking, they fell asleep. We showed Major Worth the portraits of the Adams family, in the drawing-room, and also that of General Warren. The Major combines a polished exterior with the severity of a rigid disciplinarian; his men feel that his slightest word has the force of an irrevocable decree. Mr. Adams took his seat with the ladies on the piazza, and the new standards presented by the authorities of the Town of Boston were displayed before us. The national flag is painted on a dark ground, and is never lowered except to the President of the United States. The regimental standard is painted on a white ground, with a figure of Minerva and various appropriate devices. Major Worth, wishing to exhibit the standards to the best advantage, ordered a Cadet to hold them up. The young man obeyed, and, thinking he must not move without orders, continued to stand like a statue long after the ladies and Mr. Adams had finished their survey. It was observed, however, that he made out to hold them so that he could see the ladies over them. Speaking of the presentation of colors yesterday, Major Worth said, 'I never felt my courage so severely tried as in making that speech to the Governor. I had much rather fight a battle; but, now the colors are in our hands, they shall never leave them.' He then made an unsuccessful attempt to induce Moniac, the Indian Cadet, to be introduced to Mr. Adams and the ladies. At last he gave this up, saying, 'He is too bashful.' He added: 'I have myself been taken for the Indian all along the road. People would point to me and say, 'Look there! there's the Indian!' The standards were now crossed in front of the piazza, and the band under the chestnut-tree played charmingly, giving us 'Adams and Liberty,' and other patriotic airs. Mr. Adams beat time to the music, and seemed as much delighted as any one. The Cadets were then drawn up and introduced to Mr. Adams by the officers of their respective companies. They passed over the piazza one by one, and Mr. Adams shook hands with each of them. It was very interesting to watch the varied expressions of their countenances. When they took leave, Mr. Adams put into the hands of Major

Worth a copy of his address, in his own handwriting, for which the Major said a cabinet should be made at West Point. The Cadets returned to the field opposite, where they had stacked their arms, and went through various military movements before they marched off. They were to proceed to Milton, where an entertainment was to be given them by Mr. R. Smith, in the old mansion of Governor Hutchinson. It was altogether a most interesting occasion. President Adams seemed highly gratified, and it was delightful to us to see the honors attending his old age."

Of one more act of a public nature performed by Mr. Adams I find the record. This was the generous gift of one hundred and sixty acres of land to his native town, for the purpose of establishing an academy. The deeds by which this property was conveyed were executed at my father's house, and my name appears as a witness to the documents. At the time that it was made, this endowment promised to be of greater value than it has yet turned out. No property seemed to be of more certain worth than farming lands near a large and growing centre of population. Who imagined that men then living would see the time when the food for Boston would be brought from the distant West; when a ton of produce could be moved at a cost of eight tenths of a cent per mile, and a year's subsistence could be carried one thousand miles to the laborer at the price of his wages for a single day! Not having these anticipations, the townsmen of Mr. Adams could not conceive that a half-century must elapse before a " stone school-house" could be built from the profits of the pastures which had been given for this purpose. It is only recently that the academy has risen on the site its founder designated. This was over the cellar of the house in which Governor Hancock was born; better known as that John Hancock whose name, written with such vigorous penmanship, heads the Declaration of Independence. In the deeds by which he conveyed this property the President did not confine himself to those dry technicalities which make such instruments the dreariest of literature, but said his mind freely and with characteristic strength. His old friend, Hancock, is designated as "that generous, disinterested, bountiful benefactor of his country." Lemuel Bryant, pastor of the First Church, is described as "reverend, learned, disinterested, and eloquent." His suggestions to the future masters of the academy are quaint enough to be quoted: —

"But I hope the future masters will not think me too presumptuous if I advise them to begin their lessons in Greek and Hebrew by compelling their pupils to take their pens and write, over and over again, copies of the Greek and Hebrew alphabets, in all their variety of characters, until they are perfect masters of those alphabets and characters. This will be as good an exercise in chirography as any they can use, and will stamp those characters and alphabets upon their tender minds and vigorous memories so deeply that the impression will never wear out."

New methods in education have undoubtedly superseded those in vogue in the time of President Adams; but the school that he generously founded is likely to adopt all the modern improvements. The late Dr. William R. Dimmock — one of the best teachers our country has produced — was its first master, and he gave six years of absorbing labor to the service. His was the important work of establishing the traditions of the school; and his gracious figure stands upon the background of its past like that of Dr. Arnold at Rugby. His successor was Dr. William Everett, of whose self-sacrificing devotion to the academy it is, happily, not yet time to speak.

In the cemeteries about Boston there are placed beside many of the monuments iron plates with the words "Perpetual Care" cast upon them in the most durable fashion. The Adams Academy — the worthiest monument of the distinguished friend of my youth — bears no similar inscription. Heaven forbid that such a reminder should be necessary for any citizen of his native town!

"ECLIPSE" AGAINST THE WORLD.

ON the 27th of May, 1823, nearly fifty-seven years ago, there was a great excitement in the city of New York, for on that day the long-expected race of "*Eclipse* against the world" was to be decided on the race-course on Long Island. It was an amicable contest between the North and the South. The New York votaries of the turf — a much more prominent interest than at present — had offered to run *Eclipse* against any horse that could be produced, for a purse of $10,000; and the Southern gentlemen had accepted the challenge. I could obtain no carriage to take me to the course, as every conveyance in the city was engaged. Carriages of every description formed an unbroken line from the ferry to the ground. They were driven rapidly, and were in very close connection; so much so that when one of them suddenly stopped, the poles of at least a dozen carriages broke through the panels of those preceding them. The drivers were naturally much enraged at this accident; but it seemed a necessary consequence of the crush and hurry of the day, and nobody could be blamed for it. The party that I was with, seeing there was no chance of riding, was compelled to foot it. But after plodding some way, we had the luck to fall in with a returning carriage, which we chartered to take us to the course. On arriving, we found an assembly which was simply overpowering; it was estimated that there were over one hundred thousand persons upon the ground. The conditions of the race were four-mile heats, the best two in three; the course was a mile in length. A college friend, the late David P. Hall, had procured for me a ticket for the jockey-box, which commanded a view of the whole field. There was great difficulty in clearing the track, until *Eclipse* and *Sir Henry* (the Southern horse) were brought to the stand. They were both in brave spirits, throwing their heels high into the air; they soon effected that scattering of the multitude which all other methods had failed to accomplish. And now a great disappointment fell, like a wet blanket, on more than half the spectators. It was suddenly announced that Purdy, the jockey of *Eclipse*, had had a difficulty with his owner and refused to ride. To substitute another in his place seemed almost like giving up the contest; but the man was absolutely stubborn, and the time had come. Another rider was provided, and the signal for the start was given. I stood exactly opposite the judges' seat, where the mastering excitement found its climax. Off went the horses, every eye straining to follow them. Four times they dashed by the judges' stand, and every time *Sir Henry* was on the lead. The spirits of the Southerners seemed to leap up beyond control, while the depression of the more phlegmatic North set in like a physical chill. Directly before me sat John Randolph, the great orator of Virginia; a man to be noticed more particularly in a succeeding paper. Apart from his intense sectional pride, he had personal reasons to rejoice at the turn things were taking; for he had bet heavily on the contest, and, it was said, proposed to sail for Europe upon clearing enough to pay his expenses. Half an hour elapsed for the horses to get their wind, and again they were brought to the stand. But now a circumstance occurred which raised a deafening shout from the partisans of the North. Purdy was to ride. How his scruples had been overcome did not appear, but there he stood before us, and was mounting *Eclipse*. Again, amidst breathless suspense, the word "Go!" was heard, and again *Sir Henry* took the inside track, and kept the lead for more than two miles and a half. *Eclipse* followed close on his heels and, at short intervals, attempted to pass. At every spurt he made to get ahead, Randolph's high-pitched and penetrating voice was heard each time shriller than before: "You can't do it, Mr. Purdy! You can't do it, Mr. Purdy! You can't do it, Mr. Purdy!" But Mr. Purdy *did* do it. And as he took the lead what a roar of excitement went up! Tens of thousands of dollars were in suspense, and although I had not a cent depending, I lost my breath, and felt as if a sword had passed through me. Purdy kept the lead and came in a length or so ahead. The horses had run eight miles, and the third heat was to decide the day. The confidence on the part of the Southern gentlemen was abated. The manager of *Sir Henry* rode up to the front of our box and, calling to a gentleman, said, "You must ride the next heat; there are hundreds of thousands of Southern money depending on it. That boy don't know how to ride; he don't keep his horse's mouth open!" The gentleman positively refused, saying that he had not been in the saddle for months. The manager begged him to come down, and John Randolph was summoned to use his eloquent persuasions. When the horses were next brought to the stand, behold the gentleman appeared, booted and spurred, with a red jacket on his back, and a jockey cap on his head. On the third heat *Eclipse* took the lead and, by dint of constant whipping and spurring, won by a length this closely contested race.

There was never contest more exciting. Sectional feeling and heavy pecuniary stakes were both involved. The length of time before it was decided, the change of riders, the varying fortunes, all intensified the interest. I have seen the great Derby races; but they finish almost as soon as they begin, and were tame enough in comparison to this. Here for nearly two hours there was no abatement in the strain. I was unconscious of everything else, and found, when the race was concluded, that the sun had actually blistered my cheek without my perceiving it. The victors were of course exultant, and Purdy, mounted on *Eclipse*, was led up to the judges' stand; the band playing "See the Conquering Hero comes." The Southerners bore their losses like gentlemen, and with a good grace. It was suggested that the comparative chances of Adams and Jackson at the approaching Presidential election should be tested by a vote of that gathering. "Ah," said Mr. Randolph, "if the question of the Presidency could be settled by this assembly there would be no opposition; Mr. Purdy would go to the White House by acclamation."

I have thus endeavored to describe, from my journal of that period, the first great contest between the North and the South,—a contest in which the grandfathers of many of my readers were deeply interested. It seems to have foreshadowed the sterner conflict that occurred forty years afterwards. The victory resulted in both cases from the same cause,—the power of endurance. It was, in the language of the turf, bottom against speed. The North had no braver men than were found in the Confederate ranks; it had no abler generals than Lee and Jackson. It had only greater resources. Let us hope that, as on the former occasion, the gentlemen of the South will acquiesce in a result that neither valor nor skill could avert, and that, uniting their spirit with the resources and energy of the North, we shall together advance the virtue, prosperity, and glory of our common country.

LAFAYETTE IN BOSTON.

THE visit of General Lafayette to America, nearly fifty years after the foundation of the nation which he had so generously assisted, was an event to which the world's history can furnish no parallel. The great experiment of self-government was held to be a triumphant success. Our population and prosperity had increased beyond all precedent, and our navy bore our flag over every sea. It was as if one of the dead heroes of the past, to whom the indebtedness of mankind is always acknowledged, were to be reanimated to receive the gratitude of a living world. Never was the benefactor of a people awarded a homage so universal, so spontaneous, so heartfelt, so intelligent. There are, doubtless, men living, past their threescore and ten years, who as school-boys hung upon the outskirts of the crowds which surrounded the hero. But of the grown men who occupied official positions during the visits of Lafayette to Boston, and were on this account brought into personal contact with him, I believe that I am the sole survivor. As *aide-de-camp* to the Governor of Massachusetts, I stood at the side of Lafayette on that memorable occasion when he laid the corner-stone of the monument on Bunker Hill; and when he left the State I occupied with him the back seat of the carriage, enjoying his conversation and the ovations of the towns through which we passed.

The intelligence of the arrival of Lafayette in the harbor of New York, on the morning of the 15th of August, 1824, spread through that city with a rapidity which our present methods of electrical communication could scarcely have increased. Multitudes poured into the street, in expectation of instantly beholding him. But, at the request of the city authorities, he landed at Staten Island, and waited at the house of the Vice-President till arrangements could be made for his public reception. In a letter now before me, written to my father from Paris, the General had said: "While I profoundly feel the honor intended by the offer of a national ship, I hope I shall incur no blame by the determination I have taken to embark, as soon as it is in my power, on board a private vessel. Whatever port I shall first attain, I shall with the same eagerness hasten to Boston, and present its beloved, revered inhabitants with the homage of my affectionate gratitude and devoted respect." And he remained true to his intention to "hasten to Boston," notwithstanding the urgent desire of the New York committee that he should remain on the island till the 17th, to give them more time to prepare for his reception. His words, as reported at the time, were these: "I cannot remain with you, for I must be in Boston, that I may visit Cambridge on Commencement Day, where I shall meet so many of my old friends. You know my attachment to you *all*. I am heartily glad to see you; but I must immediately visit Boston, and will return to you again." After a magnificent reception from the Empire City, Lafayette left for Boston on the 20th of August, attended by a numerous civil and military escort. As he proceeded on his way, the whole country rose to behold and welcome him. Every town and village through which he passed was ornamented or illuminated, and every testimony of gratitude and affection which imagination could devise was offered to the nation's guest.

On Tuesday, the 24th of August, as an officer of the Boston Light Infantry, I appeared on the Common at seven o'clock. About eight we proceeded to the Neck, to meet the General, who had spent the night at the seat of Governor Eustis, in Roxbury. The military was accompanied by a cavalcade of some twelve hundred horsemen. Of these the carters and woodwharfingers of the city, dressed in frocks of snowy whiteness, were very conspicuous. They had the effect of mounted priests; and, being priests of useful labor, which had built up the community, they were, no doubt, as honorable and useful as if they had received ecclesiastical ordination. At the city line, where we had a good wait, we were furnished with bread and cheese, at the expense of the municipality, and (*credite posteri!*) with free punch. The excellent Dr. Miner had not then arrived upon the scene, and we had no one to tell us that the provision of this seductive fluid was an unwarrantable employment of the city funds. Had any one proposed to provide free books at the expense of the taxpayers, there would have been much indignation. We should have been aghast at the impudence of such a proposal; but a few glasses of punch was another matter. We have changed our views here in Boston since those good old times, and changed them much for our advantage.

The first sight we caught of the General, as he drove up to the line in an open barouche, drawn by four white horses, awakened an enthusiasm which I shall not attempt to describe. The remarkable history of the man, which the events of a stirring half-century have now obliterated from the general mind, was then fresh and well known. He had sounded all the depths and shoals of honor. He had passed from every enjoyment that wealth and royal favor could bestow, to poverty and a dungeon. No novelist would dare to imagine the rapid vicissitudes which had marked his life since he had left America. Here he had joined our fathers in their glorious contest for liberty. He had freely given us his money and his blood. This was an exceptional republic which he had established. It would spurn the heartless proverb, and show itself not ungrateful.

We took up the line of march in inverted order, and, for some reason, it came to pass that I led the procession, though my military rank did not entitle me to this distinction. We passed through immense throngs, with all the noise that bells, cannon, and human lungs were capable of producing. Every countenance fairly beamed with admiration. Every one wore a Lafayette badge stamped upon blue ribbon. Here is mine, fastened upon the page of the journal which records these events. It is a little faded, but otherwise is in excellent preservation. Among the decorations I remember an arch thrown across Washington Street, inscribed with this stanza, written by Charles Sprague: —

> "Our fathers in glory shall sleep
>   That gathered with thee to the fight;
> But their sons will eternally keep
>   The tablet of gratitude bright.
> We bow not the neck and we bend not the knee,
> But our hearts, Lafayette, we surrender to thee."

The poet here hit upon the right word. It was a *surrender*, complete and without conditions. It was universal; for the population of Boston was then homogeneous and American, and the cultivated classes of our somewhat stiff and exclusive city led the wild enthusiasm of the streets. When we reached the State House, the officers of the militia were presented to Lafayette; and here I had the honor of beginning such acquaintance with the hero as a young man, totally obscure, may have with an illustrious personage of history. The same evening I met him in private at my father's house, and had the privilege of listening to his conversation with the older members of the family. George Washington Lafayette accompanied his father, with M. Levasseur, his secretary, and Colonel Colden, of New York. I fear I was too busy in committing the Latin oration that I was to give the next day to take much note of what was said. I had been on my feet since sunrise, in the character of a soldier, and must be prepared to put on a gown and talk Latin on the morrow in the character of a scholar; and so my journal shows that I did not feel equal to playing the Boswell, as I really ought to have done. One story told that evening by Dr. Bowditch, the celebrated mathematician, I am able to give. He said that, on his way to his office, whence he intended to view the procession, he was stopped on Washington Street, which he was about to cross. The military escort was passing, and he ascended a flight of steps to wait, in quiet dignity, till the show had gone by. But this was not to be; for the moment he saw Lafayette he declared that he lost all self-command. He seemed to be literally out of his senses; and when he recovered them, it was to find himself struggling with the crowd at the side of the barouche and huzzaing with all his might. Such was the confession of the great Dr. Bowditch. Those who did not have his weight of brains to keep them steady need no excuse for yielding to the excitement of the time.

I have already given some account of the memorable Commencement of Harvard, and of the master's valedictory, which my classmate, Withington, had generously relinquished to me on that occasion. I copy from my journal the entry made at the close of the succeeding day: —

"*August* 26, 1824. — Rode to Cambridge, about nine, to attend the meeting of the Phi Beta Kappa.

The procession of about two hundred members entered the church about twelve. Again Lafayette was before us. The audience was as great as the one which assembled yesterday. Mr. Ware gave a beautiful poem, with the necessary allusions to Lafayette; and then Mr. Everett pronounced an oration which surpassed all I had ever heard. When, toward the conclusion, he alluded to the noble conduct of our guest in procuring a ship for his own transportation, at a time when all America was too poor to offer him a passage to her shores, the scene was overpowering. *Every man in the assembly was in tears."*

I believe that this last expression was literally true. I have heard the great orators of my day at their best; but it was never given to any one of them to lift up an audience as Everett did upon this occasion. I can conceive of nothing more magnificent in the way of oratory. Many who have listened to Mr. Everett's polished periods during the latter part of his life may question the supreme effect he produced. They will say that he was by nature a conservative, seldom in sympathy with the heart of popular feeling, and that there was always a suspicion of a chill upon his matchless rhetoric. I can only say that the words he spoke that day in the venerable church in Cambridge were as full of fire as of music. Robertson, the historian, calls the eloquence of Cicero "a splendid conflagration." To those to whom this term has any meaning, it will give all that language can suggest of the nature of the great oratorical triumph of Edward Everett. It is just possible that among my readers there may be found some venerable man who was present upon that occasion. If so, I confidently appeal to him to say whether I have exaggerated — whether it is possible that I could exaggerate — the magnificent power with which the orator lifted that great assembly. For such a possible reader I cannot resist quoting the language of Everett, to bring back the wonderful scene we witnessed together. Those to whom the following paragraph is only so many printed words will, at least, gather from them the historical interest of the occasion which so unsealed the lips of the most cautious of orators. They may serve to justify the preservation of those reminiscences of the visit of Lafayette which I shall hereafter offer.

"Welcome, friend of our fathers, to our shores! Happy are our eyes that behold those venerable features! Enjoy a triumph such as never conqueror or monarch enjoyed, — the assurance that throughout America there is not a bosom which does not beat with joy and gratitude at the sound of your name. You have already met and saluted, or will soon meet, the few that remain of the ardent patriots, prudent counsellors, and brave warriors with whom you were associated in achieving our liberty. But you have looked round in vain for the faces of many who would have lived years of pleasure on a day like this, with their old companion in arms and brother in peril. Lincoln and Greene, Knox and Hamilton, are gone; the heroes of Saratoga and Yorktown have fallen before the only foe they could not meet.

Above all, the first of heroes and of men, the friend of your youth, the more than friend of his country, rests in the bosom of the soil he redeemed. On the banks of his Potomac he lies in glory and in peace. You will revisit the hospitable shades of Mt. Vernon; but him whom you venerated as we did you will not meet at its door. His voice of consolation, which reached you in the Austrian dungeons, cannot now break its silence, to bid you welcome to his own roof. But the grateful children of America will bid you welcome in his name. Welcome! thrice welcome to our shores! And whithersoever throughout the limits of the continent your course shall take you, the ear that hears you shall bless you, the eye that sees you shall bear witness to you, and every tongue exclaim, with heartfelt joy, Welcome! Welcome! Lafayette!"

The voice of the orator ceased and there was perfect silence. It seemed as if it could never be broken. The lift was altogether too great for immediate applause. When the response came, at last, it was something never to be forgotten.

LAFAYETTE AND COLONEL HUGER.

NOTHING could have been more perfect than the weather of that jubilee week when Boston first welcomed Lafayette. Not a drop of rain descended during the day; but during the night showers were abundant, and these laid the dust and covered the country with verdure. On Sunday it was supposed that the General would attend the Catholic Church. "Oh, no!" said he. "Let me go to Brattle Street Meeting-house and sit in Governor Hancock's pew. There I used to attend the services of my good friend, Dr. Cooper, and I should feel strange in any other place of worship." And there he did go; and the clergyman who preached upon that occasion was the historian of New England, the then Reverend and afterwards Honorable John G. Palfrey. On the afternoon of Sunday, in spite of the Massachusetts statute which made his conduct illegal, the General drove to Quincy, to dine with the venerable John Adams. But, out of respect to the day, the four white horses which drew him about were summarily cut down to two, and it is worth while to notice that from the crowds which assembled to see him pass, in the town of Quincy, there arose no sound of welcome. I mention this fact as an interesting testimony to the respect for the Sabbath that was at that time entertained by a very mixed body of sightseers. Of course, on a week-day no police would have been strong enough to repress the shouting.

The General was to stop to make a friendly visit at my father's house in Quincy, and it was an interesting moment when we saw his carriage driven down the avenue. "I have been at this house before," said Lafayette, after he had greeted us all with his tender French cordiality. "I was here during the Revolutionary War, as the guest of your great-grandfather." And there happened to be a daughter of his former host there present, my great-aunt Storer, then in her ninetieth year. She was much overcome on again meeting Lafayette, and declared that his presence took her back among the trials and sufferings of the Revolution. During this visit my sister has noted, in a journal which she has kindly lent me, that Washington Lafayette talked more than ever before and appeared to better advantage. His manners were not prepossessing, and he generally moved about as if depressed by the gigantic shadow cast by his father. His position was in some respects awkward; but on this occasion he came out of his shell, — at least to the ladies of the family. He confessed to them that he was so affected by the scenes he witnessed and the manner in which his father was received that he had great difficulty in commanding himself. His may have been one of those not uncommon characters whose extreme sensitiveness conceals itself under the mask of indifference. He was not popular; but the opinion of the time very likely did him injustice.

On Monday the reception culminated in a grand militia review, which was finer than anything which had then taken place in Boston. There were two hundred tents on the Common, beside a huge marquee, in which twelve hundred people sat down to dinner. The crowds which flocked in from the country had a peculiarity which moved the astonishment of a gentleman from New York. "Why," said he, "all these people are of one race, and they behave like members of one family; whereas with us a crowd is an assembly of all the nations upon earth." I did military duty for thirteen hours, and when at length allowed to take off my soldier's clothes, attended a brilliant reception given by the General to the ladies of the city. This was held at the house forming the corner of Park and Beacon Streets. The rooms were finely decorated, having, among other interesting objects, pictures of the first five Presidents, all taken by Stuart. But this brilliant scene was not to end the day. "After the reception," to quote from my journal, "I proceeded to Mr. W. H. Eliot's, where I was an active and efficient manager (I will not suppress the egotism) to a most delightful ball. One of the rooms was ornamented with the General's portrait, surrounded by wreaths of flowers. When the original entered, the dancing ceased at once and the band broke into a march."

And so we Boston people received the guest of America, on his first visit to our city, fifty-six years ago. As I shall have something to say of his second visit, on the memorable fiftieth anniversary of the Battle of Bunker Hill, I pass over other incidents to introduce a gallant gentleman, whose name was intimately associated with that of the hero who had won our hearts. During his visit Lafayette once exclaimed, with ardor, in my presence: "There is one man in America whom, of all others, I long to meet, — a man whom I saw but for ten minutes, and this was thirty years ago; but I saw him under circumstances which engraved his countenance forever upon my mind. I count the moments till I can embrace my good friend, Colonel Huger, of South Carolina." This gentleman was well known as the hero of the attempt to rescue Lafayette from the Austrian prison, where he was held during a miserable captivity of more than five years. The General seldom alluded to his prison life. Its details were too shocking to recall. He had been seized for the republican sentiments he was known to profess, and told that he should never leave his narrow and filthy dungeon. He was deprived of the commonest conveniences of life, and for a long time his family and friends could get no evidence of his fate. At length, the physician of the prison made a formal statement to the Austrian Government that the prisoner would die unless he were allowed to breathe a purer air. The petition was returned, indorsed with this official reply: "No; he is not sick enough yet." At length an outcry of public indignation in Europe and America forced his keepers to permit Lafayette to take occasional exercise in a carriage, accompanied by two soldiers. It was during one of these rides that his rescue was attempted. Soon after Lafayette returned to New York, my family received letters from him, introducing the gentleman he had so longed to meet.

The position of a young lawyer whose services are not demanded by numerous clients is rather discouraging. Nevertheless the situation has its advantages, as I found when it appeared that I was the only member of the family who could command the leisure to attend to Colonel Huger. It devolved upon me to drive this interesting person about the environs of Boston, and to introduce him to such gentlemen as he desired to meet. On different occasions we drove in a chaise (in those days there were no four-wheeled vehicles for two persons) to Cambridge, Roxbury, and Charlestown, and visited together Governor Eustis, Governor Brooks, Commodore Bainbridge, John Adams, and other personages of distinction. My companion had all that charm of a high-bred Southerner which wrought such peculiar fascination upon those inheriting Puritan blood. But, besides this, there was his romantic association with the attempted rescue of Lafayette; and Scott's novels, then in the full blossom of their popularity, celebrated no hero whose adventures seemed more chivalrous and thrilling. "I simply considered myself the representative of the young men of America, and acted accordingly," said Huger, modestly, when a lady expressed the feelings of admiration with which he was universally regarded. But there was no false modesty about the man, and upon proper occasions he was willing to tell the story, which every one who met him was desirous to hear. I not only heard him give the narrative more than once, but during our drives had the opportunity of questioning him upon every detail. Moreover, there is a journal before me in which his words were taken down an hour after they were uttered. From these sources I shall be able to record, in a future paper, the story of the attempted rescue substantially as it came from his own lips.

In easy conversation, one day, at my father's table, the Colonel told us something of his history subsequent to this event. He had married a daughter of I. Pinkney, Esq., and soon after purchased an estate on the high hills of Santee, about a hundred miles from Charleston, where he established his family. His wife, though very young, brought up in the gayest society, and even accustomed to the splendor of a court (her father had been our minister to England), accepted the change with cheerfulness. "And here," said Huger, "I have resided ever since, occupied in taking care of my farm and in educating a family of eleven children." He mentioned that the condition of the slaves in the part of Carolina where he lived was much less painful and degrading than on the lowlands by the seaboard. "I am not wealthy," he said, "and am contemplating a further remove toward the mountains. The land there is cheaper and richer, and I may acquire more property to divide among my children." He told us that his visit to the North was solely to meet Lafayette; but, after he had seen him, he felt a desire to see the New England States, and so had come to Boston.

Among the houses to which I took Colonel Huger, none was pleasanter than that of Professor Ticknor. This gentleman, afterward so well known in the world of letters, then enjoyed the distinction of having seen Europe; and in those days this *was* a distinction, almost as great a one as not to have run across the ocean is now. There seemed to be a cosmopolitan spaciousness about his very vestibule. He received company with great ease, and a simple supper was always served to his evening visitors. Prescott, Everett, Webster, Hillard, and other noted Bostonians — well mixed with the pick of such strangers as happened to be in the city — furnished a social entertainment of the first quality. Politics — at least American politics — were never mentioned; but diplomacy, travels, literature, and science furnished inexhaustible topics for conversation. The host was an admirable narrator, and gave his foreign experiences with such spirit that they would stick in the memory. In proof of which, there comes to me a little scene he described at Almack's, the fashionable and exclusive ball-room of London. "I was standing," said Mr. Ticknor, " by Lady Jersey, who was the patroness of the ball. It was past eleven o'clock, and the rule had been made that no one should be admitted after that hour. Suddenly there was a commotion, and word was brought to Lady Jersey that the Duke of Wellington was below and desired to enter. "Tell his Grace," said the Lady, "that I am happy in declining to admit one after whom no one will presume to apply." The story showed that British snobbishness to rank and title was not without its limits, and that a woman who is ready enough may mix a compliment with a refusal that will dull the force of the blow.

I failed to mention that during Lafayette's first visit Mr. Ticknor gave him a supper-party, which was marked by a little ceremony that had quite a foreign grace about it. A likeness of Lafayette, engraved upon bright red paper, was found under the glass by the side of each plate. As the guests seated themselves at the table, every one, except the General, took up the picture and pinned it upon some part of the dress, where it looked like the decoration of a noble order. This arrangement, if I may trust the statement of the journal before me, was devised by M. Wallenstein, a gentleman attached to the Russian legation, and whom John Quincy Adams had pronounced the most intelligent member of the diplomatic corps he ever met in the United States. Though very plain in person, Wallenstein had great personal fascination. I met him frequently about this time, at my father's house, as well as that of Mr. Ticknor. To say that he was an object of interest and attention in Boston even while Lafayette was with us, is to sound his praises to the utmost.

Wallenstein remained some years in this country, published a translation of the letters of Madame de Riedesel, and made hosts of friends. He was afterward transferred to a diplomatic station in South America, where he married a Portuguese lady, and died in 1845.

HOW COLONEL HUGER TOLD THE STORY.

I FULFIL the promise made in my last paper by giving the story of the attempted rescue of Lafayette as told by Colonel Huger when dining at my father's house in Quincy, October 3, 1825. The report, of course, is not stenographic; but as it is chiefly taken from very copious notes made at the time by my sister, Miss E. S. Quincy, the reader may rely upon its substantial accuracy.

"When I first saw Lafayette I was a child three years old. By a singular accident my father's house, on North Island, South Carolina, was the first American roof which sheltered him. Late one night in the year 1776 our family was alarmed by a loud knocking at the door. Fearing an attack of the enemy, we barred our windows and refused admittance. At length we were made to understand that the applicants were the Marquis de la Fayette and the Baron de Kalb. They had taken to their boat, to avoid British cruisers, and had been directed by some of our servants to my father's house. They were of course admitted, with every token of welcome and hospitality, and, accompanied by my father, left after a day's delay for Charleston, from whence they at once proceeded to the American army. Young as I then was, the incident made no distinct impression upon my mind."

After a short pause, Colonel Huger proceeded to the events that led to his second meeting with Lafayette.

"The merit of the contrivance to rescue Lafayette from the Castle at Olmutz belongs not to me, but to Dr. Bollmann. He was a Hanoverian physician, of great courage and address, who had been engaged by friends of Lafayette to discover his prison and attempt his rescue. Bollmann commenced his search in 1793, but for some time could only learn that the Russian Government had given Austria the custody of this dangerous republican, and that he was probably somewhere in that country. The next year, after many ineffectual attempts, he found out that certain French prisoners had been taken to Olmutz, a strong fortress in Moravia. Suspecting Lafayette might be one of them, Bollmann at once repaired to Olmutz, where he managed to make the acquaintance of the military surgeon of the fortress. Representing himself to be a physician, travelling for improvement, he inquired one day, as if from idle curiosity, whether there were any French prisoners in the fortress. 'Oh, yes,' was the reply; 'and Lafayette is among them.' Bollmann then mentioned that he had some French books with him that he would gladly lend this famous prisoner. He was informed that this would be permitted, provided the books were inspected by the proper officer. The books were accordingly sent; but in one of them, upon the margins of separate pages, Bollmann had scrawled words which, when put together, formed the following sentence: '*If you read this book with as much care as that lent your friend at Magdeburg, you will receive equal satisfaction.*' The person referred to had received an account of concerted plans for his escape from prison written in lemon-juice on the blank pages of a book. Lafayette understood the allusion, and, holding the book to the fire, soon deciphered a request to instruct his friends how to attempt his rescue. The book was then returned, and Bollmann, upon examining closely, found the words '*Hold it to the fire*' written upon one of its pages. On obeying the direction, he found that he had been understood. Lafayette informed him that he was frequently allowed to drive for his health, and, as he was personally unknown to Bollmann, he mentioned a signal by which he might be recognized if they should meet. This was all he could say. Everything else was left to the courage and ingenuity of this adventurous doctor. The volume lent and returned was the only communication he ever had with Lafayette.

"A short time after this," continued Colonel Huger, "I met Dr. Bollmann at Vienna, where he confided to me his plans and begged my assistance. I felt it my duty to give him all the aid in my power. We hired a post-chaise and a servant; also two horses, one of them trained to carry double. We then set off for Olmutz, a distance of one hundred and fifty miles. Upon our arrival, we sent the servant and the chaise on to Hoff, a post-town twenty-five miles from Olmutz, on the road we wished to travel. We mounted our horses apparently to follow him, but in fact to endeavor to meet Lafayette. Our pistols were not loaded, and we took no other arms. We had no intention of taking life to forward our design. It was the hour when we knew that Lafayette was allowed to ride. We rode toward the castle; and, upon nearing the walls, saw an open carriage, in which was seated a prisoner in a blue surtout, with an officer beside him and an armed soldier mounted behind. As we passed, the prisoner gave the signal agreed upon by raising his hat and wiping his forehead with his handkerchief. The feelings excited by this assurance that the prisoner was indeed Lafayette I can never forget. We looked as indifferent as possible, bowed slightly, and rode on. Presently we turned and followed the carriage. When it reached the open country, Lafayette alighted, on the pretence of taking exercise. He gradually drew the officer who had him in charge away from the high road. Suddenly he grasped the hilt of the officer's sword and drew it. At that moment we galloped up to his assistance. A scuffle ensued, the officer was slightly wounded, and Lafayette's coat was stained with his blood. The soldier meantime hurried back to the castle, to give the alarm. An unlucky incident here occurred. We had dismounted, and one of our horses, frightened by the sun gleaming upon the drawn swords, ran away. The officer now seized Lafayette by the collar and succeeded in throwing him. The latter exclaimed,

'He is strangling me!' We then attacked the officer, threw him, and held him down, calling to Lafayette to mount the only remaining horse and escape. I said to him, 'Go to Hoff!' a direction which Lafayette most unfortunately mistook for the English phrase 'Go off!' If I had only spoken in French, and said *Allez à Hoff*, our plan would have succeeded. Lafayette mounted and rode slowly away; but immediately returned and declared that he could not leave us in such a situation. We reminded him that not a moment was to be lost, and besought him not to frustrate our design. With great reluctance, he then galloped slowly away. We then let the officer escape, and, after much difficulty, I succeeded in catching our other horse. We mounted and attempted to follow Lafayette. But, unfortunately, the horse that he had taken was the one we had trained to carry double. The horse we were compelled to mount soon reared, stumbled, and threw us. It was impossible for us both to escape. I then insisted that Bollmann should take the horse and follow Lafayette alone. He declared that he could not leave me; but, upon my reminding him that he could be of great assistance to Lafayette, through his knowledge of the German language, of which I was ignorant, he reluctantly decided to go.

"My situation was a forlorn one. In a few moments the whole country would be in pursuit of us. But I resolved to lose no chance that remained. I hurried toward a convent, that appeared upon a neighboring hill. Soon I heard voices behind me, and took refuge in a wood. I hid myself behind a tree, determined to strike the first horseman to the ground and to mount his horse. But my pursuers were too numerous. I was instantly surrounded, seized, and carried to Olmutz."

The characteristic delicacy of Colonel Huger led him to pass slightly over his sufferings while in prison. For ten days he was treated with the utmost rigor. He was chained to the floor of a small arched dungeon six feet by eight, from which light was totally excluded. His request to be allowed to send the words "*I am alive*" to his mother was rudely refused.

Colonel Huger continued his narrative thus:—

"After the rigor of my imprisonment was abated by a removal from the dark dungeon, I discovered that Bollmann was in the apartment above me. We soon contrived to hold some communication, and from him I first learned the total defeat of our plan. He had reached Hoff; but, not finding Lafayette, he lingered on the frontier till he was arrested and sent to Olmutz. I have already explained the misunderstanding of my direction 'Go to Hoff!' which frustrated our design. Lafayette, thinking that he was only told to *go off*, wandered into the village of Zagorsdorf, where he was stopped as a suspicious-looking person, his clothes being stained with blood. We were all three brought back to Olmutz, and confined there separately, ignorant of one another's condition. When our trial came on, a young man who served as our interpreter became deeply interested in our fate, and told our story to Count Metrowsky, an influential person residing in the neighborhood. Touched by the conduct and sufferings of two men he had never seen, this nobleman gave our young interpreter the command of his purse, and the judges of the tribunal were bribed to such effect that, after an imprisonment of eight months, we were released. We had just cleared the Austrian dominions, when an order commanding a new trial reached Olmutz from Vienna. Had we been there to meet it, there can be no doubt that the result would have been a sentence of death.

"When I met Lafayette, the other day, in New York, I had not seen him for thirty years. Determined that our meeting should have no witnesses, I went to the house that had been assigned to him, early in the morning, and was admitted before he left his chamber. He remained in prison three years after the event I have related. He was told that we had been taken and sentenced to execution, but was not informed of our liberation. For months he daily expected to see us taken out to be shot."

"While Colonel Huger was speaking," writes the lady to whom the reader of this narrative is indebted for its preservation, "the countenances of his little audience round the table expressed alternate hope and fear, joy and anxiety. The interest of the most highly wrought novel was not surpassed by that of the story, as it fell from the lips of one of the chief actors, himself the best personification of a real hero we had ever seen."

Let me here say a word of the pleasant relations which for nine years I sustained with Governor Lincoln. In our many journeys about the State, — which were then *journeys;* not, as in these days, merely arrivals — he impressed me as a noble man, a kind friend, and a good officer. I mention him in this latter capacity because he was our last governor who appeared in full uniform and reviewed the troops on horseback. His aids were, of course, mounted also; and we took care to have good horses that should not be shamed by General Sumner's fine animal, "Peacock." And, as the saying is, horses and riders alike "felt their oats." We galloped past the country militia, as they appeared before us in review, feeling probably as important as the staffs of royalty whose military manœuvres are now depicted in the illustrated papers.

The second visit of Lafayette to Boston took place during the session of the General Court; and this, of course, necessitated a reception by that body. "I have been informed that the Legislature intend to receive the tribute of my personal respect," wrote Lafayette to my father; thus modestly parrying the compliment that was tendered him. "In which case it will seem proper for me to be arrived two days before the Bunker Hill ceremony. As to what I am to do, I cannot do better than to refer myself to your friendly advice; and shall hastily offer you and family my most affectionate, grateful respects." And so, according to his programme, the General arrived in time to appear at the State House on the 16th, and to make us a graceful and dignified speech, which his pretty French accent made very touching. He told us that Bunker Hill had been the pole-star upon which his eyes had been fixed, and he rejoiced in the prospect of assisting at "the grand half-secular jubilee" which was to take place the next day. I can see him as he then stood before us, looking all the better for his extended travels. A fine, portly figure, nearly six feet high, wearing lightly the three-score and ten years he had nearly completed, showing no infirmity save the slight lameness incurred in our defence at the battle of Brandywine,— such was the outward person of the General. His face, on nearer view, showed traces of the sufferings through which he had passed; but his brown wig, which set low upon his forehead, concealed some of the wrinkles which time writes upon the brow, and made it difficult to realize that he was the comrade of the bald and white-headed veterans who came to greet him. The wig, however, did him yeoman's service. Without it he could never have ridden with his hat off through the continuous receptions and triumphal entries which were accorded him.

We have lately had a surfeit of centennial anniversaries; we have come to take them indifferently and as a matter of course. They seem little more than conventional compliments to a past with which no living link connects us. How can I give an idea of the freshness and feeling with which we celebrated the fiftieth return of the day when the great battle of our Revolution had been fought? Every circumstance seemed to conspire to add dignity and pathos to the occasion. The day was simply perfect; as perfect as if made expressly for the imposing scenes it was to witness. Never before had so many people been packed into the city. "Everything that has wheels and everything which has legs," in the language of a stage-driver of the period, "used them to get to Boston." My orders were to be at the Subscription House at nine in the morning. This was the new name for the mansion at the head of Park Street, which had recently been opened as a club house, — the first, I believe, known in New England. The duty assigned me was to meet the survivors of the Battle of Bunker Hill, and to introduce them to the General, — a privilege this never to be forgotten! I passed along the line of old men, taking the name of each of them from his lips, and repeating it to Lafayette. He immediately pronounced the name after me in tones of the deepest interest, as if that of a dear personal friend, and then, advancing, grasped the hand of each veteran with tender cordiality. There was no crowd of idle witnesses to gaze upon the scene. I stood the one young man among these honored heroes. If there were dry eyes in the room, mine were not among them. It was a scene for an historical picture, by an artist who could feel its interest. Thank Heaven, it escaped the conscious posings and other vulgarities of the modern photograph! No field or staff officer of the battle survived; but there was a captain, by the name of Clark, bending beneath his ninety-five years, who brought colonial times under King George into contact with the great republic which had succeeded them. It was my duty to attach to the breast of each of these survivors a badge of honor, which was worn during the day.

The brilliant civil and military procession which escorted Lafayette and his veterans to Bunker Hill moved through crowds of spectators, who were overflowing with enthusiasm. It seemed as if no spot where a human foot could plant itself was left unoccupied. Even the churches along the route had been opened, and their windows were thronged with ladies. The contrasted feelings with which Boston had looked toward the heights of Charlestown fifty years ago was the theme of every tongue. Then, as Byron puts it, there were hurryings to and fro, and gathering tears and tremblings of distress; now there was a great nation, which had solved the problem of self-government and commanded the respect of the world. I had intended to give the scene upon Bunker Hill from my own notes and recollections; but I find in the journal of my sister so excellent a record of the occasion that I shall presently avail myself of her kind permission to copy it for my readers.

After laying the corner-stone, Lafayette positively refused to take the seat which had been prepared for him under the pavilion devoted to official personages and distinguished guests. "No," said he; "I belong there, among the survivors of the Revolution, and there I must sit." And so he took a seat among the veterans, with no shelter from the rays of a June sun.

I have already implied that the address by Everett at Cambridge was a greater display of oratory than that of Webster at Bunker Hill; but above the power of any words there was in the latter case the magnificent presence of the man. As America, in the patriotic fervors which had not then been chastened, seemed to tower superior to all other nations, so towered Webster above all other men. What a figure-head was there for the Ship of State! No man, as Sydney Smith said, could be so great as this man looked, and now he looked his very greatest. To describe him, as he stood before us, I must enlist the poets as reporters: "The front of Jove himself; an eye like Mars, to threaten and command." And below these there were the "Atlantean shoulders, fit to bear the weight of mightiest monarchies;" and, if so, then also the weight of that mightiest of republics, which was to throw them into the shade. But there was one present who awakened a higher sentiment than Daniel Webster. The occasion was to be consecrated by prayer, and the venerable Joseph Thaxter, the chaplain of Prescott's own regiment, rose to officiate. Half a century before, this man had stood upon that very spot, and in the presence of brave men, for whom that morning sun was to know no setting, called on Him who can save by many or by few for aid in the approaching struggle. What thoughts filled the minds of the patriots who had listened to Mr. Thaxter's prayer in this place! What wonderful changes surrounded their descendants! And here was again lifted the feeble voice of the old man to invoke the Unchangeable, to ask the blessing of Him who is the same yesterday, to-day, and forever. I note this prayer as on the whole the most impressive circumstance of this memorable day, and now give the narrative from the young lady's diary.

"*Friday, June* 17, 1825. — This eventful day was welcomed by the roaring of cannon, which woke us at early dawn. The whole city was soon in motion. Carriages were driving at a tremendous rate; the troops were assembling on the Common; and the streets were thronged by multitudes, hurrying to and fro. Great apprehensions were yesterday entertained with regard to the weather; but every one said, 'It must be a fair day on the 17th,' and I heard that an old man in Andover exclaimed, 'The Lord will not permit it to rain on that day.' The heavens were never more propitious. The showers of yesterday laid the dust and cooled the atmosphere, and it was indeed the perfection of weather.

"Before going to Charlestown, we arranged the house for the reception of visitors. The head of Hamilton Place was one of the best places in the city from which to view the procession, and we knew that every window would be in requisition. Two of my sisters remained home to see the parade and receive company, and some of our acquaintances arrived as early as eight o'clock. At half past eight we took our departure, escorted by my father, who walked beside our carriage to the old Hancock House, where we were to call for Mrs. Lincoln. The Governor's carriage was in waiting, and, while my father went up to attend Mrs. Lincoln, the Governor came down to the carriage, to pay his respects to my mother and exchange congratulations on the beauty of the day. Mrs. Lincoln, Miss Putnam, and my father then got into the Governor's carriage and led the way to Charlestown. On arriving there, we drove to the house of Mr. Knowles (one of the marshals), where it had been arranged that the ladies should assemble. All the rooms of the house were crowded with company, and we were received with great kindness and civility by its mistress. The ladies vied with each other in the elegance of their dresses, and their variety afforded us ample entertainment during the hour we passed there, before we were permitted to secure our places to hear the oration. We found foreigners and strangers from all parts of the Union; among them, of course, many of our acquaintances, — Mrs. Webster, Miss Sedgwick, Mr. Daniel Wadsworth, and others. The latter is a gentleman of taste and cultivation. He spoke with great enthusiasm of the visit of Lafayette to this country. 'I was in the carriage with the General,' said he, 'when he entered Hartford. Lafayette was describing to me the sufferings he underwent at Olmutz, when we came to a place where the crowd had collected to welcome him. His description was rendered inaudible by the cheers which rent the air. Lafayette bowed to the people, and then, turning to me, said, with emphasis, "*These are, indeed, the extremes of human life!*" To which I replied, "*Yes, sir; but they are extremes which no mortal but you has been permitted to behold.*"'

"We remained at Mr. Knowles's until near eleven, and then walked to Bunker Hill; my father escorting Mrs. Lincoln and my mother, and Professor Silliman Miss Putnam and myself. The stage for the orator was erected at the foot of the hill, and seats for the ladies extended in a semicircle on each side, forming a kind of amphitheatre. Above us, on the side of the hill, were seats for the soldiers of the Revolution and the multitudes who were to come in the procession. We found ourselves surrounded by an immense number of women, fashionable and unfashionable, high and low, rich and poor, all animated by one interest. The breezes came over the hill perfumed by the new-mown hay, — such as was used to form intrenchments on the day of the battle. At length the report of the cannon announced the approach of the procession, and soon the infantry appeared on the brow of the hill. The ceremony of laying the corner-stone we could not see, as it took place on the other side of the hill; but the dirge to the memory of the dead, borne by the wind in our direction, was very touching. After an hour had passed, those in the procession came forward and took their appointed seats. Just beside us were the survivors of the battle, — a company of venerable old men, covered with badges and attended with the greatest respect by the young soldiers of the present day, whose brilliant uniforms and youthful appearance formed a most striking contrast with the veterans they were supporting. Opposite were the soldiers of the Revolution, with Lafayette in the midst of them. The orator of the day ascended the stage, accompanied by the Governor and his suite and many strangers of distinction. The Masons, with their white aprons and blue scarfs and banners glancing in the sun, were upon the side of the hill, behind the soldiers of the Revolution. Next to them came the military escort and then the countless multitude. Perfect silence pervaded this vast assembly when Mr. Thaxter, the chaplain of Prescott's regiment, rose to offer prayer. His voice was tremulous with age, as he raised it here again to offer the thanksgivings of another generation. The effect of Mr. Pierpont's beautiful hymn, sung by this vast assembly, to the tune of 'Old Hundred,' and accompanied by a full band, is beyond my power of description. In the fourth verse the music died away to the softest strains, and toward the conclusion swelled again to notes of solemn grandeur.

"Mr. Webster then came forward, looking like one worthy to be the orator of such an occasion. Scarcely had he pronounced a few sentences, when he was interrupted by the shouts of the throng beyond the barriers. Their cries sounded wildly in the distance, and for some moments great apprehensions were felt that their anxiety to hear Mr. Webster would induce them to break through all restraint and rush forward upon the place where the ladies were seated. The countenances of the gentlemen upon the stage expressed deep anxiety, and some of the ladies almost fainted from alarm. We exerted all our influence to induce those about us to remain quiet. It was an appalling moment. Some of the crowd had begun to climb upon our seats and pull away the awning that protected us. If the multitude beyond had followed them, it would have produced a conflict with the military and a painful scene. The guards, constables, and marshals in vain endeavored to keep order. Mr. Webster seemed much agitated, and said, with an air of deep regret, 'We frustrate our own work.' Then, by a sudden impulse, he came forward, and with one of his commanding looks called to the marshals in a voice of thunder, '*Be silent yourselves, and the people* WILL *obey!*' The commotion ceased almost instantly, and Mr. Webster again commenced his oration."

There is no need to speak of a performance which is conspicuous among the published works of the orator. At the conclusion of the exercises we repaired to a pavilion on the summit of the hill, where more than four thousand guests sat down to dinner. The feeding of this army was as successful as such attempts usually are. The official personages, among whom I was placed, were well looked after, and it would be most ungenerous to cast any reflections upon the contractor, particularly now when no good can come of them. Patriotic toasts abounded. The sentiment given by Lafayette is interesting, as embodying the general confidence of the time, and its lack of appreciation of the slow movements of history: —

"Bunker Hill, and the holy resistance to oppression which has already enfranchised the American hemisphere. The next half-century jubilee's toast shall be: *To Enfranchised Europe!*"

DANIEL WEBSTER AT HOME.

THERE was never a more brilliant and interesting private party given in Boston than the reception by Mr. and Mrs. Daniel Webster, on the evening of the memorable 17th of June, 1825. Colonel Israel Thorndike, the neighbor of Mr. Webster, had caused a passage to be cut through the brick walls which separated their houses. This doubled the accommodation for guests, by connecting another handsome establishment with that of the host of the evening. Summer Street was as light as day, the houses were brilliantly illuminated, and a fine band was stationed a few yards from Mr. Webster's door. The rooms were filled with strangers from all parts of the country. I can notice only those few persons with whom I happened to converse or had special reason to mark.

First, there were Mr. and Mrs. Webster, who received the compliments of the hour with great dignity and simplicity. Of the lady, the journal before me declares that "she seemed highly to enjoy the success and distinction of her husband, but showed not the slightest symptom of vanity or elation." Indeed, among the most interesting spectacles of the evening was the unassuming serenity of the hosts in the midst of all the honor and congratulations which surrounded them. In alluding to the scene of the morning, Mr. Webster said: "I never desire to behold again the awful spectacle of so many human faces all turned toward me. As I looked at them, a strange idea came into my mind. I thought of what Effie Deans said, in contemplating her execution, that there would be 'seas of faces' looking up at her. There was, indeed, a sea of faces before me at that moment."

Colonel Thorndike occupied the somewhat peculiar position of guest in his own house. He was a fine-looking person, reputed to be the richest man in New England, and in this capacity was the object of much interest and attention. He was a great ship-owner, and everything he touched seemed to succeed. In Beverly, his native town, there had grown up a sort of proverb about him, to the effect that if Thorndike were to send out a pebble on a shingle it would come back a dollar. Yet, like all successful men, he had met reverses; and I remember once hearing him exclaim, with some bitterness, "If I had taken every ship I owned, brought them into Boston harbor, and burned them without insurance, I should be worth $100,000 more than I am now." This gentleman had married Miss Dana, of Marblehead,— a lady whom my father considered one of the finest women he had ever met. I well remember the words in which he congratulated Colonel Thorndike upon his engagement: "Let me tell you, sir, that you have made the very best bargain you have touched yet!" Wealth was quite as attractive in those days as it is at present, and it was deemed a happy circumstance that the intellect of the community in one of these adjoining houses should be backed by its purse in the other.

Among the interesting strangers with whom I conversed at Mr. Webster's party was Dr. S. L. Mitchell, of New York. He was a man of great learning, though of some eccentricity, and deserves the column of the "American Cyclopædia" which is devoted to his commemoration. He was then prominently before the public on account of an appeal which had been made to him to decide whether a whale was a fish. So far as I remember the case, some one had contracted to deliver a large amount of fish oil, and had offered whale oil in fulfilment of his contract. This the other parties to the bargain refused to accept, on the ground that the whale was no fish, but an animal. How the matter was decided, I have no recollection; but Dr. Mitchell had been appealed to as the best expert to be found. The Doctor expressed his delight with Boston in no measured terms. Indeed, he rolled off a quotation from Pope's "Homer" in praise of the city, which was so very flattering that I shall not set it down. It did well enough to introduce a conversation which he made very agreeable.

Literary celebrity was purchased in those Arcadian days at a much lower price than is at present set upon the article. I do not remember much about

Mr. Hillhouse's poem, called "Hadad," yet I shall venture to doubt whether it would make an author conspicuous if published to-day. Nevertheless, Mr. Hillhouse, the distinguished American poet, was pointed out as among the largest lions of the evening. I read very good verses every evening, in the Boston "Transcript," which would have crowned their authors with unfading laurels if they had only brought them to market fifty years earlier. Mr. Hillhouse was a man of great gentleness and refinement, and I afterward enjoyed his society as a visitor in our family circle. On the present occasion, however, I found more attraction in the person of a lady of his party. This was a sister of Mrs. Hillhouse (Miss Lawrence), a reigning belle of New York. With this lady I had a pleasant chat, and, as a social philosopher of three-and-twenty, was interested in comparing the taste of the two cities in the matter of feminine fascinations. There was another lady to whom I was presented, — a tall young person, of about thirty, of pleasing countenance, and wearing her hair cut short to the head. This was famous Fanny Wright, who had just returned to America, with all the glory of having written a book about us. She was destined to be still better known, at a later date, as the promulgator of unpopular theories and as the first of practical Abolitionists. The colony of emancipated slaves which she established on lands purchased in Tennessee was one of those failures which are better than many things which the world calls successful.

I do not speak of Lafayette and the survivors of the Revolution, who were, of course, at Mr. Webster's party and were prominent as the real heroes of the day. Among these survivors was Colonel Putnam, the son of General Putnam, who was conspicuous at Bunker Hill. "I was in the American army at the time of the famous battle," said this gentleman; "but my father would not allow me to accompany him to Charlestown. He chose to leave me at Cambridge to guard a Mrs. Inman, a Tory lady, who had placed herself under his protection." The evening at Mr. Webster's was a fitting climax to the exciting festival, and those who had taken part in its ceremonials had good reason to sleep soundly.

The last evening reception given to Lafayette in Boston took place on Sunday, at the house of Mr. R. C. Derby. I have noted that on this occasion the General was reintroduced to a lady with whom he had danced a minuet forty-seven years before. Strange to say, I failed to set down the lady's name, and I now find it to be gone past recovery. Mr. Derby's establishment was very stylish and fashionable; and the names of the guests, with such titles as we were so happy as to possess, were loudly proclaimed by a servant as we ascended the stairs. My sister's journal, which I have found so useful, mentions that the arrangement of the rooms was different from any she had seen before. "The principal drawing-room was large and brilliantly lighted, and opening from it was a suite of smaller apartments, some lined with paintings, others hung with silk, and illuminated by shade-lamps and lights in alabaster vases, to produce the effect of moonlight. These apartments terminated in a boudoir only large enough to hold two or three people. It was hung with light blue silk and furnished with sofas and curtains of the same hue. It also contained an immense mirror, placed so as to reflect the rest of the rooms." This, then, was the Boston elegance of 1825. Whether such arrangements would be considered effective at the present day I am not qualified to say.

Boston's farewell to Lafayette took place at the theatre; and here again I will be so considerate as to throw aside my own journal, and open that of another sister, not out of her teens, to the accuracy of whose report I can bear witness. If one cannot go to the theatre one's self, the next best thing is to hear the account that a fresh young person will give of a rarely permitted indulgence of this nature. And in this way I shall invite my readers to assist at Boston's final ovation to the nation's guest.

"We all went to the theatre early; but as soon as we reached our box my brother left us under the care of the other gentlemen of our party,— as, being aid to the Governor, he was obliged to go to the Marlborough Hotel to join his suite. We ladies seated ourselves in the front of the box, and began to look around at the decorations of the house. The pit and lower rows of boxes were already quite full, and the remaining space was filling up very fast. From the middle of the ceiling over the pit was suspended an immense gilt eagle, with its wings spread, and from this emblem diverged flags and streamers to all parts of the house. Round the gallery, in illuminated letters, were the names of all the States, and beneath the boxes those of all the governors. Over the General's box were the letters G. L. F., of immense size and appropriately decorated. Two boxes had been thrown into one for the reception of Lafayette and his suite. They were lined with green baize and decorated with flags, evergreens, and artificial flowers. The play-bills were printed on white satin. Our box was No. 3, next to the General's, and was also lined with green baize, out of compliment to the Mayor. Lafayette being at a public dinner, the play ('Charles the Second') began before his arrival. In the midst of the second scene the Governor and his aids entered the General's box. Out of compliment to the Governor, the audience arose and clapped long and loud. Soon after they had resumed their seats a loud shout from the crowd outside announced that General Lafayette was at the door. Presently the managers (who had received Lafayette at the entrance of the theatre), preceded by men in costume, bearing lighted tapers in their hands, came through the lobby, ushering in their guest. He was followed by the Mayor, Mr. Lloyd, and several other gentlemen; but George Washington Lafayette and M. Levasseur did not appear, as they were preparing for their departure. As soon as Lafayette entered the box, every one rose, and three cheers were given, which were absolutely deafening. They were accompanied by clapping of hands, stamping of feet, and beating of canes, while the orchestra burst into 'Lafayette's March.' The General reached the front of the box, bowed, laid his hand on his heart, and repeated several times, 'I am very much obliged to you, gentlemen,' and this caused renewed clapping and vociferation. At last the cry 'Down! down!' re-echoed through the house; and when all were reseated the play went on. Mrs. Henry, who was more beautiful than ever, was upon the stage when the General entered. The first play was admirably acted. When it was over, all stood up, as usual, to refresh. Lafayette shook hands with my mother, and expressed his pleasure in seeing her so near him. When the curtain rose again, a new drop-scene appeared. It represented the tomb of Washington, with divers emblematical trophies. The effect was very fine. Mrs. Powell then appeared, attired as the Goddess of Liberty, and recited a piece of poetry, winding up with a compliment to Lafayette. She appeared very well indeed, and was received with thunders of applause. Then that scene was withdrawn, and a view of La Grange was shown. This was a great surprise, and was received with repeated clapping. Lafayette seemed much pleased, and said it was a good likeness of his place. Then Mrs. Williamson, elegantly dressed, came forward and sang very well a song in honor of Lafayette. Of course, this was received with more applause, and the lady retired amid shouts of satisfaction. The after-piece, 'Simpson & Co.,' now began. Finn and Mrs. Henry again acted admirably. I never thought of Finn, but only of

Bromley; and Mrs. Henry looked more bewitching than I ever saw her. All the actors had new dresses for the occasion, and everything went off as well as possible. When the curtain dropped, Lafayette rose; and verily I thought the walls would have fallen, from the noise that ensued. As it was Lafayette's last appearance in Boston, every bow from him was received with fresh cheering. At length he turned from the audience, shook hands for the last time with the ladies of our party, and declared that he should expect to see us all in France. Then he left the box, followed by the whole house; who, meeting him at the door, gave him loud cheers as he drove off. We waited some time for the crowd to disperse, and then walked home. This evening, I think, must bear the palm, from the novelty and excitement of the scene."

I cannot suppose that the words I have quoted will give this scene to the reader as vividly as they reproduce it to me. The dead and forgotten worthies of old Boston, full of life and enthusiasm, are again crowding the theatre. Those who claim to have taken their places are to me the phantoms.

LAFAYETTE LEAVES MASSACHUSETTS.

ABOUT the year 1845, in going from Boston to New York, I fell in with a bridal party. The gentleman introduced himself, and then presented me to his wife, and to her very pretty sister, who was travelling in their company. After some chat upon indifferent subjects, the bride turned to me, with an air of well-assumed seriousness, and said: "I may as well tell you, Mr. Quincy, that I have long desired to make your acquaintance, and determined to do so when I found you were upon this boat. There is an event with which you were connected which has caused much unhappiness in our family. It is in your power to remove this unhappiness by answering a single question, '*Did you ever kiss my sister?*'" Amazed at this singular inquiry, I could only say that, without betraying the past, I should be glad, with the young lady's permission, to qualify myself to answer the question in the affirmative from that time forward. "That would not improve things," said the bride, roguishly; "for the fact is that this pert young thing has always given herself airs because, when she was four months old, and you were driving through our town with Lafayette, she was lifted up into the carriage and, as she says, kissed by the General. Now, the old people who remember the time tell us that this notion of hers is a great mistake; for they are certain that while Lafayette was shaking hands with the men on one side of the barouche, he detailed you to kiss the babies on the other." I mention this incident as one of those allusions to the visit of Lafayette which, for thirty years afterward, were testifying to the deep impression it had made upon our people. In this special case I did all that I could for the young lady, by declaring that, while candor compelled me to admit that I had kissed a goodly number of babies on the 21st of June, 1825, I had not the slightest recollection of her as being among their number.

On the morning of Lafayette's final departure from Boston, I was ordered to report myself at Mr. Lloyd's house, in Somerset Street, at seven o'clock. In company with my fellow aid, John Brazer Davis, I here passed a pleasant hour in breakfasting with the General, who was full of conversation. My journal records that he gave us highly interesting sketches of his journey through the States, and spoke with great gratification of his reception by Congress, and of its generous gift as a recognition of his services in the Revolution. "I have but one thing to regret in all my travels," he said, "and that is the loss of my little dog, who loved me so much;" and he gave us a pathetic account of his feelings when the animal was stolen during the passage up the Ohio. The conversation turned upon Napoleon, and it was evident that, notwithstanding the good reasons to detest the man which Lafayette had, he was enough of a Frenchman and a soldier to take pride in the military genius which had led his countrymen to such brilliant victories. "But the fact is," continued the General, "history will find it very difficult to get at the real Napoleon; for the man deported himself with great care when in the presence of those whom he had reason to suspect were writing diaries or memoirs. Posterity will know what poses he deemed becoming in a figure of his importance, and but little more." The remark was a shrewd one, and for fifty years after it was made at Mr. Lloyd's breakfast-table I was disposed to accept it as true. We have only just learned that all the sagacity of the Emperor could not tell him who the memoir writers were to be. There was a modest little woman, who waited upon his wife, before whom the great man did not think it necessary to keep up his posturing; and the revelations of Madame de Rémusat have amply avenged any deceptions he may have fastened upon others.

A little after nine it was announced that the carriages were at the door and that the last farewells must be spoken. "Sir, you have made us love you too much," said my father, who had come to witness the departure. "Ah! but I cannot love *you* too much," replied Lafayette, throwing his arms about him and, after the French custom, saluting him upon both cheeks. There were three open barouches, each drawn by four horses, those attached to the General's carriage being perfectly white animals of noble appearance. I rode at the left of Lafayette, and Colonel Davis had the front seat to himself. The carriages following us contained George Washington Lafayette and others of the suite. We were accompanied by outriders, and for a part of the way, at least, by a detachment of cavalry.

We left the city through throngs of people, which almost stopped the streets; and at every town and every cross-road we were received by new throngs pressing upon us to salute the guest of the nation. We made short stops for the babies to be kissed (by proxy or otherwise), and for the men (those who could get near the barouche) to take the General by the hand. Our carriage was soon filled with the flowers that were thrown into it, and there remained no space available for an additional rosebud.

Exciting as all this was, I longed for the vacant spaces upon our road, for there Lafayette would kindly answer the inquiries of his young companions and tell them of the scenes through which he had passed. He gave us a thrilling account of the mob at Versailles, on the memorable occasion when, appearing on the balcony with the Queen, he could only address them in dumb show, by kneeling and kissing the royal hand. He spoke with fervor of the beauty of Marie Antoinette, and seemed to think that this was no unimportant factor in giving events the turn they had taken. Speaking of his visit to America, he declared that nothing struck him more than the simplicity of life and the absence of accumulated capital. "What do you think," said he, "is the question which these Revolutionary soldiers, to whom I am introduced, almost invariably ask me? It is this: 'What do you do for a living?' And sometimes the inquiry comes: 'What was your father's business?' Now, everybody is working for a living in America, — that is, pursuing some money-getting trade or profession, — and the people do not understand how it can be otherwise in the older countries."

Lafayette showed great tact in the little speeches he was everywhere compelled to make, and often caused astonishment by the local information that was interwoven with his remarks. His memory was wonderfully clear in regard to the incidents of his own career; but his knowledge of the position of affairs in the villages of Massachusetts was not marvellous to those who travelled in his company. As we were approaching Andover, he said, "Now tell me all about this place and for what it is remarkable." As my boyhood had been passed in the town, as a pupil of the academy, the subject was one upon which I was thoroughly posted. I gave him several local incidents, describing especially the Theological Seminary, where the faith once delivered to the saints was held in its original purity and from whose walls many missionaries had gone forth. The General treasured the hints, and in his speech made the happiest allusion to that sacred hill from which hope had gone forth to the heathen and light to the uttermost parts of the earth. On my return through the town, I met an old gentleman who, though not connected with the institution, was deeply interested in its honor and success. "I was really surprised," he said to me, "at the particular and accurate knowledge that General Lafayette possessed in regard to our Theological Seminary. I always knew that in the religious world it was an object of great concern; but I never supposed that in the courts and camps of Europe so much interest was taken in the condition and prospects of this institution." I could not find it in my heart to dispel a delusion which gave so much innocent pleasure, and so went my way with the remark that, after the talk I had had with the General, I was not surprised at the excellence of his information concerning all that was going forward in Andover.

There was a story told about Lafayette, during his visit to Boston, which I am tempted to repeat, though I do not believe it was true. It was probably one of those apocryphal anecdotes which give the popular impressions about public characters in a pointed way. On being presented to some old soldiers, the General was heard to ask the leader of the group if he were married. Upon receiving an answer in the affirmative, Lafayette responded, with most tender emphasis, "Ah! happy man!" To the person who was next presented the same question was put; but here the reply was, "No, sir; I am a bachelor." "Oh! you lucky dog!" whispered the questioner, with a roguish twinkle in his eye. These remarks were overheard by a bystander, who taxed Lafayette with insincerity in bestowing similar congratulations under such widely different circumstances. "Is it possible," said the General, turning promptly upon his critic, "that you value the prerogative of humanity so little as not to know that the felicity of a happy man is a thousand times better than that of a lucky dog!" Certain traits of Lafayette — his way of saying pleasant things to those he met, and his graceful readiness of reply — are so happily combined in the story that it deserves to be true, and it may have had some foundation in fact.

Methuen was the last town in Massachusetts where we stopped to receive the homage of the people; and soon after we reached the State line, where we gave up our guest to the authorities of New Hampshire. Lafayette embraced his two companions at parting, and thanked us over and over again for the attention which had been shown him. To me his last words were: "Remember, we must meet again in France!" and, so saying, he kissed me upon both cheeks. "If Lafayette had kissed *me*," said an enthusiastic lady of my acquaintance, "depend upon it, I would never have washed my face again as long as I lived!" The remark may be taken as fairly marking the point which the flood-tide of affectionate admiration reached in those days.

I cannot hope to convey an adequate idea of the extraordinary spectacles represented during the visit of our nation's guest. Before us stood the very man who had crossed the ocean to a land of strangers — aliens in blood and in language — to share our desperate struggle when we were poor and weak and oppressed. It was a striking and magnificent event, one not to be repeated in the world's history. The shrewd and inexpressive New Englanders were filled with the exuberant enthusiasm of the Southern races. They rushed with the wild ardor of children to embrace a beloved parent.

Just thirty years after taking leave of Lafayette, I visited the city of Paris and stood beside his tomb. He lies by the side of his dearly beloved wife, in the little cemetery of Picpus. The entrance is through a chapel of the Nuns of the Holy Sacrament, where two of the sisters are always prostrate in prayer before the altar. They are relieved as regularly as sentinels; and day and night, through all the turbulent scenes of modern French history, their service has been unceasing. Could there be a greater contrast than between lives so spent and his whose dust they guard? The inscription upon the stone which covers Lafayette is very simple, and no word reveals the fact that he ever visited America. Surely, this is not the only memorial of him which should exist in the capital of France. Among the magnificent monuments of Paris the absence of one ought to be conspicuous to every American. Where is the equestrian statue of Lafayette which our countrymen should have placed in that city? Twenty-five years ago I asked myself this question, and determined to do what I could to cause the deficiency to be supplied. And an occasion for initiating the movement soon came. On the 22d of February, 1856, I was asked to preside at a dinner of Americans in Rome. Men of large wealth and social distinction were collected about the table. I recall Messrs. Beekman and Hamersley, of New York; Mr. Corning, of Albany; Dr. Sharpless, of Philadelphia; Mr. George B. Emerson, of Boston; and many others. Crawford, the sculptor, Page, the painter, with men of lesser fame, represented American art. This was just the occasion to introduce the proposition I had contemplated. The response was enthusiastic. Gentlemen of large pecuniary responsibility pledged themselves that funds should be forthcoming. An equestrian statue of Lafayette, by an American artist, should be placed by Americans in the city of Paris. An excellent committee was at once appointed, and I was directed to open a correspondence upon the subject with Mr. Mason, our minister to France. And here the project was brought to a sudden end. Mr. Mason wrote that the government of Napoleon III. refused to allow such a memorial to be erected in Paris. The despotism of fraud and sensuality which a band of conspirators had forced upon France had no sympathy with the pure and honorable republican.

It was a singularly graceful act in the present government of France to atone for this refusal by presenting to the city of New York the statue of Lafayette, executed by a French artist, which now stands in Central Park. It would be merely a fitting acknowledgment of this courtesy for our countrymen again to ask the privilege (which would now cordially be given) of placing in the city of Paris a statue of him who was the benefactor of two nations. No public monument can be reared of more significance, and I cannot better conclude these reminiscences of Lafayette than by commending it to the attention of patriotic Americans.

THE DUKE OF SAXE-WEIMAR AND CAPTAIN RYK.

ON July 26, 1825, the ship "Pallas" entered Boston harbor. She brought an extra complement of thirty officers, a picked crew, and one passenger, the latter being his Royal Highness, Charles Bernard, Grand Duke of Saxe-Weimar. It is not the easiest thing in the world to live up to such a title as that; but in this case the man who bore it was quite equal to the part, and I do not hesitate to say that no finer specimens of cultivated European gentlemen have ever visited America than this royal Duke and his friend, Captain Ryk, the commander of the "Pallas." The two volumes of travels which resulted from this visit testify to the accurate observation and wide interests of their author; but his previous history, added to his distinguished rank, was sufficient to make Duke Bernard's arrival in Boston a social event in those days of smaller excitements and less rapid life.

The father of the prince had been the first among German sovereigns to grant his subjects a free constitution, while our visitor was himself a distinguished officer, who had been decorated for heroic conduct at the battle of Wagram, and had been noted for conspicuous gallantry upon the bloody field of

Waterloo. The narrative of the part he bore in the latter gigantic conflict, then so recent, abounds with those romantic adventures which lend a lasting interest to their hero. He had acted as general of brigade in the service of the Prince of Orange, entering the battle with four thousand men, of whom scarcely more than one fourth survived its terrible slaughter. During the first day the Duke held his ground resolutely against a force three times as large as his own, and finally headed a desperate bayonet-charge, to gain an important position in the possession of the French. Having won his ground, he resolutely maintained it, while the supporting wing of the army was driven back as far as Quatre Bras, a retreat in which "Brunswick's fated chieftain" met his death. The next day, after a bivouac in the mud and drenched by a pelting rain, Bernard rose to the decisive battle. He was ordered to maintain a village of strategic importance, and through the long day he held his post by constant fighting and with heavy losses of men. At four o'clock in the afternoon the result was still doubtful, when the Prussians under General Bulow arrived to decide the battle. Some of these newcomers were sent to the support of Bernard and his exhausted command; but now a cruel blunder added to the horrors of the day, for the Prussians sent to the aid of the Duke mistook his Nassau troops for Frenchmen, and advanced upon them with a terrible fire. The men, spent and exhausted by their protracted fighting, were for a time demoralized by this unexpected assault. They abandoned their post and fled more than a mile before their brave leader was able to rally them. Three years after Waterloo the Duke of Saxe-Weimar entered the service of the King of the Netherlands, and was appointed military governor of Eastern Flanders; and this post he still occupied when he visited America.

I was constantly with the Duke during his stay in Boston, meeting him at parties, taking him about the city in the week and to the King's Chapel on Sunday. I have noted the excellent sermon we had from Henry Ware, from Proverbs xi. 3, and my gratification that my companion should hear so favorable a specimen of a Boston preacher. I make the following extract from my journal for August 3d : —

"Drove George Adams to Quincy about noon this day. At first we went to his grandfather's, where I was introduced to a very pretty Miss Willis, and afterward enjoyed half an hour's conversation with the old President. My father arrived later, bringing the Duke of Saxe-Weimar and his party. Old Mr. Adams was in excellent spirits. When Von Tromp, a descendant of the great Admiral, was introduced to him, he exclaimed, with the greatest enthusiasm, 'Huzza for Von Tromp! God bless Von Tromp!' In fact, I hardly ever saw the old gentleman in finer humor. The Duke, Captain Ryk, and several gentlemen dined with us. Ryk, though a thorough sailor, is a very well-informed man. He speaks all the languages of Europe, and seems conversant with the literature of each. He quoted passages from Milton and Dante, but without pedantry."

And this brief notice is all I have given of the day; but I have fortunately the privilege of consigning the reader to the guidance of a journal-writer far more accomplished than myself. My sister has kindly permitted me to copy (with some omissions) her excellent account of the old-fashioned country dinner-party that was gathered in honor of our European visitors. Here are the Duke and his friends as seen through the eyes of a young lady who little dreamed that this record would ever stray beyond the covers of her private diary.

"*Wednesday, August* 3, 1825. — My father told us that he should bring the Duke of Saxe-Weimar to dine here to-day, and, after a visit to Mr. Adams, the party drove up to the door. There is no 'And will your Highness to some *little* peer' in this case; for the Duke is considerably above six feet in height, with a finely developed figure. His face is pleasing and intelligent, his dress was perfectly plain, and he wore no orders, but carried superb and massy seals to his watch. Just behind the Duke there entered a figure in full uniform, who was introduced to us as Captain Ryk, of the ship 'Pallas.' He looked like a true Dutchman, both in face and figure. In addition to sword and epaulets, he wore two crosses hanging from two gold coronets, with which they were connected by blue and red ribbons. One was the Cross of the Legion of Honor, which he afterward told me was won fighting against the English. Captain Ryk is apparently forty, with a countenance all good-humor and animation. A third foreigner was Von

Tromp, a descendant of the famous Admiral. He is a pleasing young man of twenty-one, and has come out with Captain Ryk to study naval tactics. 'You must like Mrs. Quincy,' said my father to the Duke, 'for she is half a German.' 'What part of Germany does her family come from?' inquired our visitor. 'Kaub, on the Rhine,' was the reply. 'Ah! I know Kaub very well. There is a small island there, called the Pfalz. Have you not a view of it? There are some excellent prints.' I produced a drawing from an engraving, which the Duke pronounced very correct, and proceeded to name all the adjacent places. 'Here is the spot where the French once built a pontoon bridge across the Rhine. They built it in an incredibly short time.' The Duke then examined our Chinese drawings of Canton, and, passing to the hall, he traced upon a map of Canada the route he intended to take. Some one said that he would not find comfortable accommodations in American taverns. 'Oh! I am a soldier,' was the reply. 'If there is no bed, I can sleep on the floor; if no floor, then on the ground.'

"Meanwhile the rest of the company assembled, — Dr. Kirkland, Dr. Cooper, Mr. Everett, Mr. Saltonstall, and George Adams. Every one was brought up and presented to our guest, who, notwithstanding, insisted upon looking through a portfolio of drawings he had taken up, and commenting with great quickness of observation upon the views it contained. When, at length, he went into the other room, he called Captain Ryk to take his place, saying, 'There are drawings of that young lady's you must look at.' The Captain obeyed orders, and amused me very much by his remarks. He was as acute as the Duke, and then so infinitely odd. Taking up a view of Chingford Church, in pencil, he said: 'I like pencil; this is very pretty; but then you cannot make such fine works as with India ink. I like that, too, that way, with gamboge washed over it,' pointing to a view of Niagara from Black Rock. 'But — Whew! whew! What have we here?' taking up the likenesses of two Osage Indians, which I explained to him. 'Fine-looking fellow! Good head! Possible that is his hair, stuck up so? But I do not know that it is any more queer than for us to wear these things of gold lace on our shoulders. Do you know how to cut heads out of paper so as to throw a shadow to represent a drawing?' I said I had seen such cuttings, but could not cut them myself. He then informed me that this was one of the principal amusements of the ladies of Germany, and, taking up a piece of white paper and asking for scissors, he forthwith began to cut. In a few instants he fashioned, with the greatest facility, a head, which, being made to throw a shadow, represented Christ, after some old painting. It was, indeed, wonderful to see the adroitness with which a rough sailor performed this work. Upon my admiring it, he said, holding up his hand, 'To be sure, my hand is more used to handle the marline-spike than the scissors.' He was then about to tear the head in two; but I snatched it from destruction and told him he must give it to me. My father, who joined us, then said, 'We shall keep that head, Captain Ryk, till you are an admiral, and then we shall show it as a great treasure.'

"At the dinner-table I was seated between the Duke and Dr. Kirkland. Opposite were Dr. Cooper, Captain Ryk, and Mr. Everett. The rest of the company were below. His Highness having inquired the names of my sisters, I (to be equal in inquisitiveness) asked the name of his daughter. 'Louisa; and my two sons are William and Edward. My daughter is eight years old; my eldest son, six; my Englishman, as I call him, is two; and I presume I have another German son now, who must be about a fortnight or three weeks of age.' He then talked to me of his voyage. He had stopped on the coast of England, and visited Plymouth, Portsmouth, and Falmouth. On the British coast he was in danger from a great gale. Speaking of his travels two years ago, in England, Scotland, and Ireland, he mentioned that he had found the former a very dear country. 'The expense of travelling in England,' he said, 'is really enormous. You have to pay for everything; but I saw all their manufactories, except that of Mr. Watt, at Bolton. *There* they would not let me in. At the great houses you must always pay the servants. Many noblemen, among them the Duke of Marlborough, actually support their establishments in this way.' The remark was overheard by one of the other gentlemen, who said: 'Then the Duke equals his predecessor. I once heard that somebody was one day mistaken in the streets of London for the old Duke of Marlborough.

Wishing to be relieved from the impertinent curiosity of a crowd who were following him, he suddenly turned and threw a handful of silver among the people, exclaiming, "Now I hope you are satisfied that I am *not* the Duke!"'

"The Duke of Saxe-Weimar seemed to have a full understanding of the value of money, and said many things which showed that his possessions were by no means equal to his rank. He asked some questions about Stuart's paintings, and added, 'Is he very dear?' Indeed, the Duke was so simple and unpretending that I should have forgotten his title had I not been continually reminded of it by calls from the other end of the table: 'Will your Highness take this?' 'Shall I have the honor of a glass of wine with your Highness?' etc. I was particularly struck with the manner in which Mr. Everett pronounced the words. 'Have you visited Italy, Mr. Everett?' 'Yes, *your Highness*.' It was said with a reverence of voice and manner which appeared to me, to say the least, superfluous. I suppose Mr. Everett wished to show that he was accustomed to the manners of Europe. Of Captain Ryk the Duke said: 'He is a very clever man. He began as a cabin-boy, and has raised himself by his talents and bravery. He has been in many actions. His present situation shows the esteem in which he is held, for his ship is filled with young officers, whom he instructs in naval tactics.' In the course of the dinner, Captain Ryk described his sail through the Straits of Scylla and Charybdis. He commanded a seventy-four, and passed in perfect safety; 'not even,' he said, 'putting wool in my ears, like Ulysses, for fear of the sirens.' He spoke of the Roman Catholic relics, and described some he saw in the Cathedral at Milan. Among them there was a large stone chained to the wall. Upon asking for what it was remarkable, the monk who acted as showman replied: 'Why, that is a miraculous stone. It fell from the top of the dome without hurting a single person.' 'I suppose that was because nobody was in the church,' replied the Captain, 'and I suppose you have chained it there lest a second miracle should be performed and it should fly up again.' 'I see you are a heretic!' exclaimed the monk.

"The Duke had been asking a great many questions about the Indians, and suddenly inquired whether I had ever seen any of the skulls of their enemies which the aborigines preserve. I was somewhat shocked at this question, and turned the subject of the conversation; but the skulls seemed to have taken hold of the Duke's imagination and were not to be dislodged. He wished to investigate the matter thoroughly, perhaps from the fear that the Indians might perform some of their ceremonies upon himself; so, calling across the table to Captain Ryk, he demanded in German what was the English for *schädel*. 'Why, skull, skull,' said the Captain. Thus reassured, the Duke returned to the inquiry. 'Miss Quincy, have you ever seen any of the skulls of their enemies which the Indians drink out of?' I replied that I never had, and hoped they had given up such a horrid practice. 'I agree with you,' said Captain Ryk. 'For my own part, I very much prefer a good clean glass, like this. A skull is not a very pretty thing. How should you like to see a row of them round this table? It would be quite in the style of Ossian's heroes, to be sure. You know *they* always used skulls for drinking-cups; but they would not be very pretty nowadays.' Here the conversation was interrupted by my father, who called the attention of the company to a toast, — *The King of the Netherlands*. This being drunk with due respect, he was about to propose the Grand Duke of Saxe-Weimar, the father of our guest, when the son interrupted him, saying, 'With your leave, I will give the next toast — *The President of the United States and his venerable Father*.' After this we drank the health of his Royal Highness the Grand Duke of Saxe-Weimar, and our visitor bowed low to the company in return for the compliment to his father. Some Constantia wine was then offered. This had been brought from the Cape by Major Shaw, in the year 1792. Mr. S. G. Perkins told my father that this wine was now very valuable, worth in England several guineas a bottle, and that he must never produce it except for some very distinguished guest, such as the President of the United States. Mr. Everett now leaned forward and said, 'I beg leave to propose a toast, — *The Health of the Duchess Ida*.' This was accordingly drunk in Constantia, and it was a good notion of Mr. Everett to give the lady in the first glass of sweet wine. Unfortunately, however, the Duke made a mistake as to the author of the compliment; for, leaning forward, he bowed to Mr. Shepherd, who sat on our side of the table, opposite to Mr. Everett, and said, 'I hope the Duchess will thank you, when you visit us at Ghent, next year.' The blunder was unfortunate, but there seemed no way of rectifying it. My father then gave: *The Ladies of Rotterdam*. 'Ah!' said Captain Ryk, in an undertone, 'Von Tromp is at the bottom of that, I know. He has left his heart in Rotterdam.' The Captain then spoke of his own wife with great affection. 'I have a picture of her on board my ship,' he said, 'and it is generally covered by a curtain; but when the storms come and the winds are high I draw the curtain aside, because it does me good to see her smile.'

"The conversation turning upon General Washington, Captain Ryk said, 'When I pass Mt. Vernon, every color on my ship shall be lowered and every gun fired, and I and my men shall stand with our hats off.' The Duke then told several long stories about the proceedings of the Catholics and the way in which their plans had been defeated. At some of them he laughed, and was joined by the company; but he spoke so fast and in such imperfect English that I did not hear them distinctly enough to report. When we went into the drawing-room, the Duke seated himself before the piano. Mr. Everett, who followed us, seemed amused at his position; but, preserving all veneration of tone and manner, said, 'Ladies, cannot you prevail upon his Highness to favor us with a tune?' But our guest did not perform upon any instrument; and, after some talk about music and French masters, he went into the library. Captain Ryk, then being asked by my youngest sister to cut out something for her, took paper and scissors and produced two beautiful little flowers, a rose and a hyacinth. They were exquisitely fashioned, the leaves being arranged with the greatest taste. He laughed and talked all the time he was at work, and said, when he had finished, 'Now, you must not show these flowers to any of my men, or all my discipline would be at an end.' On his return from the library, the Duke expressed a wish to attend a family celebration, which would take place in 1833. 'That will be in eight years,' said he, 'and one of my sons will then be old enough to go to college; so I will send him to Harvard.' My mother asked if he did not intend to have his son educated at Jena, and spoke of Weimar as the Athens of Germany. 'As for Weimar,' replied the Duke, 'almost all the literary men who once made it famous are dead, and to Jena I would never send a son. No, I had rather give him a pistol and put him in the midst of a battle than send him to that university. In battle he might have some chance of escape, or at least die honorably; in Jena he would be sure to be ruined. The fashions of the place are to rebel against the government and to fight duels.' The Duke's account corresponded exactly with what Mr. Ticknor had told me of the German universities, and I liked him for speaking so openly of the faults of his country.

"At length, after all the other gentlemen had departed, the carriage drove to the door. Captain Ryk was in high spirits, laughing and talking with the girls and even beginning to sing, when the Duke said to him in German that it was time to go. The instantaneous change in his manner was very striking. All his drollery vanished, as he raised his hand to his head and made a military sign of obedience. Both gentlemen then shook hands very cordially with us all, the Captain saying that he should come and see us again before leaving Boston. I have been so taken up with the foreigners that I have said nothing of Dr. Cooper, the President of Columbia College, who is a learned and remarkable man. He has a very singular head, but is short and has the appearance of a man who has spent his life among books. Though his dress is neglected, there is much dignity in his manner, and the Duke paid him marked attention whenever he spoke. I should like to see him again, when we are more at leisure."

I have before me the account of another long summer afternoon which Captain Ryk passed with us at Quincy, on which occasion he played upon the guitar, with the skill of a troubadour; but this I am compelled to omit, together with a notice of the reception and dance he gave on board the "Pallas," in acknowledgment of the civilities he had received in Boston. I have come upon some letters from the Duke and Captain Ryk, the former writing in French and the latter in English, in which he stumbles so prettily that I must copy the story of the dog "Boston" (a noble animal, given to the Captain as a memorial of his visit) just as his master tells it. The letter was written about a year after his visit, and the "young similar dog" has done duty as a household phrase ever since.

"I have had the misfortune to lose my poor Newfoundland dog, my poor 'Boston.' One of my servants played with him imprudently with the stop of a glass decanter. The dog swallowed it. The servant dared not give me information thereof, and a few days afterward my poor 'Boston' died. I cannot tell you how deeply I feel the loss of that faithful animal. He was so beloved in my household that both my wife and children wept at his death, and I confess that I was very near to do the same. Could you find me another — a young similar dog? I will equally call him 'Boston.' The former, *stuffed*, I believe you call it (*empaillé*, says the Frenchman), still lays in my cabin, and shall remain there till a living one shall come in his place. I hope you will be able to read this letter. I am always at a loss when I write English; but, should my expressions fail, you may be sure the meanings are good and my heart beats warmly for you and your countrymen. God bless them all."

An extract from yet another letter, dated September 1, 1839, shall give us a last glimpse of good Captain Ryk: —

"I am now admiral. My breast is covered with crosses; but my heart is the same as when I lived among my Boston friends, and whenever we meet again they will find the shaking of the hand will be equally heartily as it was fourteen years ago, and that no badges of honor outside have made a change in my old-fashioned, plain Dutch heart. My new situation as governor-general of the Dutch West India Colonies gives me so much occupation that I have little time to write to my friends. Our good king (a king that even a stern republican might love and admire) has placed great confidence in me, and I must make myself worthy of it. When you have time, do write to me about my Boston friends. I have not forgotten any of them, nor the town; not even the beautiful trees on the Common."

The volume of my journal marked "1855" gives a parting look at the Duke of Saxe-Weimar. It is Sunday, the 15th of July, of the year just named; and at the close of the day I devote some pages to a description of its occurrences. Mr. August Belmont, our minister to the Hague, where I was then staying, called for me in the afternoon, and, in company with Mr. Tyson, of Pennsylvania, we drove in a New York trotting-wagon (at which the sober Dutchmen stared) to a fine sea-beach in the neighborhood. There we found a hotel, a band playing, and groups of well-dressed people regaling themselves at little tables or walking upon the sands. "All the foreign ministers are here this afternoon," said Mr. Belmont, "and there are many of the nobility of Holland." A gentle ripple of sensation ran through the company as a lady and gentleman descended from a carriage and walked upon the sands. "There is the Queen, and the old gentleman with her is the Duke of Saxe-Weimar," said one of my companions. I gazed intently upon the features of an elderly man, slightly lame and nearly blind, and could find little in common with those of the handsome officer in the prime of life whom we had fêted thirty years before. It has been said that a man will differ from his former self more than many men of the same age differ from one another. So far as the physical organization goes, this is probably true, and a feeling of overwhelming sadness oppressed me as the tall shadow passed across the beach. As etiquette prevented any approach to the Duke while in attendance upon the Queen, I had time to recall the old associations before meeting him in the evening; for that evening we did meet, and what a talk we had! The Duke was, after all, the frank and simple gentleman with whom I had strolled about an old Boston, guiltless of a foreign element, of railroads, and of transcendentalism. He gave me a rapid sketch of his subsequent life. He had passed many years in the East Indies, as commander of the Dutch forces, and had now come to end his days with his daughter, who had married a brother of the king. He told me that our good friend Admiral Ryk had died the year before, and that Von Tromp was at the head of the navy yard at Amsterdam. His remembrances of America were very vivid, and he asked with great interest concerning the subsequent histories of the friends he had made in Boston. We had met in the fashionable club-house of "The Hague," and upon this neutral ground our intercourse was easier than would have been possible under other circumstances. In fact, we talked till late into the night. The Duke called upon me before breakfast the next morning; but I missed him and we never met again. The painful impression of the infirm man is happily blurred in my memory; and when the Duke of Saxe-Weimar is mentioned I see only the symmetrical figure of the young hero who was our guest in 1825.

THE GOVERNOR AT NANTUCKET.

IF Governor Long, of Massachusetts, should visit Nantucket some summer day (as he is very likely to do), the circumstance would create no special stir in a community where life is even now a little monotonous. He might leave Boston in the morning, pass a few hours on the island, and return to a late dinner. The inhabitants would pursue their usual vocations, totally unaware that anything remarkable had taken place. It was far otherwise in the autumn of 1825, when Governor Lincoln made his memorable visit to their island. No governor of Massachusetts had ever trodden the shores of Nantucket, and the impression of the executive boot upon its sands excited the same sort of interest as the print of an unclad foot awakened in the breast of De Foe's immortal islander.

Surely it was time for a well-disposed governor to brave the fatigues and perils of the journey, in order to show himself in one of the most prosperous counties under his sway; for at that time the island contained eight thousand inhabitants, and did a greater amount of business in respect to its population than any county in the State, with the single exception of

Suffolk. And so Governor Lincoln resolved to break the spell which had held the long line of his predecessors from their thriving province; and, accordingly, his *aides-de-camp*, John Brazer Davis and myself, were commanded to hold ourselves in readiness to accompany the expedition. We were ordered to appear without uniforms, an unheard-of omission when in attendance upon the commander-in-chief; but Lincoln saw that any military reception or civil parade could not be expected in a community in which the Quakers or Friends were the predominating power, and that, with their well-known views respecting the legitimacy of war, an exhibition of the trappings even of holiday colonels would be out of taste. I feel sure that our good chief must have come to these conclusions with some reluctance. Personally he would have liked the entry upon horseback and in full uniform that was then customary for a governor. He rode well, and carried off the epaulets, gold lace, and plume with easy dignity, as the decent proprieties of his position. And this excellent Democrat lived to see a successor from the opposing party who declined to honor public occasions with the modest decoration of a shirt-collar. The tendency to cut away all graceful fringes and ornaments from our rulers is too strong to be resisted; but I doubt whether official position has gained in purity by discarding all its innocent symbolism.

On Tuesday, September 5th, at eleven o'clock in the forenoon, the Governor entered the Plymouth stage, and, with Hezekiah Barnard, Treasurer of the

Commonwealth, and Aaron Hill, Postmaster of Boston, occupied the back seat, which, as the place of honor, had been reserved for these dignitaries. The middle and front seats were then filled by Miss Abby Hedge, three young ladies whose names I have not preserved, Colonel Davis, and myself. A merry six-hours' ride we had of it, — we young people, at least. My journal tells how bright and lively was Miss Hedge, who was quite a match for a couple of colonels in readiness of apprehension, and who, when the fire of fun and repartee began to slacken, produced just the stimulant required in the form of a package of peppermints. This animated young lady afterward married a gentleman quite equal to herself in humor and good social qualities. The name of Charles H. Warren (better known as Judge Warren) could never be mentioned by his contemporaries without a smile of obligation. It has been my fortune to preside at several public dinners, — indeed, I counted up some thirty of them the other day; and, of all men, it becomes me to express a sense of the value of his contributions to the general mirth. "Is Judge Warren to be at your dinner?" was my first question to the committees who came to offer me the head of the table. "If he is to be there, and will consent to be called upon, why then I, or any other King Log, will do for a president." And quite as important was the presence of Mrs. Warren (that was to be) to the enjoyment of the bevy of careless travellers who sat face to face upon the front seats of that Plymouth coach. What cared we for the grave discussions of the Governor, Treasurer, and Postmaster, who were running the State just behind us? How soon would it be possible to complete a canal from Boston harbor to the Connecticut River? Would or would not the Commissioners report that the scheme was practicable? What then of the project of uniting Lakes Champlain and Memphremagog with our central stream, and so whitening Massachusetts Bay with the sails which this magnificent opening of the back country would necessitate? These and other questions quite as momentous were thoroughly discussed upon the back seat, and the reader might have heard all about them if the future Mrs. Warren and her fair companions had only taken passage by some other coach. In that case it is pretty certain that one of the colonels would have pulled out his note-book and appropriated some of the wisdom which his superiors were dispensing with such liberality.

We had a public reception at Plymouth, for a governor was in those days an unusual guest even in places within six hours' staging of the capital. The principal citizens assembled about our party, and performed the ceremony of hand-shaking in behalf of the less honorable multitude who had not yet learned to demand their full rights in this particular. I have heard some of our more recent public men confess that submission to the tactual privileges of their equal democrats was the bitterest trial of official position, one of them informing me that he was accustomed to devote a day to groaning with poulticed hand and bandaged arm after receiving the honors of a reception. Fortunately, the mild flavor of aristocracy still surrounding a governor saved Lincoln from this infliction, — fortunately, I say; for his Excellency had no time for poulticing, but was compelled to rise at half past three the morning after the limited hand-shaking of the reception, in order to undergo the more general shaking of the stage which bore our party to Sandwich. A noted resort for sportsmen was Sandwich in those days, and a famous inn, whose cook knew how to dress the birds which the guns of the guests never failed to furnish, added to the reputation of the town. And in this inn Daniel Webster was staying at the time of our visit, though we missed him, as he had gone off to shoot plover. The great man, however, was by no means unmindful of his duty to the head of the State, and had supplied a proxy, in the person of his friend, George Blake. "You must stay behind and see that the Governor gets the right sort of breakfast after his long ride," said Mr. Webster. And so Mr. Blake did stay, and was eminently successful in providing a meal which, garnished with his own charming manners, still lives in my memory as the ideal of all country breakfasts. After this liberal entertainment we journeyed on to Falmouth, where we arrived somewhat before noon, and there, all ready to set sail, we found the Nantucket packet; and there also we found a head wind, which positively prohibited the Nantucket packet from doing anything of the sort. Oh, those head winds! What plagues they were to those who were in a hurry to leave our harbors, and how steam has lengthened the lives of travellers by sparing them those dreary waits! We had risen at a most uncomfortable hour, to post on to Falmouth; and here we might remain a week, unless the wind condescended to blow from some quarter that would allow our vessel to get out of the bay. We accepted this fact with such philosophy as was available, listening the while to the prognostications of the skippers and frequently gazing at the heavens for such hopes or consolations as they might supply. But we were not, on this occasion, to be tried beyond our strength; for as the sun went down the wind hauled several points, and we were off. Concerning the passage, I will only observe that the Nantucket packet, although it carried the ruler of a sovereign state, could by no means transform itself into a royal yacht. We were stowed in narrow bunks, in an indiscriminate and vulgar manner, and took such repose as we might till two o'clock in the morning, when a sudden thud, followed by an unpleasant swashing sound about the sides of the vessel, brought us to our feet to inquire what had happened. "All right!" said the skipper. "Just you lie still till morning. We're aground on Nantucket Bar. That's all." Thus adjured, we thought it best to remain below, till a faint suspicion of dawn struggled into the cabin and gave us an excuse for coming upon deck. Several whaling ships, anchored outside the harbor, loomed to gigantic proportions in the gray morning. "There is Yankee perseverance for you!" exclaimed the Governor. "Would they believe in Europe that a port which

had seen no other horizon than that which bounds Nantucket. The Friends, being the oldest and most respectable body of Christians, gave their sombre color to the town and their thrifty ways to those holding its purse-strings. For instance, when it was complained that Nantucket, the greatest depot of spermaceti and whale oil in the whole world, was, likewise, its darkest corner in the evening, it was replied that it would be culpably extravagant to consume at home in street-lanterns oil that had been procured for exportation. Moreover, the reckless innovator was invited to impale himself upon one of the horns of this little dilemma: "Oil was either high or low. Now, if it was low, the citizens could not afford to pay the tax; but if it was high, the town could not afford to purchase it." After the reception, we all went to the barber-shop, not to be shaved, but to inspect the collection of South Sea curiosities of which this functionary was the custodian. And here we lingered till it was time to prepare for the grand party in honor of the Governor, which would furnish a brilliant conclusion to his visit.

This party was given by Mr. Aaron Mitchell, and was said to be the finest in all its appointments that the island had yet known. There was, of course, no dancing; but the number of beautiful and lively young women impressed me as exceeding anything that could be looked for in a similar gathering upon the mainland, and filled me with regrets that we were to sail at daybreak the next morning. My journal relates how I was expressing my feelings in this particular to a bright bevy of these girls, when Hezekiah Barnard suddenly joined our group and put in this remark: "Friend, if thou really wishest to tarry on our island, thou hast only to persuade one of these young women to put a black cat under a tub, and surely there will be a head wind to-morrow." This sailors' superstition, of which I had never heard, was the cause of much pleasantry. The ladies united in declaring that there was not a black cat in all Nantucket, they having been smothered under tubs, to retain husbands and brothers who were bound for the southern seas. At last Miss Baxter ("the prettiest girl in the room," says my record) confessed to the possession of a black kitten. But, then, would this do? Surely, a very heavy and mature pussy, perhaps even two of them, would be required to keep a governor against his will. Yes; but then an aide-de-camp could certainly be kept by a kitten, even if it were not weaned, and Miss Baxter had only to dismiss the Governor from her thoughts and concentrate them upon his humble attendant, and the charm would work. I do not know whether young people talk in this way now, or whether they are as glad as Miss Baxter and I were to find some topic other than the weather to ring our simple changes on; but I should refrain from personal episodes in this historical epic, which deals with the august movements of the Governor. It is well for us chroniclers to remember that the *ego et rex meus* way of telling things once got poor Cardinal Wolsey into a good deal of difficulty.

"Wind dead ahead!" were the words with which Mr. Burnell called me, the next morning. "The Governor must spend Sunday on the island, and we will show him a Quaker meeting and Micajah Coffin." An account of both these objects of interest finds its place in my journal. At the Friends' Society we sat for nearly an hour in absolute silence, and this seemed to me very favorable to reflection and devotional feeling. There was something in the absence of any human expression in the awful presence of the Maker which struck me as a more fitting homage than any words or ceremony could convey. It was only when two women felt themselves moved by the Spirit to address the assembly that my feelings underwent a quick revulsion, and I acknowledged that, for the majority of Christians at least, a trained and learned clergy would long be indispensable. After meeting, the Governor and his staff paid a visit of ceremony to Micajah Coffin, the oldest and most respected citizen of the island. At a time when the rulings of etiquette were far more stringent than at present, it was doubted whether the representative of a sovereign state could properly call upon a private person who had not first waited upon him. Lincoln's decision that this case should be an exception to all general rules was no less creditable to the magistrate than gratifying to the islanders; for good Friend Coffin, then past ninety, was at times unable to command his memory, and his friends had not thought it right to subject him to the excitements of the reception at the Insurance Office. For twenty-two years this venerable man had represented Nantucket in the Massachusetts General Court. In his youth he had worked at carpentering and gone whaling in a sloop, bringing home on one occasion two hundred barrels of sperm oil, which made his owner a rich man. These latter particulars I learn from Mr. William C. Folger, of Nantucket, who remembers Mr. Coffin as "a tall old gentleman, dressed in the style of a past age." And one thing more Mr. Folger mentions, of which the significance will presently appear: "Benjamin Coffin, the father of Micajah, was one of Nantucket's best schoolmasters for about half a century." I had been looking in vain through college catalogues to explain a singular circumstance which my journal relates; but the appearance of Benjamin Coffin the schoolmaster suggests the true solution of the difficulty. When this patriarch of Nantucket was presented to the Governor, it made so little impression upon him that he instantly forgot the presence of the chief magistrate; and yet a moment afterward he astonished us with one of those strange feats of memory which show with how tight a grip the mysterious nerve-centres, of which we hear so much, hold what has been committed to them. For, having a dim consciousness that something out of the common was expected from him, the venerable man turned suddenly upon Postmaster Hill, and proceeded to harangue that very modest gentleman in a set Latin speech. It was one of those occurrences which might appear either sad or droll to the bystanders, and I hope it does not reflect upon the good feelings of the party to mention that we found its comic aspect quite irresistible. There was poor Mr. Hill, overcome with mortification at being mistaken for the Governor, and shrinking from fine Latin superlatives, which, under this erroneous impression, were discharged upon him. And when the Postmaster, at the conclusion of the address, felt that he was bound in courtesy to make some response (which, of course, could not be in the vernacular), and could hit upon nothing better than "*Oui, Monsieur, je vous remercie,*" the climax was reached, and even the Governor was forced to give audible expression to his sense of the ridiculous. And thus it was that testimony was given to the good instruction of Master Benjamin Coffin. The father had undoubtedly taught his son Latin as a spoken language, as the custom formerly was. The lessons were given in the first half of the eighteenth century, and here am I, in the concluding fifth of the nineteenth, able to testify to the thoroughness of the teaching.

Micajah Coffin lived for little more than a year after the visit of Lincoln. "In his old age," says Mr. Folger, "he took an interest in visiting the sick and aiding them in procuring native plants suited to cure or at least to relieve their various maladies." I learn, also, that in his rambles about Nantucket, when he met a face that was unknown to him, he was accustomed to stop and give this challenge: "Friend, my name is Micajah Coffin. What is thine?" It was the robust assertion of a personality of which there was no reason to be ashamed, and testifies to the reasonableness of the high esteem in which his character and services were held among his fellow-islanders.

Early Monday morning we left Nantucket with a breeze which carried us to New Bedford in six hours. The Governor's reception in that town, the courtesy of the selectmen, the magnificent hospitalities of the Rotches and Rodmans, my space compels me to omit. One word, however, of the picture presented by the venerable William Rotch, ninety-three years of age, standing between his son and his grandson, the elder gentlemen being in their Quaker dresses and the youngest in the fashionable costume of the day. "You will never see a more ideal representation of extreme age, middle life, and vigorous maturity than is given by these three handsome and intelligent men," said Governor Lincoln to me, as we left the house. Up to this date, at least, his prediction has been verified.

A JOURNEY WITH JUDGE STORY.

IN the beginning of the year 1826, Judge Story invited me to accompany him to Washington, whither he was going to discharge his duties upon the Supreme Bench. My acquaintance with this distinguished man began when, as an undergraduate, I dined with him in Salem, during a visit to that town. As a boy I was fascinated by the brilliancy of his conversation, and now that I was at the base of the profession which he adorned I regarded him with peculiar reverence. I remember my father's graphic account of the rage of the Federalists when "Joe Story, that country pettifogger, aged thirty-two," was made a judge of our highest court. He was a bitter Democrat in those days, and had written a Fourth of July oration which was as a red rag to the Federal bull. It was understood that years and responsibilities had greatly modified his opinions, and I happened to be present upon an occasion when the Judge alluded to this early production in a characteristic way. We were dining at Professor Ticknor's, and Mr. Webster was of the party. In a pause of the conversation, Story broke out: "I was looking over some old papers this morning, and found my Fourth of July oration. So I read it through from beginning to end."

"Well, sir," said Webster, in his deep and impressive bass, "now tell us honestly what you thought of it."

"I thought the text very pretty, sir," replied the Judge; "but I looked in vain for the notes. *No authorities were stated in the margin.*"

The invitation to go to Washington with Judge Story did not imply any promise of attention after we arrived in that city, as he was careful to point out when I received it. "The fact is," said he, "I can do very little for you there, as we judges take no part in the society of the place. We dine once a year with the President, and that is all. On other days we take our dinner together, and discuss at table the questions which are argued before us. We are great ascetics, and even deny ourselves wine, except in wet weather." Here the Judge paused, as if thinking that the act of mortification he had mentioned placed too severe a tax upon human credulity, and presently added: "What I say about the wine, sir, gives you our rule; but it does sometimes happen that the Chief Justice will say to me, when the cloth is removed, 'Brother Story, step to the window and see if it does not look like rain.' And if I tell him that the sun is shining brightly, Judge Marshall will sometimes reply, 'All the better; for our jurisdiction extends over so large a territory that the doctrine of chances makes it certain that it must be raining somewhere.' You know that the Chief was brought up upon Federalism and Madeira, and he is not the man to outgrow his early prejudices."

Before I begin my journey with Judge Story, I have been asked to say a word of my previous travels. I had visited Washington in 1807, accompanying my father, who was a member of Congress. I well remember the intolerable roads, and the flat-bottomed boats in which we crossed the Hudson and the Susquehanna, and that, on returning, we took a sloop between New York and Providence. No wonder that the statesmen of that day foretold the dissolution of the Union, from the vast extent of territory it occupied, and the consequent time and expense involved in assembling representatives. They thought they had all the data for calculation, and that it required only moderate powers of reasoning to see the result. Let us take heed by their example when we are tempted to characterize as Utopian the co-operative solution of the difficulties between labor and capital by which we are at present beset. The dream of no enthusiast can appear so incredible to us as the prophecy that, within a life then existing, a representative from the Pacific Coast might reach Washington with far less fatigue and expense than was incurred by the representative from Boston would have seemed to the gentlemen in powdered hair and pigtails whom I dimly remember in Washington. The city itself presented a forlorn appearance. Blocks of houses had been commenced; the speculators had failed; and unfinished buildings, without doors or windows, were in every street. I recall all this very distinctly, because there was a print of the "Ruins of Palmyra" which I pointed out to my parents, on our way home, with the exclamation, "Why, there's a picture of Washington!" This innocent blunder was considered a most felicitous characterization of the general appearance of the city, and for years after the "Ruins of Palmyra" was used in the family as a convenient synonym for the capital of the nation.

Nineteen years after, when I made the journey with Judge Story, stages ran regularly between New York and Boston. They left the latter city at three in the morning, and at two o'clock a man was sent round to the houses of those who were booked for a passage. His instructions were to knock, pull the bell, shout, and disturb the neighborhood as much as possible, in order that the person who was to take the stage might be up and dressed when it reached his door. Light sleepers in the vicinity were made painfully aware when the stage was expected, and were often afflicted with an hour of uneasy consciousness, till it had rumbled through the street and taken up its passenger. In the mean time the inmates of the stage waited through the dreary hours preceding daybreak, till they could see the faces of their fellow-travellers and commence that intimate acquaintance with them which a ride of some days seldom failed to effect. People who never talked anywhere else were driven to talk in those old coaches; while a ready conversationalist, like Judge Story, was stimulated to incessant cerebral discharges. When the sun at length revealed our fellow-passengers, they turned out to be Mr. and Mrs. McCobb, from Maine, who were escorting to Washington the Misses Cleaves, two young ladies who, as we were privately informed, were heiresses, and were to make their *début* in the society of the capital.

Besides these, there was Mr. John Knapp, brother-in-law to Chief Justice Shaw, of Massachusetts. He was a lawyer, somewhat diminutive in stature, who was on his way to Washington to argue before the Supreme Court. He was fully awake to the good fortune which gave him one of the judges as a fellow-traveller, and succeeded in making an agreeable impression upon us all. My journal mentions a very funny account he gave of an employment which, in his earlier days, he had combined with that of legal adviser. He was held by his neighbors to possess a very pretty talent for composition, and it came to pass that he was constantly called upon to write love-letters of the most confidential and tender character. He had thought of establishing rates of charges to correspond with the fire and pathos that was required in these productions, and might have created a permanent business, had the noble profession of the law failed to support him. "But the worst of it is," said Mr. Knapp, glancing at the young ladies, "I have glowed with such fervors on behalf of other people that I seem to have lost the capacity of feeling on my own account, and, consequently, have remained a wretched bachelor to this day." Lest we might consider his success limited to amatory literature, Mr. Knapp went on to tell us of a sea-captain of his acquaintance who engaged him to write his epitaph. "This was, to be sure, somewhat out of my line," said the little lawyer, "and I might have failed without discredit; but the fact was, I gave my employer such satisfaction that he actually had my epitaph cut upon a gravestone, and enjoined it upon his executors to add nothing but the date when the time came to set it up."

Judge Story was one of the great talkers at a period when conversation was considered a sort of second profession. At dinners, when the time was limited and other distinguished men were present, he sometimes talked too much; but in the coach he could not pour himself out too abundantly for the pleasure of his listeners. He had spent part of the previous summer in travelling with Daniel Webster, and had added a fresh stock of observation and anecdote to his abundant *repertoire*. There was only one thing he did not talk about, and that was law. As the expressive phrase goes, he "sunk the shop;" though this same "shop" would have been a subject most interesting to at least two of his companions. A person who did not know Judge Story might have taken him for one of those agreeable individuals who are so well informed in all departments that they can be great in none. If required to find the most learned jurist of the age in that coach, such a person would have pitched upon Mr. McCobb or Mr. Knapp. Certainly, this courteous gentleman, all whose reading seemed to be poetry and *belles-lettres*, could not be the man. It was sarcastically said of Lord Brougham, when he was Chancellor of England, that, if he only knew a little law, he would know a little of everything. But this bitter saying was nothing but an inversion of the tribute Judge Parsons received from John Lowell, who declared that Parsons knew more law than anybody else, and more of everything else than he did of law. The compliment is so neat that we forgive its extravagance; but it is certainly as applicable to Story as to the elder jurist. I can give no better idea of the intimate relations developed in the old stage-coach than by mentioning that before night the Judge was favoring us with recitations of original poetry. They were not brief selections either, and were rolled off with evident confidence in their excellence. Subsequently, Judge Story came to the conclusion that the Muses were not favorable to his invocations, and actually bought up and burned all attainable copies of a poem called the "Power of Solitude," which he once committed to the press. But a conviction of sin in this particular had not yet reached our learned companion. He found occasion to quote Pope's lamentation, "How sweet an Ovid was in Murray lost!" and evidently thought that the stanza might find an American application. Cicero, John Quincy Adams, and other great men never quite accepted the fact that their abilities and application gave them no foothold upon Parnassus; and if Judge Story was at one time not free from the delusion which afflicted these his distinguished peers, he was at least mistaken in good company. He had the knack of rhyming with ease, and it was said that he would sometimes beguile the hours of tedious argument to which he was compelled to listen by making his notes in verse.

As we jogged on, the conversation fell upon novels, and, this being a subject we could all talk about, it remained there for a good many miles. After the tribute to the powers of Scott, which was a matter of course, Judge Story spoke of Mrs. Radcliffe in terms of great admiration, and wished she could have had some of the weird legends of Marblehead upon which to display her wealth of lurid imagery. Miss Burney's "Evelina" he thought very bright and fascinating, while the conversations of Maria Edgeworth were Nature itself, and yet full of point — the duller speeches of her characters being simply omitted, as was proper in a work of art. On a subsequent occasion, I heard him place Jane Austen much above these writers, and compliment her with a panegyric quite equal to those bestowed by Scott and Macaulay. "It is only the nature of their education," said the Judge, "which puts women at such disadvantages and keeps up the notion that they are our inferiors in ability. What would a man be without his profession or business, which compels him to learn something new every day? The best sources of knowledge are shut off from women, and the surprise is that they manage to keep so nearly abreast with us as they do." I think that I am safe in saying that Judge Story was alone among the prominent men of that day in the adoption of views respecting women very similar to those afterward proclaimed by Mr.

Mill. He would not admit that sex or temperament assigned them an inferior part in the intellectual development of the race. It was all a matter of training. Give them opportunities of physical and mental education equal to those enjoyed by men, and there was nothing to disqualify them from attaining an equal success in any field of mental effort. Whether his views were drawn from reliable data and have been sustained by subsequent experience are questions upon which a writer of reminiscences need not enter; but it seems due to all parties to say that many of the theoretical opinions published by Mr. Mill were anticipated by Joseph Story.

The first night of our journey was spent at Ashford, in Connecticut, where we arrived late in the evening; and here the bother of the wild-cat currency, as it was afterward called, was forced upon our attention. The bills of local banks would not circulate beyond the town in which they were issued, and when Judge Story, who had neglected to provide himself with United States notes, offered the landlord a Salem bill, in payment for his supper, the man stared at it as if it had been the wampum of the Indians or the shell-money of the South Sea Islanders. "This is not good," said the host, "and I think you must know it." "I know it *is* good," retorted the Judge, testily; "and I'll tell you how I know it. *I made it myself.*" This reply, of which the landlord could make nothing, unless it were the confession of a forger, did not mend matters; and it was fortunate that I had provided myself with some national notes, which ended the difficulty. The explanation may have been that Judge Story, as president of some Salem bank, had signed the bill in question, though I have not at hand the means of verifying the fact that he held such an office. Our present system of currency, which makes the bills of petty banks good throughout the nation, and indeed in all civilized countries, is a blessing which the present generation cannot fully appreciate.

Another day, and we reached New Haven, where we passed the night. The early hours of Sunday that we were allowed in this city I spent in visiting the churches, in attendance upon the Misses Cleaves, "who, being fresh from boarding-school" (so says my journal), "are somewhat romantic." May it chance that either of these fair young creatures (for so they must be to me) are yet living? May it happen that either of them survives to read this narrative of our journey with the great Judge? Were they also keeping journals? It is just possible that the publication of this paper may bring me some news of their lives during the fifty-four years since we parted company.[1]

---

[1] It resulted in a correspondence with the venerable Mrs. A. C. Dummer of Hallowell, Maine, the survivor of the sisters mentioned in the text. "Little did I think," wrote this lady, "that, when taking the journey alluded to, which was the first great event of my life, 'being fresh from boarding-school and somewhat romantic,' I should be reminded of it after a period of fifty-four years by one of the party who enjoyed the privilege of the friendly intercourse, the pleasure, and instruction derived from the unlimited fund of conversation and knowledge possessed by Judge Story. During the long course of years since that time, each member of that stage-coach party has been held in pleasant remembrance."

Leaving New Haven at ten in the morning, we reached Stamford about dark. The day following we drove into the great city in time for a late dinner. It seemed quite incredible! We had left Boston early Friday morning, had driven all the way, and here we were, Monday evening, actually dining in New York. It need not be said that we congratulated ourselves upon living in the days of rapid communication, and looked with commiseration upon the condition of our fathers, who were wont to consume a whole week in travelling between the cities.

FROM NEW YORK TO WASHINGTON.

WHEN Judge Story and his companion reached their lodgings at Mrs. Frazier's boarding-house, on the afternoon of the 30th of January, 1826, they were met by a solemn announcement. New York had succumbed to the influenza. Everybody had been, was, or was going to be sick with it. This mysterious disorder, travelling in the path of the Asiatic cholera, was now making the tour of America, some parts of which it visited with great severity. It was known as "the winter epidemic" in Philadelphia, and in the South, where it was very fatal among the negro population, as "the cold plague." The simple faith in the power of medicine was in those days quite touching, and for the question "What ought I to do?" which sensible persons now ask when disorder threatens the body, there was substituted the inquiry "What ought I to take?" The answers came thick and fast, and here are a few of them. Take linseed and licorice, also barley water, also a mixture of vinegar and sugar candy, also wine of antimony, then try senna, and, above all things, practise no short-sighted economy in the matter of blue pills. I declined to fortify my system with any of these admirable doses, for it was evident to me that everybody was not sick, after all. There was Cooper, for instance, — "Cooper, the noblest Roman of them all," as Charles Sprague called him in his Phi Beta poem upon Curiosity, — he, at least, had no influenza, for the bills announced that he was to play one of his best Shakespearian parts, *Mark Antony* in "Julius Cæsar," that very night. And, for further assurance, no sooner had we seated ourselves at Mrs. Frazier's dining-table than Cooper himself stalked into the room and took a place in our neighborhood. He was a fine-looking man of about fifty, and we found his conversation to be that of an educated gentleman, with just that dash of easy Bohemianism which young people find attractive. Americans can never feel about any other actor as we once felt about Cooper, who came to our shores in the last century and had created our conceptions of the greater characters in the Shakespearian drama. I have before me some letters written from Boston, in 1807, which testify to the fascinations of Cooper's acting at that date. They mention that the fashionable circles of the town could make nothing of *Hamlet* until Cooper came to show them what Shakespeare meant by that mysterious personage. About the time I met him in New York he was much admired in *Romeo* (Miss Kelly being the *Juliet*), a part which he played much better than when he was a young man. And so theatre-goers matched a saying of Edmund Kean's, that only a young man could play *King Lear*, by declaring that it required an old one to give the best representation of the boy-lover of Verona.

After dinner, I repaired to my uncle's house on the Battery, then the ornament of New York and surrounded by the wealth and fashion of the city. Everybody there was down with the influenza; but one of my cousins, less afflicted than the rest, insisted upon getting up to go with me to Mrs. Hamilton Holley's splendid ball, which it would never do for a stranger to miss. And a splendid ball it was! — or was meant to be. Handsome rooms, a fine band of music, and a good supper. There was but one drawback, — there were no guests. Six ladies, says my journal, and a few more gentlemen were the only influenzaless persons in the polite society of New York; and one of these six ladies was from Philadelphia. This was Miss Anna Gillespie; and much amusement we had together over this ball, which was no ball, in the arrogant metropolis. We had been brought by our respective friends as humble provincials to gaze upon social glories we could never emulate, and much innocent fun was the result. A trifling bond of union like this will put young people on easy terms for an evening, and when I left Mrs. Holley's ball, at one in the morning, it was with the feeling that for me, at least, the influenza had not despoiled it of agreeable incidents.

Of our journey to Philadelphia I copy from my journal this brief notice: —

"*February* 1, 1826. — We left our lodgings at five o'clock this morning, and, after waiting an hour for the ferry-boat, crossed to Powles Hook, breaking the ice all the way. Our party consisted of Judge Story,

Judge Thompson (who talked incessantly about pleading), a navy officer, and three ladies of uncertain reputation, with whom the said navy officer held high converse all the way. We had an opposition stage at our heels, and consequently drove very rapidly; but our detention at the ferry was so great that it was between eleven and twelve before we put up at the Mansion House."

The next day I saw something of Philadelphia, and in the evening three acts of Kean's *Hamlet*, which I left, with great reluctance, to attend a supper-party at Mr. Nathaniel Amory's, "where I found everything in the Boston style, and could hardly believe, when I saw the jolly face of my host, that we were both so far from the land of our fathers. Here I met Messrs. Vaughan, Hopkinson, Meredith, with other notables of the city." On returning to the Mansion House, late in the evening, I found Judge Story prostrated with the influenza, and, of course, unable to continue our journey to Washington. He begged me to abandon him to his fate, and to leave the next day, as we had intended. This I refused to do, as we were travelling companions for better or for worse, and it was clearly my duty to remain and take care of him. A delightful week in Philadelphia rewarded me for this consideration. As soon as the Judge was convalescent the great lawyers and mighty men of the city thronged to call upon him, and most interesting discussions went on in the sick-chamber. Of these I regret to say I made no notes, although my journal implies that the talk of those eminent lawyers, Sergeant and Binney, would have been well worth reporting. Both of these men I heard in court during my visit. Sergeant was dull in his manner, giving a stranger no adequate impression of the depth and force of reasoning which had made him famous. His rival, Binney, on the contrary, had all the qualities which take at a glance. He was fine-looking and exceedingly graceful; his speaking was easy and often rose into eloquence. The men seemed to be pretty nearly abreast in the estimation of the bar.

I soon had another distinguished patient; no less a person than Henry Wheaton, at that time reporter for the United States Supreme Court, and engaged in the preparation of those twelve volumes of decisions which will keep his name greener than all the good diplomatic work he afterward performed. He arrived at the Mansion House terribly afflicted with the prevailing epidemic, and, at the recommendation of Judge Story, who was now getting better, put himself under my care. In a day or two he so far recovered as to be no small addition to the distinguished circle which held its sessions in the Judge's parlor. My journal gives some notices of Philadelphia society: of a dinner at General Cadwallader's, and of a young man's supper-party at the house of Mr. ——. Of the latter entertainment the entry reads thus: "We met about eight; looked over caricatures and played cards until nine. We were then summoned to an elegant supper, about twenty of the first young men of Philadelphia being the guests. They were not intellectual, and were in a fair way to be drunk when

I left them at midnight." Probably nothing better could be said of the gilded youths of New York or Boston at that period of little literature and much conviviality. I find a notice of an evening at the theatre, whither I was taken by Mrs. Cadwallader, and where I was greatly surprised to see women admitted to the pit. The *Beatrice* of the play — I suppress the name of the actress, as she has long been past criticism — I find vulgar and coarse; but the *Dogberry* of Jefferson (grandfather to *Rip Van Winkle*) was a revelation of the power of comic acting. It was magnificent. I tell how I stopped to laugh over it on my way home. I could not get rid of that superb patronage of *Goodman Verges,* and of the monstrous inflation of the "rich fellow enough, who knew the law and had had losses."

On Sunday I listened to preaching from Dr. Abercrombie, at St. John's Church, and heard some discussion of a singular ecclesiastical privilege which then existed in Philadelphia. This was the right to obstruct the streets by chains during the hours of divine service. There were petitions going about for the repeal of the act of legislation which permitted proceedings which the objectors seemed to think worthy of the imaginary Blue Laws of Connecticut. It was alleged that doctors visiting their patients, and other travellers upon errands of mercy, were put to sore inconvenience by these chains across the highways. They were, moreover, typical of that fetter between Church and State which the Genius of America was supposed to have shattered. To all which it was answered that a state which compelled no one to attend religious exercises must, at least, protect from annoyance those who choose to do so; that medical men and the very few lawful travellers might well be required to go a little out of their way for the good of large classes of the community; and that, as all other travellers were breaking the law by being out at all, it was the height of impudence to ask law-makers to consider their convenience while doing so. How the dispute was settled I am unable to say. It seemed to me one of those cases in which appearances which excite the imagination of any part of the community should have been avoided. Philadelphia is so built that the inconvenience of going round a block or two, to avoid disturbing worshippers, must have been scarcely appreciable; but the chains did have a bad look about them, and proper police regulations should have prevented their employment.

On Thursday, the ninth day of February, Judge Story and Mr. Wheaton were pronounced well enough to proceed on their way to the capital, provided they broke the journey and avoided the chill and exposure of the early morning. They accordingly left Philadelphia by a private conveyance, and I was to overtake them, the next day, by the more fatiguing but more economical transportation of the regular stage. As the brief account of my progress toward Washington seems to require no abridgment, the contemporary record shall be copied.

"*February* 10, 1826.— At three o'clock this morning the light of a candle under the door and a rousing knock told me that it was time to depart, and shortly after I left Philadelphia by the Lancaster stage, otherwise a vast, illimitable wagon, with seats without backs, capable of holding some sixteen passengers with decent comfort to themselves, and actually encumbered with some dozen more. After riding till eight o'clock, we reached the Breakfast House, where we partook of a good meal and took up Messrs. Story and Wheaton. We then proceeded through a most beautiful tract of country, where good fences and huge stone barns proved the excellence of the farming. The road seemed actually lined with Conostoga wagons, each drawn by six stalwart horses and laden with farm produce. At Lancaster, the largest inland town in the United States, we changed stages and company. From that place to York our party consisted of Langdon Cheves, formerly president of the United States Bank, Mr. Buchanan, a member of Congress from Pennsylvania, Mr. Henry, another member from Kentucky, Judge Story, Mr. Wheaton, and myself. I found the additions rather amusing men, and we rode together till some time after dark, when we reached York, found good accommodations, and are ready to turn in, it being about ten o'clock.

"*February* 11. — After being detained till near ten by the non-arrival of the stage from Harrisburg, we started for Baltimore, and, after a tedious ride through a hilly country and over bad roads, we reached 'Barnum's' at eleven o'clock to-night. We were much fatigued and wanted to go to bed; but Barnum, who is a great friend of Judge Story, and knew him when he (Barnum) kept the Exchange Coffee House in Boston, would keep us up for canvas-backs and a bottle of capital wine. We sat talking over these delicacies till near one o'clock.

"*February* 12. — We left Baltimore at nine o'clock in the morning, and reached Washington about three in the afternoon. At the recommendation of Mr. Cheves, I accompanied him to Miss Hyer's on Capitol Hill, where I found a delightful party of gentlemen, consisting of Thomas Addis Emmet and David B. Ogden, of New York; Rufus G. Amory, of Boston; Captain Stockton, of the navy; Captain Zantzinger, of the army; and, last and least, so far as bodily presence goes, my old travelling companion, Mr. John Knapp. I suppose it was only because he had retained Mr. Emmet that he dared to come to the same table with Captain Stockton, the defendant in the 'Marianna Flora' case, whom he is bound to make out a fierce and terrible fellow indeed. I called this evening upon Mr. Webster, and through his hands received a letter from home. He was not in himself; but I spent a pleasant hour with Mrs. Webster and Mrs. Blake."

I had come to Washington at an interesting time. John Quincy Adams, perhaps the best-trained executive officer this country has ever possessed, occupied the Presidential chair. Henry Clay was Secretary of State, — an office he should never have accepted, as the charge of corrupt bargaining with the man whom he had made President was sure to be made. Shortly after the inauguration, had been heard the first threatenings of the conflict which thirty-four years later was to deluge the country with blood. During the previous May, Governor Troup, of Georgia, had addressed a message to his legislature complaining of "officious and impertinent intermeddlings with our domestic concerns," and closing with an exhortation to "step forth, and, having exhausted the argument, to stand by your arms." A combination of brilliant, if unscrupulous, political leaders, about which a new party was to crystallize, had opened its batteries upon the administration and was thundering forth the grossest charges. The situation must be remembered in order to understand such notices of public and social life at Washington as my journals may enable me to give.

VISITS TO JOHN RANDOLPH.

I WILL begin my account of Washington with some notices of the remarkable man whom of all others I most desired to see. This was John Randolph, a good friend and correspondent of my father's, though two men more utterly dissimilar in temperament and opinions can scarcely be imagined. I shall first give some report of the part he took in the private conversations to which I was admitted, and afterward describe two memorable occasions when I heard him in the Senate.

I left a card with a letter from my father at "Dawson's," on Capitol Hill, the lodgings of Mr. Randolph, soon after my arrival. With great promptness, he sent me a note, in which he alluded to the trying political scenes through which he had passed with my father, and declared the "sentiments of great esteem and regard" which he cherished toward him. Describing himself as "an old and very infirm man," he begged me to waive ceremony, and visit him either before the meeting of the Senate or between its adjournment and eight o'clock in the evening, which hour, he was careful to mention, was his bedtime.

About ten the next morning I called upon Mr.

is a satire on the weakness, folly, and wickedness of man worthy of the Prince of Darkness." Soon after this climax a stout gentleman, about seventy years of age, came in to accompany him to the Capitol, and Randolph introduced me in these words: "I have pleasure to make you acquainted with the ablest man in Washington, Mr. Macon, of North Carolina." This gentleman was much admired by Randolph, who in his will paid him the still higher compliment of being "the best and purest and wisest man that I ever knew." The fact that Macon had opposed the adoption of the Constitution, on the ground that it gave too much power to the General Government, was sufficient to endear him to this ardent Virginian, who was always protesting against its aggressions.

Before I visited Mr. Randolph again, I had listened with admiration to his wonderful improvisations in the Senate, and had determined to get at his views about the oratory of Patrick Henry, of which I had heard John Adams speak in terms of some disparagement. I accordingly put a question which I supposed would call out a panegyric upon the orator of Virginia. I asked who was the greatest orator he had ever heard. The reply was startling, from its unexpectedness. "The greatest orator I ever heard," said Randolph, "was a woman. She was a slave. She was a mother, and her rostrum was the auction-block." He then rose and imitated with thrilling pathos the tones with which this woman had appealed to the sympathy and justice of the bystanders, and finally the indignation with which she denounced them. "There was eloquence!" he said. "I have heard no *man* speak like that. It was overpowering!" He sat down and paused for some moments; then, evidently feeling that he had been imprudent in expressing himself so warmly before a visitor from the North, he entered upon a defence of the policy of Southern statesmen in regard to slavery. "We must concern ourselves with what is," he said, "and slavery exists. We must preserve the rights of the States, as guaranteed by the Constitution, or the negroes are at our throats. The question of slavery, as it is called, is to us a question of life and death. Remember, it is a necessity imposed on the South; not a Utopia of our own seeking. You will find no instance in history where two distinct races have occupied the soil except in the relation of master and slave." I brought away only these few fragments of an elaborate defence of the course which he and other Southerners felt compelled to pursue; but they give its nature with sufficient clearness.

I again ventured to touch upon the subject of oratory, and this time Mr. Randolph broke into a disquisition upon the nature of the illustrations which a speaker might draw from literature. I regret that I can give so little of what he said; but so much as I have preserved is substantially in his own words: "It is a great blunder for a speaker to allude to books which are not familiar to his audience. A quotation from Horace or Juvenal will do in the British Parliament. The members are all graduates from Oxford and Cambridge, and they understand it. But what folly it would be to quote the classics to an average American audience! I know of only three books with which all decently educated Americans are familiar. These are the Bible, Shakespeare, and Milton. Now I want you to notice a fine passage from Burke, which I will repeat, and you will find that he has used thought or language from these three books in its construction." Mr. Randolph then recited the following passage from the author he had named: —

"Old religious factions are volcanoes burnt out. On the lava and ashes and squalid scoriæ of old eruptions grow the peaceful olive, the cheering vine, and the sustaining corn. Such was the first, such the second condition of Vesuvius. But when a new fire bursts out a face of desolation comes on, not to be rectified in ages. Therefore, when men come before us and rise up like an exhalation from the ground, they come in a questionable shape, and we must exorcise them and try whether their intents be wicked or charitable; whether they bring airs from heaven or blasts from hell."

I said that I did not remember this passage, and asked where I could find it. "Go to the Congressional Library," was Mr. Randolph's reply, "look in the third alcove, on the right-hand side, third shelf from floor, fifth volume on the shelf, page 336, about half-way down." I made a memorandum of the direction, went to the library, and found the passage exactly where he had placed it. [Having lost the original memorandum, I have given the page from my own copy of Burke, which may or may not correspond with that in the library; but Mr. Randolph's direction was just as explicit as I have written it.] Of course, such a feat of memory might have been an accident or a trick. In Mr. Randolph's case I am convinced it was neither. No one could have heard him in debate or conversation without being impressed with the tenacious clutch of his memory upon all that had come within its range. A fluent talker without abundant stores to draw upon soon betrays himself. Others may have had as great a capital; but this man's wealth was, so to speak, all on deposit, and he could command it in an instant.

Mr. Randolph spoke of the Waverley Novels, and declared Scott to be a mere romancer, who drew men as we should like to see them, but by no means as they are. "Fielding, on the contrary, holds the mirror up to nature; his characters are flesh and blood. There are Blifil and Black George types of character repeated in every age." A week or two after this, Mr. Randolph's remarks were vividly recalled to me by the use he made of these fictitious personages in the Senate of the United States. In one of his outbursts of indignation, he called the union of the President and Henry Clay "the coalition of Blifil and Black George; the combination, unheard of till now, of the Puritan and the blackleg." According to the ruling sentiment at Washington, there was but one result which could follow such language as this. Mr. Randolph and Mr. Clay must exchange shots, and so they did; Mr. Clay's ball cutting Mr. Randolph's coat near the hip, and Mr.

Randolph's ball burying itself in a stump in the rear of Mr. Clay. On the second round Randolph received the shot of his antagonist, which was happily without effect, and then, raising his pistol, fired into the air. "You owe me a coat, Mr. Clay," said he, advancing and holding out his hand. "I am glad the debt is no greater," was the reply. And so ended an affair which Mr. Benton places among "the highest-toned duels" that he ever witnessed.

I spoke of the death of Mr. Gaillard, of South Carolina, and of the eulogium of his colleague, Mr. Hayne, on announcing it to the Senate. "Gaillard was our oldest senator," said Mr. Randolph, "and is greatly to be pitied, — to be pitied, not because he died, but because he died in this place. I have been ill here and have feared death; feared it because I would not die in Washington, be eulogized by men I despise, and buried in the Congressional Burying-ground. The idea of lying by the side of ——. Ah, that adds a new horror to death! I have done what I could to guard against this calamity by directions to my executors; but who knows what may happen?" When I rose to take leave of Mr. Randolph, after a long and most agreeable visit, he shook my hand very cordially and said, "As the son of a valued friend of mine, it has given me great pleasure to talk with you. I mean to talk *to* you, for I have given you no chance to say five words this evening."

As I have mentioned the death of Mr. Gaillard, I will close with a word about his funeral, which I fear I attended in no better character than that of a sightseer. It was held in the Senate Chamber; but except the members of a committee, who, having the arrangements in charge, attended officially, there were neither mourners nor senators. Dr. Staughton, the chaplain of the Senate, assisted by Mr. Post, who held that office in the House, performed the service. They wore long white scarfs, which also decorated the committee, as well as the doctor of the deceased, who, contrary to the rulings of medical etiquette, was among the few stragglers who looked in upon the ceremony. I have never seen the color white used as mourning upon any other occasion, and am at a loss to explain its significance. The chilly indifference with which these last services over the oldest senator of the nation were regarded struck me very painfully. They had given Congressmen a holiday, and that was enough. But the indifference of the Senate Chamber was, at least, better than the *burlesque* of the streets; for this is the term my journal applies to the funeral procession which it describes. This consisted of some sixty hacks, in every stage of shabbiness and dilapidation. They carried no passengers; but the hats of the drivers were bound with broad bands of snowy whiteness, which descended half-way down their variously colored backs. A thick fog of the most depressing sort filled the atmosphere as this wretched pageantry escorted the mortal part of poor Mr. Gaillard to the congressional sepulchre. Truly, John Randolph's feelings about the mortuary rites of Washington were not to be wondered at. "*Leur luxe est affreux*," shuddered Talleyrand, in reference to the taste of that generation of our countrymen with which he was acquainted. He would have had no occasion to use a less vigorous adjective in contemplating the *pompe funèbre* of an American senator in the year 1826.

RANDOLPH IN THE SENATE.

I HAD two opportunities of listening to Mr. Randolph in the Senate, and was completely fascinated by his extraordinary gifts as a talker; for it was not oratory (though at times he would produce great oratorical effects) so much as elevated conversation that he poured forth. His speeches were charming or provoking, according to the point of view of the listener. To a senator anxious to expedite the public business, or to hurry through the bill he had in charge, Randolph's harangues upon all sorts of irrelevant subjects must have been very annoying; but to one who was not troubled by such responsibilities they were a delightful entertainment. There was no effort about the speeches. They were given with absolute ease, the speaker constantly changing his position, turning from side to side, and at times leaning against the rail which enclosed the senatorial chairs. His dress was a blue riding-coat with buckskin breeches; for he always rode to the Senate, followed by his black servant, both master and man being finely mounted. His voice was silvery in its tones, becoming unpleasantly shrill only when conveying direct invective. Four fifths of what he said had the slenderest possible connection with the subject which had called him up; but, so far as the chance visitor was concerned, this variety only added a charm to the entertainment.

On the 14th of February, 1826, the introduction of a bill for surveying a portion of Florida with a view to a canal route brought Mr. Randolph to his feet. This project was favored by the other representatives of the South, and it was easy to see how provoked and embarrassed they felt by opposition in a quarter so unexpected. But Randolph, who had always strenuously denied the power of Congress to make internal improvements in the States, would not willingly concede it in the case of the Territories. He could not find it written in the bond that the money of the people should be poured out for local improvements anywhere.

Johnston, of Louisiana, put in a reply, in which he used Mr. Randolph as a Southern ally with great tenderness, but intimated that, as Cuba commanded the key to the Gulf of Mexico, its possession by a first-class naval power would be highly injurious to Southern interests. The canal would be in some sort a protection against this dire possibility.

"If all constitutional restraints are to be pushed aside, let us take Cuba and done with it!" said Randolph, in reply. Johnston's special pleading was dubbed an *argumentum ab inconvenienti*, and he was urged to consider the *consequences* (the word was uttered with significant emphasis) which might ensue. Here Randolph paused and looked his fellow

Southerners well over. Could they not see that, by taking this bait of internal improvements to strengthen their peculiar institution of slavery, they opened the way for the General Government to interfere to its disadvantage? The words were unspoken, but the look conveyed their meaning with perfect clearness He concluded in a strain of the bitterest irony: "But what care we for consequences? Only the timid and the purblind look to consequences! No, sir; your gallant statesman, mounted on his Rosinante and fairly in the lists, looks to no consequence — [a pause] *except to his own consequence!*"

The sarcasm provoked no angry retort from Hayne, of South Carolina, who now entered the debate with the grace and forbearance of a polished gentleman. He believed in drawing a distinction between state and territory, and took occasion to say that South Carolina had spent nearly two millions in making her own canals and roads. The Territories resembled the District of Columbia, over which no one doubted that the authority of Congress was paramount.

Mr. Randolph replied by holding up a copy of the Constitution, in a somewhat theatrical style, and declaring that it was like the Bible, which his friends found useful for preserving their receipts and deeds, but which they never opened. He disposed of the comparison to the District of Columbia very effectually, showing that the omnipotent sovereign authority that Congress might there exercise was widely different from the power to make needful regulations which was conceded over the Territories. The authors of the Constitution, he said, never suspected how their political machine would work; and, after pointing out their misapprehensions in this particular, he disposed of these worthies by exclaiming, with a superb wave of the hand, "And such is political foresight!"

Interesting as was Mr. Randolph's part in this debate on the canal question, my friends assured me that I had not yet heard him at his best, or worst. But it was my good fortune to be present in the Senate some two weeks afterward, when he gave what was universally allowed to be one of the most characteristic speeches he ever made. This was in reference to the Panama Mission, an absorbing topic of public interest and one which created on both sides feelings as intense as have ever been shown in our national legislature. The condition of certain South American states had recently been changed from that of subject colonies to independent republics, and the project was formed of assembling on the Isthmus of Panama a congress, at which each of them should be represented, to deliberate upon subjects common to all. The United States were asked to take a leading part in this assembly, and the invitation had been accepted, and plenipotentiaries appointed by the Executive. The Northern States warmly approved this course, which seemed to be in the line of what should be the national sentiment. The monarchies of Europe had formed a "Holy Alliance" to crush liberty in the Eastern Hemisphere. What could be more suitable than for the republics of the West to unite in a much holier union to maintain it? By the South this interrogation was met by the cry that a fearful crisis was at hand; and while some of its more astute representatives confined their scruples to questions of constitutional law and national policy, John Randolph and the hotter spirits blurted out the real objection to the scheme. The South would never consult with nations who had put the black man on an equality with the white, and, horror upon horrors! were known to have mulatto generals in command of their armies. From this opposition arose the party which finally placed Jackson in the presidential chair; a party whose stock in trade at this time consisted of bitter vituperation of the administration, and at the head of which Randolph took his natural place. John Quincy Adams — to his lasting honor be it said — refused to remove from high offices men who had joined a party which imputed to his administration all that was corrupt and base. They had a right, he declared, to support such men and measures as they saw fit; and he would never punish a man for any criticism upon his own political acts, however offensively it was conveyed. The debate in the Senate upon the proposition to send ministers to the congress at Panama had been held with closed doors. This was the custom when the appointments of the Executive were considered, and consequently there was no audience for the stirring appeals which rumor attributed to Randolph. But the fiery Southron had no notion of confining a vehement expression of his feelings to a petty senatorial group. He must address a larger assembly, and he saw how to make the opportunity. On the 1st of March he suddenly sprung a resolution upon the Senate which called upon the Executive to communicate information concerning the views of the South American republics relative to the emancipation of slaves. The demand was, of course, absurd, as the President could possess no information upon the subject that was not open to any inquirer; but it served the purpose of abolishing the secret session, and admitting the public to hear Mr. Randolph's views about the Panama Mission and about a great many other things besides.

He began with sarcasm. It was well known that the President of the United States meant to send ministers to the congress that was to assemble at Panama. He fervently hoped that these ministers would labor under none of the odious and exploded prejudices which revolted the over-fastidious Southern gentleman and repelled him from associating on terms of equality with persons of African descent. He hoped that the ministers who had been appointed were prepared to sit down humbly with the native African, the mixed breeds, and the Indian, and to take no offence at the motley mixture. General Bolivar, whom somebody had called "the South American Washington," was then handled without gloves. "I remember, sir," said Mr. Randolph, "that when the old Earl of Bedford was condoled with by a hypocrite on the murder of his son, Lord Russell, he indignantly replied that he would not exchange his dead son for the living son of any man on earth. So I would not give our dead Washington for any living Washington, or (whatever may be the blessings reserved for mankind in the womb of time) for any Washington who is likely to live in your time, Mr. President, or in mine." After pouring out his usual wealth of illustration and miscellaneous knowledge, Mr. Randolph took up Cuba, from which island he asserted that the whole country on the Gulf of Mexico could be invaded with row-boats. If other states were to take possession of this island, the genius of universal emancipation would proclaim its anathema against the white population; and then what would be the consequence to the Southern States? "This is one of those cases," he exclaimed, "in which the suggestion of instinct — the instinct of self-preservation — was worth all the logic in the world. It is one of those cases in which our passions instruct our reason!"

But Mr. Randolph's great effort (if I may so call a performance which to him was evidently no effort at all) was reserved for the next day. He announced that he should ask for the consideration of his resolution immediately upon the meeting of the Senate, and that meant that another speech would be forthcoming. I was early upon the spot, and for two hours held my attention fixed by his various and fluent improvisations, his cutting irony, his terribly sincere, although absolutely undeserved denunciations. His memory and imagination seemed inexhaustible. He would take a subject (almost any which happened to get in his way), turn and twist it about, display it in some fantastic light, and then, with scorn, push it aside. That famous dictum of the Declaration of Independence concerning the equality of men, which thirty years after Rufus Choate styled "a glittering generality," Randolph pilloried as "an idle fanfarronade." The pernicious falsehoods contained in these general expressions were in a certain sense true, and so were especially misleading. He compared Mr. Jefferson's statement to that of a person who should say that the soil of Scotland was as rich as that of Kentucky, because there was no difference in the superficial contents of the acre.

During a pause in the discourse Hayne rose, and urged the speaker to postpone his call upon the Executive, at the same time complimenting him warmly upon his speech.

Taking up the word, Randolph declared that he could make no regular speech. Not that this was to be regretted; for, like many other regular things, regular speeches were apt to be exceedingly dull. The general effect of such speeches was a want of any effect whatsoever. What he did was to imitate an Italian improvisatore, taking up subjects that he had well thought out. He considered that the world had been greatly injured by parliamentary eloquence, which was no qualification for government. Fox, to be sure, was a statesman, as well as a debater; but the dialectics of Pitt had been the curse of England. He was admirably qualified for a professor of rhetoric, and might have held that chair at Cambridge in Old or New England (a thrust at Mr. Adams, who had been professor of this art in Harvard College); but as a statesman he was a tyro and his great measures all failed.

In concluding, Randolph told a story of some wiseacre who was sent to search the vaults of the Parliament House at the time of the Gunpowder Plot. This mythical personage reported that he found fifty barrels of powder, and had removed twenty-five of them and hoped that the rest would do no harm. "The step you are about to take," exclaimed the speaker, the characteristic outstretched forefinger pointing the emphasis, "applies the match to the powder; and, be there twenty-five barrels or fifty barrels, there is enough to blow, not the first of the Stuarts, *but the last of another dynasty* sky-high, sir! Yes, sir, sky-high!"

And sky-high rose the voice of Mr. Randolph, as if to follow Mr. Adams in his aerial flight. There was no savor of the ridiculous in this passionate climax. The speaker's thorough-going sincerity prevented such a suggestion. The old saying that language was given to man to conceal his thoughts has a percentage of truth in it. Most men are conscious of selecting and modifying the products of the mind, with a view to their suitable presentation. The interest of Randolph's speeches was that he simply exposed his intellect and let you see it at work. It was like catching Webster or some other great orator in his library and looking over the rough notes he had rejected. There one might find figures of rhetoric a little too showy for good taste; blunt expressions of opinion which had been softened and draped in ambiguous phrases. It is possible that such a survey might increase our admiration for the artist, at the expense of our respect for the man. But after hearing Randolph speak or converse, the feeling was that you had come in contact with the essential personality of this Virginian Hotspur, and that there was much there which justified the affection that his friends felt for him.

A gentleman whom I met in Washington had returned with Randolph to his plantation after a session of Congress, and testified to me of the affection with which he was regarded by his slaves. Men and women rushed toward him, seized him by the hand with perfect familiarity, and burst into tears of delight at his presence among them. His conduct to these humble dependants was like that of a most affectionate father among his children, and it is well known that, when he could no longer protect them, he emancipated them by will and provided for their support in a free State.

The time has not yet come to estimate with impartiality the class of Southern gentlemen to which Randolph belonged. Many of them were men of great ability and singular fascination of manner. Once accept their premises (and these premises were to them as the axioms of mathematics), and they are knightly figures fighting upon that side of the irrepressible conflict which protected their families and the civilization, such as it was, which had produced themselves and the high-spirited caste into which they were born. The incendiarism which would light the torch of servile insurrection and plunge their fair possessions into barbarism seemed to them far worse than that which fired warehouses and dwellings, which a few months of labor might replace. It is unnecessary here to enlarge upon their errors or delusions, which every school-boy now deems himself able to expose. Of Mr. Randolph I saw too little, and I look with sincere regret upon this kind note from him, interleaved with my journal and written the day I left Washington. It bids me come and dine with him at "a confectioner's shop near the Seven Buildings." There I should have met a small circle of his friends, with the consequence of much satisfaction to myself at the time, and possibly to the readers of this paper half a century later.

COMMODORE STOCKTON.

THE gentlemen whom I met at Miss Hyer's boarding-house were for the most part considerably older than myself, and I became really intimate with only one of them. To Lieutenant Stockton — or, as he was commonly called, Captain Stockton — there was much to unite me. A few years my senior, he was a lifetime before me in experience. Our fathers had fought together in the thinning ranks of Federalism, and had imbued their sons with the sentiment that it was honor enough to perish with that failing cause, and that no future party could so claim the allegiance of intelligent gentlemen. In Captain Stockton himself there centred elements of romance which are seldom possible to our prosaic modern life. His cruises about the world were in the exciting times of war and piracy, and he had penetrated a part of Africa where no white man had ever set foot. Of hairbreadth 'scapes he had had a generous allowance. He had fought duels when the sentiment of his profession called for this test of personal valor; and, with a nobler courage, he had thrown the cat-o'-nine-tails into the sea, declaring that the lash was not necessary to govern men who were sailing under a competent commander.

I became very well acquainted with Stockton. We took long rambles together about Washington; and, after my return from its evening festivities, we would sit long into the night, gently sipping a medicine which the doctors of the capital thought destructive of the influenza germs which were lying in wait for the unwary. Of course, I am fitting their opinions to a modern phrase; for they knew nothing about the germ theory in those days, but fought disease with such antidotes as observation commended. Not knowing the Latin name under which their prescription may figure in the pharmacopœia, I am obliged to give it the bald English translation of whiskey punch. The hour was, of all the twenty-four, best adapted to confidences, and it is possible that the medicine contributed a little to the easy flow of the narratives. Had Sindbad the Sailor been a man of unimpeachable veracity, I am willing to allow that those who listened to the story of his voyages, as it fell from his own lips, might have been more astonished and interested than was the companion of Captain Stockton; but with this notable exception, surely no mariner of thirty ever had adventures more remarkable, or told them more modestly and agreeably.

I remember the fine spirit with which Stockton gave the story of the expected engagement with the British ship "Plantagenet." "This was just off the harbor of New York," he said. "We had been cruising about the seas for months, and were spoiling for a fight. The 'Plantagenet' was to windward, and we could not go to her; but Rodgers backed his topsails and fired a gun as a signal to her to come down. Our guns were then shotted and our decks cleared for action. The Britisher had a heavier weight of metal than we, and Rodgers's plan was to take her by boarding. Some of us had to go to the maintop, armed with rifles and a couple of howitzers. Up aloft I was in command; below every man was at his post; and then — we waited and waited. Rodgers kept walking up and down the deck, and the creak of his boots was the only sound that broke the silence. Suddenly the Commodore called out to me, 'Mr. Stockton, we expect great things from you to-day, sir!' I was but a young fellow then, and when he said that, I would have got into a gun and been shot off, if that would have given us the victory. What Shakespeare says about the interim between the acting of a fearful thing and the first motion we had reason to understand. The delay was a hideous dream, just as he calls it. We waited and waited; but the 'Plantagenet' would not accept our challenge. Well, Rodgers had a British colonel down below, whom he had taken out of a prize; so, when he could stand it no longer, he sent down his compliments and begged him, if he were at leisure, to step on deck for a few moments. 'Now, sir,' said the Commodore, handing him his glass, 'oblige me by looking that British man-of-war well over. Does she carry more metal than the "President"?' 'I he did, sir.' 'Well, sir, I've challenged refuses. What do you say to that?'

'I don't know what to say to it, sir; but this I do know, that if I ever get to England I will take no rest till the commander of that vessel is hanging at his own yard-arm.' Well, the end of it was that the commander of the 'Plantagenet' was tried in England; but got off on the ground that his crew were in such a state of mutiny that he could not give battle."

I can give only a few salient points from narrations which deserved much fuller reporting. But what no reporting can give is the joyous, patriotic temper with which the gallant officer gave his spirited accounts of the humbling of the British flag upon the ocean during the war which began in 1812. His adventures on board the "Guerrière" and the "Spitfire," and the capture of the Algerine pirates, given as I heard them, would make the fortune of a star lecturer; but of these neither my notes nor my memory permit me to furnish reliable fragments.

But Stockton's most wonderful feat was his journey into an unknown portion of Africa, in the interest of the scheme of colonization, which finally resulted in the settlement of Liberia. His route lay through swamps and jungles which no white man had ever passed; and the end of the expedition placed him in the power of savages who were inflamed against him as an enemy to their business of supplying victims for the slave-trade. He was surrounded by five hundred or more negroes, breathing vengeance and threatening the instant extermination of his small party. "I thought I would get in a speech," said

Stockton, "before I went down. I had brought along an interpreter, who translated every sentence while I was thinking over the next. I was speaking for my life, and I think I was eloquent; but I used only one gesture. My hand held a pistol at full cock, pointed at the head of the chief. I told them that upon the first attempt at violence that man should drop, and that the Almighty would visit a worse punishment upon the rest of them, if they dared to molest a stranger who had come to do them good." The end of it was that the savages quailed at the threat, and became perfectly submissive. Stockton thought that moral cowardice was not peculiar to the civilized races. It might be excited in savages, if one happened to hit upon an appeal which could reach them. However this may be, it is certain that the effect of the speech did not cease when the chief was no longer under fire. The pledges then made were faithfully carried out, and the adventurous mission accomplished its purposes.

Something more than a hundred years ago the question whether duelling was consistent with moral duty was raised in the presence of Dr. Johnson. Old General Oglethorpe, Boswell tells us, fired up at the doubt implied in this inquiry. "Undoubtedly," said he, "a man has a right to defend his honor." Although the great Christian moralist was indisposed to settle the question in this off-hand way, he admitted that the practice might be justified in the then existing state of public opinion. He reasoned that it was never unlawful to fight in self-defence;

and, so long as the notion prevailed that an affront was a serious injury and a man lost social standing by putting up with it, he might be permitted to challenge the aggressor. In 1826 the dominant opinion of Washington was in accord with that of Dr. Johnson. I have already mentioned that the Secretary of State, charged with the interests of a mighty nation, felt obliged to peril his own life and to risk taking that of another man because foolish words had been spoken in debate. It was admitted, indeed, that duelling was an evil; and so was war an evil; but as the higher civilizations could not be maintained without recourse to arms, so the unsullied character of a gentleman — the priceless outcome of these civilizations — could not be preserved unless he was ready to hazard life in its defence. It would not be difficult to point out the defect in an analogy which was specious enough to justify a temporary phase of human opinion; and this opinion, strong as it was in the civil circles of the capital, was held with tenfold tenacity in the army and navy. To say, then, that Stockton in his younger days was a duellist amounts to little more than to declare that Washington was a slaveholder. In these times a knight-errant would be quickly dismounted and driven to the House of Correction in the prisoners' van. Place him where he belongs, and he stands out as the type of a hero. A gallant and chivalrous officer of the American navy, when this century was in its teens, was bound to risk his life in a duel when the honor of his profession demanded it. His ideas of duty in such a matter were very different from ours; but, such as they were, we can admire the pluck and consistency with which a man like Stockton accepted the course they indicated. The entire conscientiousness of the man shone through the accounts he gave me of his adventures upon the field of honor, and neither of us were troubled by scruples which might have presented themselves when the blood moved less rapidly and a more sober generation was conducting the world.

An insult to the gentlemen of the American navy, written in a book that was seen by everybody, was shown to Stockton, when his ship, the "Erie," arrived in the Bay of Naples. It bore the signature of a British officer then in that port; and the young Lieutenant, without more ado, declared that the fellow should eat his words or fight him. A friend properly accredited was despatched to the British ship, and, after a good deal of demur, the author of the outrage was got ashore and consented to fight at long range. Their pistols were discharged at the proper signal, and Stockton's ball struck his adversary in the leg, whereupon the fellow bellowed out: "You have hit me. Are you satisfied now?" "No," said Stockton; "I am not satisfied until you write me an apology for the language you have used." Whereupon his fellow Britons declared that their man, having given satisfaction, was exempt from further proceedings. He had vindicated his honor, and that was enough. The American party by no accepted this decision, and said several unpleasant things about the cowardice which prompted this miserable subterfuge.

I now come to the most marvellous duelling adventure in which Stockton was engaged; and this I shall give as I heard the story told by its hero, one day after dinner and in the presence of several gentlemen who were lingering about the table. Since writing out the narrative given below, I have found in the Boston City Library an anonymous life of Stockton, apparently written for some political purpose and published in 1856. The writer gives an account of this duel from hearsay and "according to his remembrance." The narrative differs from mine in several respects, and omits some striking particulars, which I am certain that I heard from the principal actor. There must exist materials for an authentic life of the brilliant Commodore, and a most interesting book it would be. Neither my memory nor my journals are infallible; and if any particulars are misstated (which I do not believe to be the case), they are offered as subject to correction by a responsible biographer.

The scene was at Gibraltar, and there had been a previous duel between Stockton and a British officer attached to the station, who, however, was not *the* officer from whom the affront to be avenged had really come. There had been charges and counter-charges, negotiations and criminations, till finally the American officer in command put a stop to proceedings by an order that none of his subordinates should go ashore while the ship remained in that port. The lull was only temporary. After a short cruise, the "Erie" returned to Gibraltar, and this time the real offender was forced by the public opinion of his fellows to give the Yankee Lieutenant the meeting he had demanded. A guaranty was required by Stockton that the British authorities of the town should not be informed of the duel, with a view to ordering his arrest; and a pledge was given that there should be no interference. "Under these circumstances," said Stockton, "I went ashore without distrust. The flag had been grossly insulted by a British officer, who was now backed up by his comrades. I was the only unmarried officer on board the 'Erie,' and my duty was, of course, clear. The governor of the fortress, during our previous visit, had announced that he would hang any Yankee who came ashore for the purpose of fighting; and although it was not probable that he would have dared to carry out the threat, he would have been ugly enough, had he caught me. It was arranged between our seconds that, upon landing, we should be conducted to a retired place, where the duel might come off without interference. British honor was pledged to this, and, believing it still to be worth something, I was rowed ashore, accompanied by my second and the ship's doctor." The graphic description of what followed must be given in a feeble outline. The Americans were conducted to a spot near the top of the rock, where they met the opposing party. It then appeared that no immediate fighting was contemplated, for the Englishmen began to enter upon a discussion, and to raise frivolous objections to the recognized code of duelling. Stockton, seeing that all this tended to delay, and suspecting treachery, suddenly declared that he would waive all rights, and fight at once upon whatever terms his opponent chose to exact. After such a declaration no retreat was possible. The ground was measured, shots were exchanged, and the British officer fell wounded. Stockton advanced to inquire into the nature of the injury, and then the wretched man was shamed into a confession that treachery had been practised, and that instant flight was necessary, if his opponent would avoid arrest. Upon this the Lieutenant started for his boat, running at full speed. His way lay through a passage cut out of the rock, which gave access to the beach below. Upon turning a corner, when about half-way down, he was confronted by a file of soldiers, drawn up to oppose his passage. The officer in command was a pursy little fellow, who seemed to enjoy hugely the discomfiture of his supposed captive. There stood this merry gentleman upon a parapet which guarded the road, and which was raised a few feet above it. His squad was ranged in a line with him, completely cutting off the passage. There was not a moment for delay; the situation was desperate; it could be met only by a resolve as desperate. The officer was off his guard and was chuckling with delight. Now was the instant for a dash. Now stiffen the sinews, summon up the blood, and there was yet a chance for liberty. Instead of making the surrender which was expected, Stockton sprang at this cheerful officer.

He grappled with him; he got his head under his arm; he jumped with him from the parapet, and in a moment the two men, clasped together, were rolling over and over down the side of the rock. Presently the parties separated, the Englishman rolling one way and the American another. At length Stockton managed to stop his dizzying and perilous descent, and dropped a number of feet to the beach below. Covered with blood and dirt, with his clothes nearly stripped from him, he accosted a gentleman who was taking his morning ride upon the beach, and begged the instant loan of his horse. This request the rider not unnaturally declined. Whereupon he was seized by the leg and pulled from the saddle. His assailant instantly mounted the horse, and, putting him to his speed, made for the boat. He looked up for a moment, and saw the soldiers running about in a distracted manner; most of them tearing down the road, to cut him off. Stockton, however, reached the boat, gave the order to pull for the frigate, and then fainted. He did not recover consciousness until he found himself in his berth on board the "Erie."

These events were related at the persistent request of others. They were given modestly, but with great spirit. There were at that time living witnesses to the escape, and the facts connected with it were well known. I have already said that we must regard Stockton's duels from the point of view of the profession to which he was devoted. The highest officers of the navy sanctioned this barbarism as a duty to which a brave and honorable man might be called.

Only a few years before my visit to Washington four American Commodores left the city on this miserable business. Decatur and Barron were the principals; Bainbridge and Elliot acting as seconds. The brave and gallant Decatur, the pride of the American navy, there met his death. It is not necessary to resort to Christian ethics to condemn a practice which has cost such valuable lives; but let us do justice to the high-minded men who were victims of an infatuation which we have left behind us.

THE SUPREME COURT AND THE "MARIANNA FLORA."

THE day after my arrival at the capital I called upon Judge Story, at the Supreme Court, as he had requested me to do. Immediately upon adjournment he presented me to the Chief Justice and Judge Bushrod Washington, both gentlemen whom I had much desired to meet. The first view of Judge Marshall was not impressive. He struck me as a tall man who regretted his height, because he had not the knack of carrying it off with ease and dignity. His manner was so simple as to be almost rustic; and, were it not for the brilliancy of his eyes, he might have been taken for a mere political judge instead of the recognized expositor of the Constitution. Judge Story had already hinted that Marshall would be disappointing to a stranger, adding that only his associates on the Bench could appreciate his real wisdom and greatness. The Chief Justice spoke of his sympathy with my father in the good cause of Federalism, and referred to the venerable sage of Monticello as "Tom Jefferson," pronouncing the name with an interrogative emphasis, which, without compromising judicial impartiality, showed that, in the opinion of the speaker, the verdict of the competent upon that important personage had not yet been rendered. Marshall was held in extraordinary esteem by all political parties, and the Virginians were especially proud of him. Like all really great men, he never troubled himself about dignity and had the simple tastes and ready sympathies of a child. He hated slavery, but prophesied that it could only cease through a social convulsion. He thereby proved himself wiser than most of the enlightened men of his time, who confidently looked to economical causes to destroy this anomaly. A few days after my introduction to the Chief Justice, I spoke of him to a gentleman from Richmond, whom I met at an evening party. "People in Washington don't begin to understand him," said he. "Why, do you know, I have met Marshall carrying his dinner through the streets in an open basket!" This act of humiliation was more impressive to a Southerner than to one of Northern birth, and perhaps I did not exhibit the astonishment that was expected. But the Virginian (whose name I cannot recall, though I can bring the man distinctly before me) had a climax in reserve, of which he delivered himself with impressive emphasis: "*Yes, sir; and I have seen that man walking on his hands and knees, with a straw in his mouth!*" This was sufficiently removed from the actions usually associated with the ermine, and was startling to one who could not supply the explanation that would have instantly occurred to a Southerner. The game of quoits was at that time as universal at the South as was croquet a few years ago upon Northern lawns.

Disputes constantly arose, which required that the distances of the quoits from the hub should be accurately determined, and a straw, which was commonly at hand, was the accepted instrument for measuring. Judge Marshall, who was a great lover of the game, would not shirk any of its duties. Hence the singular position in which his fellow-citizen represented him.

Through Judge Washington, the men of my generation were brought, as it were, within speaking distance of the Father of his Country. He was not to us the statuesque, passionless figure which I am told that he has since become. Here was a man who had called him "Uncle George," had joked with him, and plagued him, as young people will plague older relatives who are responsible for their good conduct. For Bushrod Washington was more than the nephew, he was almost the adopted son, of his uncle. He resided at Mt. Vernon, which he had inherited, as the representative of the name, as well as the nearest relative, of its former possessor. He struck me as being somewhat too small a man for an ideal judge, and he took snuff too frequently to be credited with those personal austerities which are not unbecoming in magistrates. But his manner to me was very kind and pleasant. He spoke of his friendship for my father, and of the visits he had received from him at Mt. Vernon.

One of these visits was in the spring of 1806; and although I was in Washington at the time, I was too young to remember the circumstances. But, like many events which happen in childhood, and for some years after are constantly referred to in the family circle, it seems as if I remembered all about it. The scene of my father's only ghost story — if so it may be called — was laid at Mt. Vernon; and this alone was sufficient to make the occasion memorable to a boy. The chamber in which his uncle had died was assigned by Judge Washington to his guest; the host, as he withdrew, mentioning the rumor that an interview with Washington had been granted to some of its former occupants. If this were true, my father pondered upon the possibility that he might be found worthy to behold the glorified spirit of him who was so revered by his countrymen. And during the night *he did see Washington*, and this is all I have to say about it. If I gave the particulars, I should feel bound to give a full explanation of them by Dr. Hammond, or some other expert in cerebral illusions; and this would occupy too much space for an episode. It may be worth while to say that nothing my father saw, or thought he saw, was useful in confirming his faith in a spiritual world. His assurance in this matter was perfect. He believed that brain action (if that is the correct expression) was at times set up in us by friends no longer in the flesh, and that his own life had been guided by these mysterious influences. Shortly before his death, he spoke of reunion with those he had loved, as men speak of what they know, not as they speak of what they hope or believe. There was a custom connected with the hospitalities of Mt. Vernon in Judge Washington's time which is worth noting, because it would be scarcely possible among persons of refinement at the present day. Guests of the family were not only conducted to the tomb of Washington, but were invited to pass through its portal, and to touch the receptacle of his remains. It stood beside that of Mrs. Washington, on a slightly raised platform, other members of the family being placed against the sides of the sepulchre. When my father visited the place, in 1806, the velvet cover of the coffin was hanging in tatters, it having been brought to this condition by the assaults of relic-hunters. "Care not to strip the dead of his sad ornament," sings my classmate, Mr. Emerson; and, surely, of all fetiches with which the imagination contrives to associate the august spirits of the great, such miserable shreds and patches are the most vulgar. But it is time to leave the Judges, and pass to a scene in the tribunal over which they presided.

Saturday, the 18th of February, 1826, was an interesting day for Captain Stockton and his friends. The case of the "Marianna Flora" had at length been reached by the Supreme Court. Already opposing decisions had been pronounced by lower courts, and now the highest bench would decide whether Stockton was justified in the course he had thought it right to pursue. The facts of this interesting case, so far as they can be gathered from evidence that was sometimes conflicting, may be condensed into a narrative something like this. On the 5th of November, 1821, the United States schooner "Alligator," under the command of Lieutenant Stockton, encountered the "Marianna Flora," a Portuguese vessel, commanded by Captain De Britto, an elderly officer, who had passed many years of service. De Britto, supposing the American schooner to be a pirate or privateer, from whom an attack was to be apprehended, caused his ship to lay to and prepare for action. Stockton, on the contrary, observing that the vessel carried no colors to show her nationality, but only a flag which seemed to be displayed as a signal of distress, ordered provisions to be got ready, in case they were needed, and directed his course toward the stranger. He then went below, to work up his longitude, which he thought his neighbor might want. A ball which De Britto sent whistling past the "Alligator" soon dissipated these suppositions; and for some time the schooner, although displaying the American flag, was raked by shot, which her position prevented her from answering. The wind was very light, and it was long before Stockton could obtain a position from which to make an effective reply to the fire that was poured upon him. His guns were short pieces of ordnance, called carronades, and were useless at a long range. When, at length, the American was in a position to return the cannonading with effect, the Portuguese color was suddenly hoisted by the attacking ship. This Stockton did not think himself bound to regard; but proceeded to pour volley upon volley into this belligerent stranger, till her color came down quite as quickly as it had gone up. She had struck her flag to the "Alligator," and was, so the commander considered, his lawful prize. In his opinion, De Britto intended to commit an act of piracy, and wished to plunder what he supposed to be an unarmed merchantman. A prize crew was put on board the "Marianna Flora," the sailors of that vessel being confined in irons, and the order was given to make sail for Boston, for adjudication. Seven weeks were consumed in this winter voyage; and dreary weeks they must have been to the miserable Portuguese mariners, who lay fettered in the hold. The case was brought before Judge Davis, of the District Court; the owners of the "Marianna Flora" claiming that Stockton had committed an unlawful act and demanding heavy damages. They brought evidence which clearly established the fact that no wrong was intended on the part of De Britto. He had commenced and maintained his fire upon the "Alligator" under the conviction that he was repelling an enemy. To be sure, the American flag had been displayed by Stockton; but then any pirate might do that, and there was a naval ceremonial of an affirming gun, which the "Alligator" was said to have omitted. The decision of Judge Davis was in favor of the claimants. The act of Stockton in sending in the vessel, though perfectly conscientious, was severe and unnecessary. Damages were awarded to the owners of the Portuguese ship for the losses they sustained, and to the crew for their seven weeks of captivity.

An appeal was instantly taken, and the case was brought before the Circuit Court, Judge Story being upon the bench. The decision of Judge Davis was reversed. The capture being lawful, — for this the lower court had admitted, — Stockton was justified in sending the "Marianna Flora" to the United States for adjudication. He might have released the vessel, — possibly it might have been commendable to have done so; but he was not *bound* to grant such release, and the whole question of damages was disposed of by denying this obligation. So decided Judge Story. Would the full Bench confirm that decision, and so disperse the cloud which threatened the reputation and fortune of Stockton? The question was one of painful interest to the friends of this brave officer, and I felt unpleasantly nervous when my travelling companion, Mr. John Knapp, began to open the case for the Portuguese complainants and to reflect severely upon the course of the commander of the "Alligator." George Blake, the district attorney, replied for Stockton, and (so says my journal) surprised me by a power of speech which I did not suppose he possessed. He had not finished when the hour for adjournment arrived. Early Monday morning I repaired to the court-room, where I met Mr. Webster and Mr. Blake, with their respective wives. "These ladies would come to hear their husbands bestow their dulness upon the Court," said Mr. Webster to me; "and now you shall take care of them and entertain them, if we fail to do so." I was, accordingly, seated by these ladies, who took such creditable interest in the arguments that there was no occasion to whisper social gossip for their diversion. Blake's close was even better than his opening; and then rose Webster, who proceeded against poor Mr. Knapp with the confidence of a giant. "It is the *aggressor*," he said, — and the indignant emphasis he threw upon the word was in itself an argument, — "it is the *aggressor* who comes before this Court masquerading in the character of a plaintiff and asking redress for a supposed injury done to himself." And then a pause, that the absurdity of the position of his antagonist might sink in and be vividly realized. "The capture was made in repelling an act of piratical aggression, for so Lieutenant Stockton supposed it to be; and only a judicial examination could show that it might have been otherwise. The suffering party had himself furnished the occasion for any discomfort to which he may have been subjected. It was a *damnum absque injuria* — a damage without a wrong — and it is futile to pretend that it was anything else." So ran the drift of the argument, which was earnest and eloquent and was not concluded till the following day.

The final appeal for the plaintiffs was given by Thomas Addis Emmett, then an old man (he died the following year), but full of Irish fire and feeling. My journal declares that his brogue, which was very evident in the warmer passages, was a marked addition to their force and eloquence. Being a fellow-boarder with Mr. Emmett, I had much conversation with him. He had told me some of the romantic incidents of his early manhood, which resulted in his long imprisonment in Scotland and had finally banished him from British soil. "I think him the most interesting man of his age whom I have ever seen." This is how I characterized him in my contemporary record, after one of these free talks. What a pity, it seemed to me, that he should be on the wrong side; for the right side was, of course, that of my friend, Captain Stockton. But Emmett went at his work, as I suppose a lawyer should, as if *his side* was the right side, beyond all question. He began by laying down the proposition that every ship navigating the ocean in time of peace might appropriate to her temporary use so much of its waters as she deemed necessary for her protection. He drew a lively picture of the pirates which infested the seas, and declared that, if the right to approach *in invitum* were allowed, merchantmen might as well be broken up for firewood. The conduct of the "Marianna Flora" was justifiable. The first fault was committed by the "Alligator," in not following the raising of her flag with an affirming gun; and then in approaching the stranger against her consent. After the capture the ship's papers should have shown Stockton that his prize was an innocent merchantman, — armed, indeed, against pirates, but armed for no purposes of aggression. In substance this was the amount of the plea for the plaintiffs. The wealth of illustration by which it was embellished and the earnest and hearty rhetoric of the advocate there was no phonograph to preserve.

The opinion of the Court was pronounced by Judge Story, some weeks afterward, and may be read in the eleventh volume of "Wheaton's Reports." It vindicated Captain Stockton. Mr. Emmett's doctrine of non-approach was pronounced novel and unsupported by authority. While every vessel had the right to use so much of the ocean as was essential to her movements, no exclusive right beyond this could be recognized. A ship-of-war, like the "Alligator," sailing under the authority of the government, might approach any vessel descried at sea, for the purpose of ascertaining her real character. The Court denied that the mere fact of approach excused the hostile attack of De Britto. He had said that he lay to in order to meet a supposed enemy by daylight and because he dreaded the peril of a night attack; but all this could not have been known to Stockton, who was acting from a humane motive and in the line of his duty. He was justified in taking possession of the "Marianna Flora," because she attacked him without cause or provocation.

This opinion delighted me at the time; to the friends of Stockton it fully vindicated the wisdom of the Court and the beneficence of the law which it expounded; but in re-reading it to-day, I find at one point a lack of equity which, if the Court was powerless to prevent, might at least have been noticed with regret. How fared it with those unhappy sailors who, through no fault of theirs, had made a seven weeks' voyage in irons and to whom the District Court had mercifully awarded five hundred dollars? Surely, if justice was to be wrought among men, these unfortunates had claims upon somebody; but the learned judge remarked that in their case no privilege of appeal was allowed, because the sum of five hundred dollars was insufficient to entitle the parties in interest to be heard before the Supreme Bench. A mere bagatelle, truly! Only a fraction of what Crœsus might spend for a single evening of festivity, yet possibly as important to those roughly used mariners as the larger stakes which opened the courts to the capitalists, their employers. It is no disrespect to the majesty of the law to mention that it has not yet sloughed off all its barbarisms. So long as the punishment of a money fine is accepted from the rich and the alternative imprisonment is exacted from the poor, the equality of all men before the law is but a sounding phrase. As for those Portuguese fellows fettered in the hold, they ought to have known that their sad plight was only a *damnum absque injuria;* and when they were prevented from following their masters to the highest court, they should have consoled themselves with that sage morsel of law Latin, *De minimis non curat lex.*

WASHINGTON SOCIETY IN 1826.

I.

DR. HOLMES has declared, with all the solemnity of verse, that, for reasons which to him are good and sufficient, he never dares to write as funny as he can. Following so excellent a precedent, I will confess that I do not mean to make this paper on the social life in Washington as entertaining as I could. For hasty gossip and uncharitable strictures upon individuals (such as a young fellow may set down in a journal intended for no eyes but his own) are certainly amusing; but their publication, either by the writer or his executors, is, as it seems to me, almost never justifiable. The mention of the names of ladies, even when one has nothing but what is pleasant to say of them, is only to be sanctioned by a certain unwritten statute of limitations, which, after the lapse of half a century, seems to allow a certain discretion in this particular. It will, however, be necessary to make but few reservations in telling what I saw in Washington society in 1826.

And first come the dinners. On Friday, February 17, I find an account of a dinner at Mr. Webster's. The occasion was absolutely informal and very pleasant. Besides myself, Henry R. Storrs, of New York, and Rufus Greene Amory, of Boston, were the only guests. Webster carved the beef and was in a charming humor. He told some good lawyer's stories, and gave us a graphic account of the burning of his house in Portsmouth, in the winter of 1813. "Though I was in Washington at the time," he said, "I believe I know more about the fire than many who were actively at work on the spot. Besides, here is Mrs. Webster, who was burned out. She will correct me if I am wrong." He told us that all he possessed in the world was lost, there being no insurance upon house or furniture; but as more than two hundred buildings were consumed in the fire, some of them belonging to those less able to make a living than himself, he felt he had no right to murmur. He was, nevertheless, troubled about the loss of his library. His books were full of notes and associations, and could not be replaced.

"I think there was something in the house which Mr. Webster regretted more than his books," said his wife, with an amused expression, which showed her remark was not to be taken quite seriously. "There was a pipe of wine in the cellar, and I am sure that Mr. Webster's philosophy has not yet reconciled him to its loss. You see we were young housekeepers in those days. It was the first pipe of wine we ever had, and the getting it was a great event."

"Let us be accurate, my dear," said Mr. Webster, with one of those pleasant smiles of his which fairly lit up the room. "Undoubtedly it was a pipe of wine when we bought it; but then it had been on tap for some time, and our table was not without guests. If I had you upon the witness stand, I think I should make you confess that your pipe of wine could scarcely have been more than *half a pipe* at the time of the fire."

I suppose that there was nothing said at that dinner so little worth preserving as this trifling family jest; yet the sweet and playful manner of Webster has fixed it indelibly upon my memory. That manner I cannot give, and it was everything. It somehow carried one of those aside confessions of the absolute affection and confidence existing between this married pair which were so evident to those admitted beneath their roof. A congenial marriage seems to be essential to the best development of a man of genius, and this blessing rested upon that household. It was like organ-music to hear Webster speak to or of the being upon whom his affections reposed, and whom, alas! he was so soon to lose. I am sure that those who knew the man only when this tenderest relation had been terminated by death, never knew him in his perfect symmetry. Whatever evil-speakers might choose to say about the subsequent career of Daniel Webster, he was at that time "whole as the marble, founded as the rock." He was on the happiest terms with the world, which had crowned him with its choicest blessing, and stood forth in all respects as an example and a hero among men.

I will repeat an anecdote which I think that Webster gave at that dinner, though, as I made no note of it, it is just possible that he told it in my presence at some later date. The conversation was running upon the importance of doing small things thoroughly and with the full measure of one's ability. This Webster illustrated by an account of some petty insurance case that was brought to him when a young lawyer in Portsmouth. Only a small amount was involved, and a twenty-dollar fee was all that was promised. He saw that, to do his clients full justice, a journey to Boston, to consult the Law Library, would be desirable. He would be out of pocket by such an expedition, and for his time he would receive no adequate compensation. After a little hesitation, he determined to do his very best, cost what it might. He accordingly went to Boston, looked up the authorities, and gained the case. Years after this, Webster, then famous, was passing through New York. An important insurance case was to be tried the day after his arrival, and one of the counsel had been suddenly taken ill. Money was no object, and Webster was begged to name his terms and conduct the case. "I told them," said Mr. Webster, "that it was preposterous to expect me to prepare a legal argument at a few hours' notice. They insisted, however, that I should look at the papers; and this, after some demur, I consented to do. Well, it was my old twenty-dollar case over again, and, as I never forget anything, I had all the authorities at my fingers' ends. The court knew that I had no time to prepare, and were astonished at the range of my acquirements. So, you see, I was handsomely paid both in fame and money for that journey to Boston; and the moral is, that good work is rewarded in the end, though, to be sure, one's own self-approval should be enough."

I may be pardoned for taking from my journal of later date another after-dinner story which I heard Mr. Webster tell with great dramatic effect. One of the party mentioned that a president of one of the Boston banks had that morning redeemed a counterfeit bill for fifty dollars, never doubting that his signature upon it was genuine. This incident led to a discussion of the value of expert testimony in regard to writing, the majority of our company holding it in little esteem. Mr. Webster then came to the defence of this sort of testimony, saying that he had found it of much value, although experts were like children who saw more than they were able to explain to others. "And this reminds me," he said, "of my story of the tailor. It was a capital case that was being tried, and the tailor's testimony was very important. He had been called to prove that he made a certain coat for the criminal; and he swore to the fact stoutly. Upon cross-examination he was asked how he knew that the coat was his work. 'Why, I know it by my stitches, of course.' 'Are your stitches longer than those of other tailors?' 'Oh, no!' 'Well, then, are they shorter?' 'Not a bit shorter.' 'Anything peculiar about them?' 'Well, I don't believe there is.' 'Then how do you dare to come here and swear that they are yours?' This seemed to be a poser, but ⸻ met it triumphantly. Casting a look of contempt upon his examiner, the tailor raised both hands to heaven and exclaimed, '*Good Lord! as if I did n't know my own stitches!*' The jury believed him, and they were right in doing so. The fact is, we continually build our judgment upon details too fine for distinct cognizance. And these nice shades of sensibility are trustworthy, although we can give no good account of them. We can swear to our stitches, notwithstanding they seem to be neither longer nor shorter than those of other people."

I had been listening to Mr. Storrs that morning, in the House of Representatives, where he greatly distinguished himself, as I shall hereafter have occasion to notice; but if he said anything at the dinner, I find no reference to it in my notes. Mr. Amory seems to have made more impression upon me, and I mention the amusing account he gave of his adventures on the road from New York; for there *were* adventures ere the discovery of the art of packing travellers like herrings in a box, and thus making their experiences as identical as are those of the fishes so transported. Mr. Amory had undertaken the journey on horseback, and had fallen among highwaymen, who were as high-toned and chivalrous as those of the dime novel. They took his money, indeed, and bound him to a tree; but these acts seem to have been strictly professional, and he told how the thieves regretted, with abundant courtesy, that they were compelled to put an old gentleman to any inconvenience. "I an old gentleman!" exclaimed the narrator. "Could not the fellows have been content with theft, without adding libel?" And the merry old soul led off a contagious laugh at his own pleasantry. How the bonds of Mr. Amory were finally loosed my journal does not chronicle, so I must leave him tied to the tree, confident that a reader of the slightest imagination will find some good way to release him, and to bring him safely to Mr. Webster's dinner-table.

I dined twice at the White House; the first time informally, with Charles King and Albert Gallatin. The latter gentleman scarcely said anything, owing, perhaps, to the constant and amusing utterances of the President and Mr. King, who talked as if they were under bonds to furnish entertainment for the party. The next occasion was a state dinner, of forty ladies and gentlemen, very splendid and rather stiff. My place was next a pretty Miss Bullett, of Kentucky; but, to say the truth, the conversation rather dragged between us, until I discovered that we had a mutual friend in Larz Anderson, of Cincinnati. I had known Larz well in college, and remember when he arrived in Cambridge, a small, flaxen-haired boy, accompanied by two companions from the distant West. They had come all the way from Kentucky on horseback, their effects being borne in saddle-bags behind the riders. There was no public conveyance, the roads were execrable, and this manly mode of travelling was then the only way of getting to Harvard. Now, I happened to have a story to tell about our friend Anderson, which I felt sure would gratify the pride of a Kentuckian; and as I have not recorded a word of what my fair neighbor said to me, I can only fall back upon what I said to her, and the substance of my tale might be written out thus: —

Oxford Street, in Cambridge, is at present a very decorous thoroughfare, not at all adapted to the wild sport of turkey-shooting, for which purpose the ground it occupies was used when I was in college. We stood with our backs to the site of Memorial Hall, and discharged rifles, at long range, at a turkey which was dimly discernible in the distance. A small fee was demanded for the privilege of shooting, and the turkey was to be given to any one who could hit it. But, except for some chance shot, like that made by Mr. Tupman when out rook-shooting, it was safe to predict that nobody would hit it. The usual end of a Harvard turkey-shooting was the departure of the proprietor of the turkeys with all his birds and all our sixpences. Still there was the excitement of a lottery about it, if nothing else. The ball, if discharged, must strike somewhere; and, if so, why might it not happen to strike the turkey? The logic was simply irresistible. A fowl of that magnitude would be a most desirable addition to the meagre fare furnished by the college commons; and so the rifles cracked, with small result to the students and splendid profits to the turkey-man. One day a little tow-headed fellow appeared on the field, and desired to take part in the sport. Though he seemed almost too young to be trusted with a rifle, the master of the fowls (foreseeing future gains) was quite willing he should try. He must first receive proper instructions about the holding and pointing of his piece, and then there would really be no danger. Young Larz received the directions with great good nature, raised the rifle, and down went the turkey. The man stared in amazement, and then broke into a smile. "Try it again, young one," said he. "'Most any one can throw sixes once, you know." Another bird was procured, the ball flew to the mark with the same result, and a second turkey was added to the banquet upon which his friends would regale. "Well, where in" — the United States, let us call it — "did *you* come from?" exclaimed the master of fowls, who began to realize that his occupation was gone.

"I came from the State of Kentucky, sir," answered Larz Anderson, proudly; "and next time you meet a gentleman from that State, just remember there's not much you can tell him about a rifle. That's all."

And thus it was that our good friend Anderson broke the ice between pretty Miss Bullett and myself at that solemn dinner of high state, fifty-five years ago. I suppose the other eight-and-thirty people found something to say; but it is evident they were not talking for posterity. Neither their words nor their names appear in my journal. That record only makes it evident that a state banquet of the period was, in a general way, a frigid affair, but was capable, nevertheless, of considerable mitigation if one were well launched in conversation with a fair young lady from Kentucky.

I enjoyed the hospitality of the Vice-President, who, contrary to custom, had come up to the capital and was actually doing the work of his place. The usage had been for the holders of this office to stay quietly at home, draw their salaries, and allow some senator to preside in the Upper House. But Calhoun proclaimed that he would receive no emoluments from an office without assuming its responsibilities, and, whether constrained by this just sentiment or to look sharply after his political fortunes, had established himself at the capital and was one of its principal figures. He was a striking-looking man, then forty-four years old, with thick hair, brushed back defiantly. He had joined the bitter opposition to the administration; and though his position prevented him from publicly assaulting the President, he ruled that John Randolph was not to be called to order for so doing. Mr. Calhoun, with the foresight of a politician, was accustomed to make himself agreeable to young men appearing in Washington who might possibly rise to influence in their respective communities. It was probably with a view to such a contingency that he favored me with a long dissertation upon public affairs. He never alluded to the subject of slavery, though it was easy to see that reference to this interest shaped his opinions about tariffs, state rights, internal improvements, and other questions, with which, on the surface, it had small connection. The concluding words of this aggressive Democrat made an ineffaceable impression upon my mind. They were pronounced in a subdued tone of esoteric confidence, such as an ancient augur might have used to a neophyte in his profession. Substantially they were these: " Now, from what I have said to you, I think you will see that the interests of *the gentlemen* of the North and those of the South are *identical*." I can quote no utterance more characteristic of the political Washington of twenty-six than this. The inference was that the "glittering generalizations" of the Declaration were never meant to be taken seriously. *Gentlemen* were the natural rulers of America, after all. It has taken all the succeeding half-century to reach a vital belief that the people, and not gentlemen (using the word, of course, in its common and narrow sense), are to govern this country. It will take much more than another half-century before the necessary and (in the end) beneficent consequences of this truth shall be fully realized. I may here mention that I have rarely met a lady so skilful in political discussion as was Miss Calhoun, the daughter of the Vice-President. I do not feel certain that it was during this visit to the capital that I made her acquaintance, — it may have been at a subsequent period; but I well remember the clearness with which she presented the Southern view of the situation, and the ingenuity with which she parried such objections as I was able to present. The fashionable ladies of the South had received the education of political thought and discussion to a degree unknown among their sisters of the North. "She can read bad French novels and play a few tunes on the piano," said a cynical friend of mine concerning a young lady who had completed the costly education of a fashionable school in New York, " upon my word, she does not know whether she is living in a monarchy or a republic." The sneer would never have applied to the corresponding class at the South. These ladies were conversant with political theories, and held definite political opinions. Yes, and they had the courage of their opinions too, as the war abundantly testified.

One of the pleasantest dinners that I attended in Washington took place at Miss Hyer's boarding-house. It was given by the gentlemen lodgers, who, by a small subscription, added a few dishes to the ordinary bill of fare. Mr. Webster and Senator Mills, of Massachusetts, were among the guests, and when, after the removal of the cloth, some Bordeaux wine was added to the customary Madeira, the conversation was easy and animated. It was Mr. Webster's saying that dinners were agreeable in inverse ratio to their state and formality, and on this occasion he certainly proved that French cooking and cut-glass were no necessary adjuncts to a brilliant party.

For the benefit of younger readers, it may be well to mention that the use of wine and spirit was practically universal at the time of which I am speaking. Nobody thought it possible to dine without one or the other. At the boarding-houses and hotels every guest had his bottle or his interest in a bottle. In the early days of the Sound steamers, decanters of brandy, free to all, were placed upon the table, as part of the provision necessary for a meal. What a beneficent change in public sentiment has been wrought! Much as yet remains to be done, the advocates of temperance should be full of courage, by remembering what has been accomplished.

As the present paper has had so much concern with Mr. Webster, I will conclude it by giving an incident which occurred some years afterward, and which will show the overwhelming effect which his mere personal presence wrought upon men. The route between Boston and New York by the way of New Haven had just been opened, and I was occupying a seat with Mr. Webster when the cars stopped at the latter city. Mr. Webster was not quite well, and, saying that he thought it would be prudent to take some brandy, asked me to accompany him in search of it. We accordingly entered a bar-room near the station, and the order was given. The attendant, without looking at his customer, mechanically took a decanter from a shelf behind him and placed it near some glasses on the counter. Just as Webster was about to help himself, the bar-tender, happening to look up, started, as if he had seen a spirit, and cried "Stop!" with great vehemence. He then took the decanter from Webster's hand, replaced it on the shelf whence it came, and disappeared beneath the counter. Rising from these depths, he bore to the surface an old-fashioned black bottle, which he substituted for the decanter. Webster poured a small quantity into a glass, drank it off with great relish, and threw down half a dollar in payment. The bar-keeper began to fumble in a drawer of silver, as if selecting some smaller pieces for change; whereupon Webster waved his hand with dignity, and with rich and authoritative tones pronounced these words: "My good friend, let me offer you a piece of advice. Whenever you give that good brandy from under the counter, never take the trouble to make change." As we turned to go out, the dealer in liquors placed one hand upon the bar, threw himself over it, and caught me by the arm. "Tell me who that man is!" he cried with genuine emotion. "He is Daniel Webster," I answered. The man paused, as if to find words adequate to convey the impression made upon him, and then exclaimed in a fervent half-whisper, "*By Heaven, sir, that man should be President of the United States!*" The adjuration was stronger than I have written it; but it was not uttered profanely,—it was simply the emphasis of an overpowering conviction. The incident was but a straw upon the current; but it illustrates the commanding magnetism of Webster. Without asking the reason, men once subjected to his spell were compelled to love, to honor, and (so some cynics would wish to add) to forgive him. No man of mark ever satisfied the imagination so completely. The young men of to-day who go to Washington find a city of luxurious appointments and noble buildings, very different from the capital of muddy streets and scattered houses with which I was familiar. But where is the living figure, cast in heroic mould, to represent the ideal of American manhood? Can the capital of to-day show anything so majestic and inspiring as was Daniel Webster in the Washington of 1826?

II.

THE evening parties of Washington were the social features of the place at the time of my visit. The company assembled about eight, and began to break up shortly after eleven, having enjoyed the recreations of dancing, card-playing, music, or conversation. Everybody in the city who occupied the necessary social position appeared at these gatherings; and, being at the age when the tinsel of Vanity Fair is at its full glitter, I enjoyed them highly. My first Washington party was at Mrs. Wirt's, where I was taken as a stranger by Mr. and Mrs. Webster. My journal mentions the ladies who impressed me sufficiently to appear in its record. I talked, it seems, with Miss Henry, a descendant of the Virginian orator; and with Miss Wirt, the daughter of the house. Both these ladies impressed me very favorably, and I tell how the former played finely upon the piano and harp and sang simple songs, to the satisfaction of the guests. Mrs. David Hoffman, of Baltimore, I describe as "pretty, learned, and agreeable." With her I have a brief talk, and am then presented to a lady whose beauty was the admiration of Washington and whose name was, consequently, upon every tongue, — at least something like her name; for society had decreed that this fair woman should be known as Mrs. Florida White, her husband being a delegate from our most southern territory. And splendid in her beauty Mrs. White undoubtedly was, and it was only natural that the impressible young gentleman from Boston should feel highly gratified when she proposed to promenade the rooms with him, and that he should emphasize this fortunate circumstance in the account he gives of Mrs. Wirt's party.

Next comes my notice of a ball, at which I first saw a lady who at that period was the acknowledged chief of the elegant and fashionable young women of our country.

"*February* 16, 1826. — I spent this evening at a ball given by Mrs. Johnston, of Louisiana. I was to have gone there with Everett; but the death of his brother prevented him from appearing. Accordingly I accompanied Mr. Cheves, and found a crowd in comparison with which all other crowds that I have experienced sink into nothing. We were jammed so closely that it was impossible to see the faces of those who stood at our sides. I had a striking exemplification of this fact by finding a lady hanging upon my arm who was unable to look up to see who I was. I, on my part, exerted all my skill in craniology in a vain attempt to discover who she might be. It was only after a considerable time that we made each other out. The lady proved to be a Mrs. Atkinson, from Louisville, and a good laugh we had together on discovering the mistake. As there was no dancing, I contented myself with moving in the current round the room, first conducting Mrs. White, and afterward Mrs. Hoffman. By the latter lady I was introduced to Miss Cora Livingston; and I must be able to paint the rose to describe a lady who undoubtedly is the greatest belle in the United States. In the first place, she is not handsome, — I mean not *transcendently* handsome. She has a fine figure, a pretty face, dances well, and dresses to admiration. It is the height of the *ton* to be her admirer, and she is certainly the belle of the country. Mrs. Livingston, the mother, is a fine-looking woman, extremely polite and well-bred. She seems to be wholly absorbed in her daughter, and is constantly watching her movements."

I suppress much that might be said about my acquaintance with this charming Miss Cora. That I was greatly fascinated with her my journal confesses upon nearly every page. I called on her betimes the morning after Mrs. Johnston's ball (I had fortunately letters to her father), attended her to other balls, visited her frequently, and was fairly to be numbered in her large circle of admirers. At the public ball at Carracci's Assembly Rooms, where all Washington was present, I note my gratification in the honor done me by Miss Cora in reserving for me the first cotillon, and add that, " as a matter of course, every one gathered about our set, to admire the grace of my fair partner." And, the dance being finished, I tell how I walked about the room with her, and how she graciously introduced me to several of the lesser beauties. "And now," said she, "I am going to perform one of the greatest acts of heroism of which a woman can be capable. I am going to present you to my rival." So saying, Miss Cora divided a group of gentlemen, who had gathered about Miss Catherine Van ⸺er, of Albany, — "a tall, genteel girl," says my journal laconically, "and said to have a fine mind and a rich father." This lady, it appears, was considered a belle who might possibly compete with Miss Livingston; but if I did not warmly protest against the possibility of the rivalship that was hinted at, I was far less enthralled with this latter lady than the evidence before me seems to indicate. I puzzled that night over the mystery of the attraction exercised by this exquisite specimen of womanhood, and wrote out a theory upon the subject, which is too crude for quotation. When I took leave of Miss Cora, on leaving Washington, there was perhaps a little feeling on both sides. We had been much together — meeting nearly every day, in fact — and in an innocent way had become very pleasantly intimate. We acknowledged that we might never meet again: Boston and New Orleans were then far apart; and so the lady turned, I suppose, to the scores of young fellows who were coveting her smiles, and I bore away an image of loveliness and grace never to be erased. But we did meet again; and if the reader will kindly suppose thirty years to have elapsed, I will tell him how. From this shelf of old journals I select the volume for 1856, and open to the record of Saturday, the 30th of August. I am now with some friends on the North River, and am taken to Montgomery Place, to see the fine arboretum belonging to Mr. Barton. And Mr. Barton himself meets us at the door of his house, and, although lame from the gout, walks with us about the garden, and points out his choicest trees. At last comes the invitation which fills me with a nervous apprehension: "Will you come into the house and see Mrs. Barton?" Yes, I was to see what remained of the lovely Cora Livingston. The picture of what she had been was perfect in my mind and remains so to-day. "Surely, never lighted on this orb, which she hardly seemed to touch, a more delightful vision!" Burke's famous apostrophe to the Queen of France is none too good for the queen of American society in 1826. She was as graceful as a bird, and her step was so elastic that, as Hawthorne says of one of his characters, motion seemed as easy to her as rest. I will not describe the old lady, in cap and dress of studied simplicity, to whom I was presented by Mr. Barton. My nap had lasted ten years longer than Rip Van Winkle's, and this was the penalty. The reflections which arise under such circumstances have been written for all time by the author of Ecclesiastes, and it is unnecessary to repeat them. "You would not have known me!" said Mrs. Barton. I could only be silent. "Come into the next room, then, and you shall see the Cora Livingston you knew in Washington." A full-length portrait of a young lady, in a ball dress, hung upon the wall. Yes, fixed upon the artist's canvas was the lovely being who shone upon the society of the capital thirty years before. I wonder where that portrait is now, and whether those who may daily see it have a proper sense of their privilege! Some years ago the venerable Mrs. Barton passed to the world of spirits; but before her death an arrangement was made by which the four folio Shakespeares she possessed came to the Boston City Library. Interesting old volumes they are; highly prized by the many owners through whose fingers they have slipped; and containing, as we all know, some good descriptions of what is delightful in woman. But there will be one association the less with them when I am no longer able to climb the stairs which lead to Bates Hall. There will be no one left to tell how their last private possessor once seemed to fill the most perfect outline of a charming woman that the poet has drawn.

And now let us go back again to the Washington of 1826. At the public ball of which I have spoken I saw the waltz introduced into society for the first time. The conspicuous performer was Baron Stackelburg, who whirled through its mazes with a huge pair of dragoon spurs bound to his heels. The danger of interfering with the other dancers, which seemed always imminent, was skilfully avoided by the Baron, who received a murmur of appreciative applause as he led his partner to her seat. The question of the decorum of this strange dance was distinctly raised upon its first appearance, and it was nearly twenty-five years later before remonstrances ceased to be heard. How far the waltz, and its successors of a similar character, may be compatible with feminine modesty, is a question which need not here be discussed. It is sufficient to say that, socially speaking, it has proved an unmitigated nuisance. It has utterly routed the intellectual element that was once conspicuous even in fashionable gatherings. It has not only given society over to the young and inexperienced, but, by a perverse process of unnatural selection, it has pushed to the front by no means the best specimens of these.

I find in my journal an account of a ball at the house of Baron Durand de Mareuil, the French minister. The decorations were very elegant and displayed the perfection of French taste. I mention talking with Miss Morphin, of Kentucky, Miss Tayloe, and other young ladies; also my introduction to Mrs. A. and Miss B. (for these initials will do to represent them), — "the former being a beautiful creature, who is bound to a great, clumsy fellow of a husband; the latter very pretty, but ignorant of everything except accomplishments, and vain and susceptible of flattery to any amount." It is thus that our fair sisters are sometimes entered in the private records of young gentlemen. But the finest ball I attended was given by Mr. Vaughan, the English minister. Here the dancing was in a large room on the second floor, in order that the lower hall might be given up to the supper. A table of liberal dimensions, profusely laden and constantly replenished, was the feature of the evening. Another ball at Mr. Obregon's, the Mexican minister's, "given under the patronage of Mrs. and Miss Livingston," is duly recorded, as well as many lesser parties, by persons holding no official position. It is unnecessary, however, to give further particulars of these festivities. Many agreeable and sensible people, both men and women, were to be met. The society was exclusive and a proper introduction was rigorously required. General Jackson's administration swept away much of the graceful etiquette which was characteristic of the society as I saw it. Then set in the era of universal hand-shaking with everybody who could get to Washington, and social barriers were carried by the unrefined and coarse. Gambling was considered a reputable pastime for gentlemen, and a room at most parties was reserved for this purpose. Card-playing for high stakes was usual among prominent politicians and men in office. The enormous increase of wealth without labor which had come to fortunate speculators since the peace of 1815 seemed to make the invocation of chance almost a legitimate business. It was said that an original proprietor of a single share in the Charlestown Bridge Company had received in 1826 not only principal and interest, but a surplus of $7,000. Certain lands in Pennsylvania, purchased in 1814 at sixty-two cents an acre, were selling at $400 an acre. Such facts as these, and many similar to them, in which the gains were not so enormous, seemed to make speculation honorable and respectable, and the controlling spirit of the time found one of its outlets in games of chance.

Among the notable matrons whom I met in Washington, perhaps the first place must be accorded to Mrs. Peter, of Georgetown. She was a granddaughter of Mrs. Washington, an intelligent and ardent Federalist, and from the heights of Tudor Place looked down upon the democratic administrations of Jefferson and his successors in a spirit of scornful protest. She was accustomed to speak of them as "our present rulers," much as a French Republican under the Second Empire might have spoken of the men who had seized his country against its better will. This patriotic lady had named her three daughters America, Columbia, and Britannia, — the latter, it was said, as a significant rebuke to the Gallic proclivities of the third President. Of these young ladies the name of Miss America alone appears in my journal. When presented to her, I could not avoid an awkward and yet comical consciousness of the august nationality which the lady in some sort symbolized. An introduction, followed by the usual sequences, seemed almost such a desecration as one would be guilty of who proposed to shake hands with the Goddess of Liberty and entertain her with ball-room gossip. If my memory is to be trusted, Mrs. Peter's appearance in Washington society was confined to extra-official circles. For a quarter of a century the good lady had hoped against hope for a Federal President, in whose court she might conscientiously assume the commanding place to which descent and talents entitled her. Our hold upon political parties is now so narrowed that it is difficult to realize the uncompromising sternness with which the original Federalists kept the faith. To them party had the character of a church or a religion; and I cannot better illustrate this last remark than by quoting the words of Elisha R. Potter, of Rhode Island, a gentleman whom I constantly met at Miss Hyer's table in Washington, and with whom I made part of my journey home. He had been a member of Congress in the last century, and had served again during the War of 1812. He was one day giving me a pathetic description of the gradual fading out of the Federal party, and of the pluck with which the standard was followed after the day was lost. "I remember a time," he said, "when we found ourselves in a minority of eleven, and some timid soul had called a sort of meeting, to see whether it were worth while to continue the opposition. Some were disposed to be dispirited, and I was asked to say a few words to brace them up. Well, it came upon me to say only this: 'Friends, just remember that we are as many as the Apostles were after Judas had deserted them. Think what *they* did, and fight it out.' That did the business. We did fight it out and fell fighting for the good cause." There spoke the uncompromising spirit of Federalism.

Mr. Potter was one of the largest men I have ever seen, excepting, of course, the professional giants in the service of Mr. Barnum. He told me that he generally paid for two seats in a stage-coach, and suffered much if he neglected to do so. But the wit and intelligence of the man were in fair proportion to his goodly bulk. I had taken the pains to write out a humorous story of his illustrative of Washington life; but my literary adviser inexorably draws his pen through it, as not adapted to general perusal. Mr. Potter was one of the men who carry about them a surplus of vital energy, to relieve the wants of others. The absurd inquiry whether life were worth living never suggested itself in his presence. I well

THE HOUSE OF REPRESENTATIVES.

THE popular branch of the national legislature was the most interesting sight that the capital had to offer to those who journeyed thither in 1826. The day of read speeches (prepared, perhaps, by persons outside of Congress) had not arrived; neither had it occurred to any one to ask leave to print prosy documents which had not even been read. The excitement of brisk debates, conducted by able men, was constantly to be had; and the elaborate speeches were eloquent or logical appeals, designed to make or change votes. My very first morning in Washington was devoted to the House, and the discussion gave me the opportunity of hearing Webster make one of those massive appeals for loyalty to the spirit, as well as the letter, of the Constitution which distinguished his public career.

A movement to put a breakwater in the Delaware was in contemplation, and, as a means toward the successful prosecution of this end, Miner, of Pennsylvania, introduced a resolution requesting the President to lay before Congress a statement to show the net amount of revenue derived from imposts and tonnage from ports within the Bay of Delaware for the past thirty-four years. Also the President was requested to furnish the amount of expenditures for lighthouses, beacons, and other public works made in that bay. This was to be followed by like information in respect to receipts and expenditures within the Bay of Chesapeake, as well as similar figures appertaining to the harbor of New York. Now, the request for the increase of knowledge embodied in these resolutions seemed to me so harmless and even so laudable that I marvelled at the evident displeasure of Webster while they were being read. Could it be that his practised eye had detected a cat concealed in this measure of apparently innocent meal? It was even so, and the moment the reading ceased the great man rose, and, with the air of one not to be trifled with, demanded full information of the motives with which the call had been made. And so the motives had to appear, though the mover of the resolution covered them with all the gloss of which they were susceptible. The hard fact was that the Delaware breakwater was wanted by his constituents, and he thought that these revenue statistics would establish a claim which Congress could be moved to recognize. Was it not pertinent, he asked, to show how the receipts and expenditures of this commercial district compared with those of others? "No," exclaimed Webster; "not if you mean us to infer that, because the port of Philadelphia has yielded such and such sums to the revenue, it is *therefore* entitled to have its wishes complied with in the matter of the breakwater. I oppose a call based upon such principles."

And then he added with a mighty scorn, which seemed to settle the question, "*They are the very essence of local legislation!*" Whereupon Wurts, of Pennsylvania, came to the assistance of his colleague, and (to follow out the metaphor) smoothed the meal so carefully over the pussy, whose slumbers had been disturbed, that it almost seemed doubtful whether she could still be beneath that placid surface. An amendment was, of course, proposed, and the debate became general, Wood, of New York, and other members taking part in it. The closing speech was made by Webster, and was pointed and effective. He began by disclaiming any hostility to the breakwater. The project, on its own merits, deserved serious consideration. But he wanted no information concerning the revenue collected in the port of Philadelphia. That revenue was paid wherever consumers of the imported products happened to reside. "The gentlemen in charge of this resolution," said Webster, with his imperative emphasis, "are pushing the argument of State against State; *and I bar all such reasoning.*" He proceeded to a *reductio ad absurdum*, sarcastically proposing to find out how much revenue was received at other ports, and then to make appropriations to each correspond to the figures of the custom-houses. "If the breakwater is wanted," he concluded, "let it be shown on other grounds. If it is wanted at all, it is wanted as a *great national work* and must be urged upon *great national considerations.*" As soon as Webster resumed his seat the question was called, and the resolutions rejected by a handsome majority.

The speech was absolutely unprepared, and was not a great one; but it was eminently characteristic of the man. It illustrated that exquisite sensitiveness to any disrespect to the paramount majesty of the Union, which would allow no slur, however subtle and indirect, to pass unchallenged.

On the morning of Thursday, February 16, the galleries of the House were filled at an early hour. It was known that the most sensational orator of the time, George Macduffie, of South Carolina, a bitter opponent of the administration, was to ask a hearing of his countrymen. The occasion gained interest from the fact that a young lady to whom the orator was very attentive, and whom, I believe, he afterward married, was conspicuous in the gallery. "See! there is Miss —— opposite. Depend upon it, Mr. Macduffie will outdo himself to-day," said one of the ladies of my party, as we took our seats. And these same ladies whom I attended were Miss Mease and Miss Helen; the former remarkable for her powers of conversation, the latter a niece of Mrs. Adams, whom I had often met in Quincy.

Macduffie was certainly an orator, if earnestness and fluency can make one. His effort (and it may well be so called, for he gesticulated all over) lasted the greater part of two days, and was always lively, if never conclusive. He was not guilty of sawing the air with his hand, after the manner which Hamlet deprecates, for he preferred to pound that element with tightly clenched fists. "Will not those fists of Mr. Macduffie fly off and hit somebody?" whispered

Miss Helen to me, during one of the tempests or, as I may say, whirlwinds of his passion. Such were the remarks of the friends of the administration upon the over-emphasis of this high-talking Southerner.

To understand the motive of this violent speech, it is necessary to remember that in 1824 the choice of President fell upon the House of Representatives, and an executive was elected to whom a majority of the electors and presumably of the people were opposed; in other words, the majority of the House had overruled the majority of the nation. Here was a situation capable of rhetorical treatment of the intensest sort; and the fact that the administration of Mr. Adams was one of the most honorable which the nation has enjoyed had no power to stay the sound and fury of partisan calumny. The House had resolved itself into a Committee of the Whole on the State of the Union, and was sitting to consider certain resolutions formally moved by the gentleman from South Carolina. It was proposed to amend the Constitution, so that a uniform system of voting by districts should be established in the States, and to prevent the election of President from ever devolving upon either branch of Congress. Under the guise of an amendment to the Constitution, a proposition was made to alter the relation between the States upon which the original compact of union had been based; and this because, after nine successful presidential elections, there had come one failure. As the report of Macduffie's speech may be read in the Congressional Records of the time, I shall attempt no sketch of its argument. The drift of it was that, because of the idolatrous homage rendered to the Constitution, the rights of minorities were in grievous peril, and this was a matter of serious concern to this very democratic slaveholder; but, after all, he argued, the Constitution was aimed at ascertaining the popular voice in the election of President, and, if it missed the mark, it must of course be set to rights. And then the equality of representation of the States in the Upper House was glanced at, and pronounced a wrong which the larger communities would not always tolerate. "In throwing the election into the House," said the orator, "we expose ourselves to those arts of political courtship which the ambitious have ever been prone to practise. The little arts of a dinner or a condescending smile are the means by which cunning aspirants address themselves to the vanity and foibles of those who fall within the sphere of their fascination. The People [properly spelt by the reporter with a large P] cannot be reached by these arts!" And then Macduffie went on to show how Mr. Adams, destitute of the confidence of this virtuous and discriminating People, would be forced to buttress himself with patronage, and to introduce a corrupt civil service, like that employed by the Roman emperors. How has history answered these unworthy surmises? Three years later the People seated Andrew Jackson in the presidential chair, and the pure and efficient civil service maintained by President Adams was degraded to a position which is the shame of America to this day.

Mr. Macduffie's harangue, though one of the famous incidents of the time, would be scarcely worth the notice here accorded to it were it not necessary in order to emphasize my delight with the reply of Henry R. Storrs, of New York. "A very masterly speech," says my journal. "He spoke like a statesman, and commanded the attention of the House by his manly eloquence and cogent reasoning. He descended to none of the meretricious arts to provoke applause, but met the full responsibilities of the situation." I had never heard a parliamentary speech that was so vigorous, or which seemed to come from a man so thoroughly equipped. Storrs swept down upon Macduffie's hasty assertion that the Constitution was aimed simply at ascertaining the popular voice in the election of President. The pure democratic principle was to be found in no branch of the government, not even in the House of Representatives. The nation was based upon a mixed principle, in which the rights of independent States were commingled with those of the people at large. And then came a cutting proposition to the Southern gentleman, who, in his enthusiasm for pure democracy, was disposed to sink the rights guaranteed to the States as separate communities. With telling effect Storrs pointed his finger at the peculiar Southern institution, and showed that its stability would be at an end the moment that the people of all the States were melted into one mass, and the voters of the South had no advantage in representation. He begged that Macduffie would proceed to complete his amendment on his own principles, and abolish a state of things which gave the white men of his section a much greater weight than those of the North. The *argumentum ad hominem* was never more remorselessly put, and the "sensation" which ran along the galleries was a deserved tribute to the acumen and eloquence of the member from New York. Mr. Storrs was, after Daniel Webster, the most impressive man in a Congress which fairly represented the best intelligence of the country. To hear him speak was to carry away a lasting memory of eloquence and ability; yet, for some reason, he missed the position of conspicuous leadership which men of far less power have easily maintained. His friends used to account for this by saying that Storrs had a judicial way of looking all round a subject, which deprived him of that absorbing enthusiasm for one particular view of it upon which political prominence depends. His reasoning, they said, was strong enough to convince every one but himself; but he could never believe that his own arguments quite closed a question, and he was sincere enough to let the world know that this was the case. A biography of Mr. Storrs was once in contemplation. It was to have been the joint work of William C. Noyes and William H. Bogart, and the latter has told us that, after the death of Mr. Noyes, the journal of Mr. Storrs had been given to the Buffalo Historical Society. Whether it has ever been published I have no knowledge.

I was fortunate in hearing the elaborate speech by William S. Archer, of Virginia, upon the Macduffie resolutions, as it was a fine specimen of Southern eloquence, as well as very sensible in its general drift. The name of this gentleman was seldom mentioned without the addition of an adjective borrowed from Dr. Young's "Night Thoughts," a poem which at that time was familiar to everybody who read poetry at all. "Insatiate Archer! would not one suffice?" sung the royal chaplain, thus apostrophizing the last enemy of man. The quotation was altogether too felicitous to escape attention when the member from the Old Dominion made more speeches than were thought necessary upon some question before the House; and so it came to pass that in the social Washington of 1826 it was as natural to speak of *Insatiate* Archer as of *Daniel* Webster or of *Henry* Clay. Mr. Archer's rhetoric, though a little too brilliant for Northern taste, was certainly effective, and his unequivocal condemnation of the radical changes in the Constitution which Macduffie had demanded was sustained by a vigorous argument. Nevertheless, about the matter upon which the feeling of the day was most excited he was with his friend from South Carolina. He saw small hope for the Union unless the Constitution were so far amended as to prevent the election of President from devolving upon either branch of Congress. Waxing very eloquent over the perilous jurisdiction of the House in the appointment of the executive magistrate, he finished a compromise speech which commanded the attention, as it largely appealed to the sympathies, of his audience.

The gallery of the old House of Representatives was, in fact, not a gallery at all, it being simply a platform, raised a foot or two above the floor of the hall, which gave the honorable members an excellent opportunity of attending to the ladies who had come to listen to them. The huge pillars by which it was divided rendered it difficult to secure a place from which the whole assembly could be seen, and it followed that it was highly important to know who the speakers were to be before selecting seats. It was a serious drawback to the interest of a debate that some of the participants must necessarily be concealed; but then the debates were interesting enough to overcome this drawback, for Congress was at that time fairly thrust up to the true theory of its character, and it was an education to have the freedom of the galleries. Men who could think on their feet and who were keen to take advantage of any slip in the arguments of their opponents were sent as the ablest mouthpieces of different phases of public sentiment. To a New Englander, a debate in the House was like a glorified town-meeting. There was all the alertness of mind which is so conspicuous in that primal assembly, accompanied with an ability which could fairly grapple with the national problems presented for solution. Prejudice and passion, of course, there were; but the unjust war upon the administration was well fought. From their point of view, the assailing partisans were patriotic men. Grant the premises that the Southern States were their country and slavery was its life-blood, and their favorite epithet, "chivalrous," need not be withheld from the leading spirits of the opposition. Men will soon come to believe what they wish to believe. A few downright phrases of Mr. Adams ("Paralyzed by the will of our constituents" was one of them) were torn from their context to represent him as a monarchist conspiring against the liberties of the nation. Meantime the "Old Roman" (as Jackson was absurdly called) was marching upon the straggling provincial town which then did duty as the capital. He would reward his friends and punish his enemies, who were also, of course, the friends and enemies of mankind. The verdict of history has already been given upon the administration of the younger President Adams. It was tried as by fire, and came out as gold from the furnace.

THROUGH BALTIMORE TO BOSTON.

AT seven o'clock on the morning of the 4th of March, 1826, all the company at Miss Hyer's boarding-house made their appearance at an uncomfortably early breakfast, to take leave of Martin Brimmer, of Boston, Captain Zantzinger, and myself, who were booked to leave Washington by the early stage. The breakfast, however, might as well have been postponed to a more seasonable hour, for the stage did not appear for an hour after it was due, and, to say the truth, did not appear even then. What did arrive was a nondescript sort of conveyance, which looked more like a hearse upon a gigantic scale than any modern vehicle with which I am acquainted. There were about a dozen passengers who wished to go North, and we were told that the combined weight of this unexpected multitude had broken down the regular coach, and hence we were served this melancholy substitute. It was raining violently, and my journal relates how we were forced to climb in over the horses' backs, in the most irregular and awkward fashion. For an hour we travelled in absolute darkness and discomfort; and then, the rain having ceased, the leathern curtains were rolled up, and I

Mr. Oliver's, we called upon Mr. Hugh Thompson, and finally ended the evening at Dr. Stuart's, the father of my attentive friend; and the result of it all was that when I returned to Mrs. West's establishment, late in the evening, I found myself engaged for ten days of constant festivity, comprising balls, dinners, morning calls, a fox-hunt, a "cotton cambric," and such other not-specified entertainments as would be forthcoming to fill the intervals; and any social meetings more hearty, easy, friendly, and in all respects agreeable than those which characterized the Baltimore society of 1826 it has never been my fortune to attend. My stay seemed like a long English Christmas, — such a one, I mean, as we read of in books. The beauty and grace of the ladies and the charming ease of their manners were very taking to one reared among the grave proprieties of Boston. I paid two visits to Charles Carroll (the signer of the Declaration of Independence), and dined with him and Mr. Gallatin at Mr. Caton's, where the service, though the most elegant I had ever seen, in no wise eclipsed the conversation. The ladies of the family, Mrs. Caton and Mrs. MacTavish (mother and sister, as my journal is careful to mention, to the Marchioness of Wellesley), were fine-looking women and bore the impress of refinement and high breeding. Old Mr. Carroll, courtly in manners and bright in mind, was the life of the party. He was then in his ninetieth year, but carried himself as if thirty years younger than his contemporary, John Adams. I have never seen an old man so absolutely unconscious of his age. One reason may have been that Carroll was very spare in his person, and had no surplus pound of mortality to weigh down the spirit. On terminating my first call upon this very active patriarch, he started from his chair, ran down-stairs before me, and opened the front door. Aghast at this unexpected proceeding, I began to murmur my regrets and mortification in causing him the exertion. "Exertion!" exclaimed Mr. Carroll. "Why, what do you take me for? I have ridden sixteen miles on horseback this morning, and am good for as much more this afternoon, if there is any occasion for it." On leaving the house, General Stuart told me that Mr. Carroll made it a point of etiquette to see every guest well over his threshold. "But you should see him when there are ladies!" he added. "The old gentleman will then run into the street and throw down the steps of the carriage, before the footman has a chance to reach them." At Mr. Caton's dinner Carroll was rich in anecdotes of Franklin and other great men of the Revolution; but my journal, which finds room for much of the petty gossip of the younger society of Baltimore, gives them no record. He spoke with great respect of my venerable friend John Adams, giving me a Maryland view of this eminent personage, which was, so to speak, somewhat softer in outline than that obtaining in Massachusetts. In social meetings of those days men talked much of the past, because there was none of the varied and inexhaustible present which steam and telegraph now thrust upon their attention. Let it be mentioned that, when I met Mr. Carroll at this dinner-table, not a word had been heard from Europe for fifty-eight days. If the reader considers this single fact in its full bearings, he will appreciate the changes in the objects of human thought and interest which these physical marvels have wrought.

It is only modest to mention that the attention I received in Baltimore was due not to my own deservings, but partly to the regard in which my father was held by the Federalists of the city, and partly to the wish to acknowledge the civilities which Bostonians had shown to strangers on the occasion of the Bunker Hill celebration of the previous summer. I had dinner invitations from Robert Gilmore, John Hoffman, George Hoffman, Robert Oliver, and so many others that, when the latter gentleman insisted on my dining with him any day when I was not engaged elsewhere, he added, pleasantly, that there was really no hospitality in giving an invitation under conditions which made its acceptance plainly impossible. One little incident connected with these Baltimore dinners forcibly reminded me that I was not in the latitude of Boston. I was engaged to dine with Mr. ——, one of the principal citizens, but received a polite note from him regretting that the party must be postponed, as his nephew had just been shot in a duel.

Of the evening parties it will not be necessary to copy the records in full. A brief specimen will show their character.

"*Wednesday, March 8.*— Spent the evening at Mrs.

Bozeley's ball, where I was greatly struck by the beauty of the ladies. The principal belles were Miss Clapham, Miss Gallatin, and Miss Johnson. This last lady has one of the most striking faces I ever saw. It is perfectly Grecian. And this, added to her fine figure and graceful movements, presented a *tout ensemble* from which I could not keep my eyes. I was introduced to her, and found her manners as bewitching as her person. She was all life and spirit. After finishing the first dance, I discovered a corner, where we sat for nearly an hour, keeping up an easy, laughing sort of conversation. This would have occasioned observation elsewhere; but here no one seemed to notice it except the gentleman who wished to dance with her, so I had a very comfortable time. When we were obliged to separate, I tried to dance with Miss Clapham, but found she was engaged. I could only represent to her partner that I should never have another opportunity of dancing with this lady, whereas he would have many others; but he was inexorable and refused to give her up, so I did the next best thing in standing by her and talking to her during all the intervals of the dance. After it was over, I retired, well satisfied that the reputation of Baltimore for the gayety and beauty of its ladies was fully deserved."

There is no use in multiplying extracts like this. It is the old, old story of maidenly fascinations upon a young man. Let me hope that the intuitive sympathy of a few youthful readers will give piquancy to the foolish words which chronicle experiences once so vivid. At yet another ball my journal tells how I was introduced to Miss ——, "the great belle of the city," and testifies that I found her "pretty, agreeable, and sensible." And then there is written some idle gossip of the young fellows of Baltimore about this fair lady. The question with them was: Why did not Miss —— marry? She was nearly as old as the century, and had had annual crops of eligible offers from her youth up. There must be some explanation; and then excellent and apparently conclusive reasons why the lady had not married and never would marry were alleged, and these were duly confided to the guardianship of my journal. It is apropos to this lady that I shall be generous enough to relate a subsequent awkwardness of my own; for it enforces what may be called a social moral, which it is useful to remember. A few years after this (that is, they *seemed* very few years to me), a gentleman from Baltimore was dining at my house. During one of the pauses of conversation, it occurred to me to inquire after the former belle of his city, about whom I had heard so much speculation. Expecting an immediate acquiescence in the negative, I carelessly threw out the remark: "Miss ——, of Baltimore, I believe, was never married." No sooner were the words uttered than I saw that something was wrong. My guest changed color and was silent for some moments. At length came the overwhelming reply "Sir, I *hope* she was married. *She is my mother.*" And so the moral is, that we cannot be too cautious in our inquiries concerning the life, health, or circumstances of any mortal known in other years and bounded by another horizon.

I was introduced to Lucien Bonaparte, brother of Napoleon, whom I first met at a superb dinner at Mr. George Hoffman's. Christopher Hughes, our minister to the Netherlands, was of the party, and drew Bonaparte into general conversation, for the benefit of the table. Morally speaking, Lucien was one of the best of the family, and in society appeared as a man of varied experience and accomplishment. His title of "Prince," which sounded strangely to my ears, was brought in by those who talked with him quite as often as was necessary; yet, as the man had had the chance of being a king, and had declined royalty for very creditable reasons, no one could grudge him the poor papal princedom of Musignano, which satisfied an ambition to which richer fields were offered. Among the subjects of discussion was the recent action of the New York Legislature inaugurating common schools. Would this Yankee notion spread further? It might do for New England, where property was pretty equally divided, but would be very unjust where this was not the case. That the rich should be taxed to give education, without discrimination, to the children of their poorer neighbors, was decided to be simply preposterous. The grounds upon which this appropriation of the taxpayer's money may be justified were apparently not perceived; and, indeed, it was impossible that the characteristic institution of the Puritans should at that day be acceptable to the gentlemen of a milder latitude.

THE REVEREND CLERGY.

THE narratives which I have hitherto offered the reader have been taken from or suggested by my journals written during the decade commencing with 1820, a period so remote as to be historical to all who are now carrying on the active work of the world. The decades beginning with 1830 and 1840 are richer in incident, as I came into more intimate contact with distinguished contemporaries and took a humble part in forwarding that great revolution which followed the introduction of locomotion by steam. But the diaries which chronicle these things have not the savor of relating to an extinct condition of society, which is characteristic of those from which extracts have hitherto been taken; and before leaving the decade following 1820, I have been urged, by the friend by whom my journals have been read, to give some illustrations of the social life in Boston which they present.

The progress in scientific discovery and mechanical invention, which has distinguished the last half-century beyond any other since the world began, has swept us past many comfortable traditions which controlled our society when I first knew it. In the third decade of the century Boston was a synonym for certain individuals and families, who ruled it with undisputed sway and, according to the standards then recognized, governed it pretty well. On the topmost round of the social ladder stood the clergy; for although the lines of theological separation among themselves were deeply cut, the void between them and the laity was even more impassable. Dr. Channing, the pastor of my father's family, upon hearing that I had joined a militia company, spoke to my mother on the subject, and alluded to a personal grievance with a bitterness of tone which caused his words to be long remembered. "Your son, madam," he said, "is to be greatly congratulated, for he will now have the satisfaction of seeing men as they really are; and this is an inestimable privilege which has always been denied to me. The moment I enter any society, every one remembers that I am a clergyman, puts off his natural self, and begins to act a part. My profession requires me to deal with such men as actually exist, yet I can never see them except in disguise. I am shut out from knowledge which is essential to my work." And so strongly did this eminent man feel the disadvantage under which he labored that he made it the subject of an address from the pulpit. I find, in my journal for January 8, 1826, an abstract of a sermon preached that day upon "Sanctity of Persons," wherein Dr. Channing thought it necessary to maintain the thesis that ministers, merely in virtue of their office, were no holier than the rest of mankind, and that the reverence accorded them should not differ from that due to Christian laymen whose influence tended to the elevation of our characters.

The absence of the able religious press which at present exists gave great weight to the utterances of the pulpit, and my journals contain always a notice and often a pretty full report of the Sunday discourses. A brief mention of some of these old sermons may be found interesting. On Sunday, June 17, 1821, I find that the venerable Mr. Norton, of Weymouth, preached at the First Church in Quincy, and that he saw fit to address his remarks, not to potential presidents of the United States, as it would have been polite in him to do, but to *servants*. The domestics of the family in those days often worshipped with their employers, and the good old minister saw no reason why a fact of social existence recognized everywhere else should be ignored by the pulpit. "I am Abraham's servant," was announced as the text, and surely, thought the preacher, there was nothing unbecoming an honorable and self-respecting man in this statement; for the Scriptures are at pains to inform us how good a servant was he who thus bluntly declared his office. "Mark, in the first place," quoth Mr. Norton, "the dignified mission with which he was intrusted. It was to choose a wife for Isaac. Observe, in the second place, his self-denial in refusing to eat until he had told his errand, though he must have been very hungry after his long journey. In the third place, note that we hear nothing of his visiting any of the sights of Nahor, though to a stranger they must have been attractive, and doubtless the friends of Rebekah would have feasted him had he chosen to tarry for this purpose." Those acquainted with the sermons of the time can imagine the picturesque treatment that naturally belongs to these different heads. The resulting moral was shot point-blank at such servants and apprentices as were present to receive it. While Mr. Norton thought it improbable that they would be employed in delicate matrimonial negotiations, like the servant of the text, he was quite confident that there would never be lacking opportunities of showing fidelity in the condition of life to which their Maker had called them. Perhaps I should apologize for bringing this rusty old homily from its sixty years of silence. It is little adapted to that fair world of railroad presidents, popular politicians, and successful speculators which all young Americans are now on their way to adorn.

My journal for Sunday, November 11, 1821, is devoted to an account of services held by John Newland Maffit, a Methodist preacher, who attracted great attention and was claimed by his admirers to be the successor of Whitefield. On the morning of the day I attended a baptism by immersion of some fifty adults, most of them young women, who had been converted by his appeals. The ceremony took place in Charles River, near the site of the Massachusetts General Hospital. For some reason or other, Mr. Maffit could not administer the rite. With an earnest half-whisper, that was very impressive, he pronounced a benediction over each of his converts, as he handed them to an older minister, who led them into the water. Those who were baptized seemed under great excitement, and took their chilly November plunge without shrinking. They all sang with fervor as they waded back to the beach. It was no easy matter to hear Mr. Maffit preach, for the crowds which thronged to the Bromfield Street Meeting-house packed the aisles of that building so closely that the minister had been forced to enter by a ladder placed at a back window. I was so much struck by the services of the morning that I determined to hear this famous preacher, and by dint of great perseverance succeeded in doing so. My journal thus describes him: "Mr. Maffit is a little black-haired man, with the scar of a harelip, which has been sewed up. His wonderful power lies in his fluency and his imagination. In the afternoon his text was from Acts vii. 22: 'And Moses was learned in all the wisdom of the Egyptians.' In the evening he preached upon Nebuchadnezzar's dream. He is very rapid in his enunciation, never hesitating for a word or pausing for an instant. He has a fine voice, and it is pleasant to hear him." I then speak of his utter want of method, and the adroit way in which he disguised it by a rapid rush of utterance in the places where a want of proper sequence would otherwise have been marked. "His self-possession is amazing, and when he made some ridiculous mistake he hurried on and took no notice of it, and so nobody else did."

It is not unlikely that the abundant incense offered at the shrine of Mr. Maffit drew from Dr. Channing an excellent sermon from 2 Corinthians xiii. 9, of which my journal for the following Sunday contains a report. It was a rigid examination of the duties of ministers, showing the temptation which assailed those possessing certain gifts of voice and manner to substitute the startling effects which produce immediate applause for more effective methods of dealing with sin. The warning, if it was intended for one, was timely; for the much-flattered Mr. Maffit got into trouble the very next year, and appeared in court, prosecuting Joseph T. Buckingham, editor of the "Galaxy," for a libel. My father, who was judge, ruled that the defendant might be allowed to prove that his allegations were true and that they were published for justifiable ends, since the specific reservation of the liberty of the press under the Massachusetts Constitution annulled the doctrine of the common law, that the truth could not be put in as evidence under a libel. Owing to this ruling, Mr. Maffit lost his case before the civil court; but it is due to him to say that the ecclesiastical court, which subsequently considered his alleged offences against decorum, found that while he "had exhibited mournful evidence of want of judgment and prudence," no more serious charge could be sustained against him. This was doubtless a correct view of the case, and furnishes one warning more of the jealous scrutiny to which the ways of a popular preacher are subjected. The Christian usefulness of this impulsive and eloquent Irishman was forever marred by his imprudence.

I was on intimate terms with Dr. Channing and often visited him. I recall a conversation I had with him about this time in relation to Maffit or some other modern Whitefield. "To compare any man that this generation has heard to Whitefield is on its face absurd," said Dr. Channing. "Could any of them move such cold and competent critics as Garrick and Gibbon? Now to Whitefield's eloquence we have expert testimony, which places him far above all uninspired preachers. Would the most consummate actor of his day and the philosophical scoffer at the religion Whitefield preached have been touched by anything short of the light and sincerity of genius?" I then repeated to Dr. Channing a remark made in my presence by my great-aunt Storer, at which he seemed much struck, saying that it was in perfect accordance with the traditions of Whitefield which had come to his knowledge. Mrs. Storer, who had heard this great preacher upon Boston Common, was asked to give the company some idea of the effect he produced upon her. Her reply was substantially this: "I remember that in the course of one of his sermons (it was preached just after sunrise) he quoted the words, 'If I take the wings of the morning and dwell in the uttermost parts of the sea.' Well, his voice was like that of an angel when he uttered them, while his arms rose slowly from his sides with an indescribable grace. I should have felt no surprise to see him ascend into the air. That would have been no miracle. The miracle was rather that he remained on earth."

My journals abound in abstracts of Dr. Channing's sermons, which, although far too lengthy for quotation in these papers, have at least the interest of showing how much matter the average hearer could bring home from those wonderful services. Testimony of mine to the thrilling impressiveness of his voice would be utterly superfluous. "I could form no idea of eternity," said a lady to me, "until I heard Channing say the words 'from everlasting to everlasting,' and then it overwhelmed me. They were as full of spiritual discernment as the simple exclamation of Whitefield, which Garrick said he would give a hundred guineas to imitate." I may give some notion of the sustained elevation of Channing's pulpit utterances by mentioning that when he had occasion to make some ordinary request from the sacred desk, the descent of his manner excited a sense of the ridiculous. "I should like to have those in the back pews come forward and occupy the pews near the pulpit." What is there in this simple and proper request to raise a smile? And yet, when Channing made it, after one of his impassioned discourses, the effect was somehow as comically incongruous as if *Prospero* should follow his grand speech about the dissolution of the great globe itself by asking *Ariel* to serve him with chops and tomato sauce. The fact is, that the man who loomed to such gigantic spiritual stature in the pulpit was not a great pastor. With all his interest in education, he did not personally come near the average youth of his congregation. We revered him and were very proud of him, but the distance between us was impassable. I am speaking of him, of course, as he appeared to the very young. A timid young girl, who went on a fishing excursion with her pastor in 1815, gave me this specimen of the way in which the good man sought to enter into conversational relations with her. The party had been out for some hours, and at length the shy Mr. Channing seemed to feel that it was his duty to say something to the daughter of one of the principal supporters of his church. He accordingly sidled up to her, and thus began: "Do these waves look to you as if they were moved by the wind, or as if each wave was propelled by the impulse it receives from the one following it?" An admirable question this. Indeed, it will look so well in print that the point of the story may be missed. Nothing could be better to introduce that body of useful information which oppresses the fathers of the Franks and the Rollos, and of which they are bound to relieve themselves at any sacrifice; but, excellent as the inquiry was, it shut up the young girl most effectually, for it testified to the awful distance which separated her simple thoughts from those of her pastor. To ask whether his young friend were not hungry and did not hope there would be chowder for luncheon, would not have been a dignified opening; yet easy relations, valuable to one of the parties at least, might thus have been established. There is no harm in admitting (nay, it is often encouraging to remember) that men full of genius and goodness have had their human limitations, like the rest of us. Channing's gift was that of a preacher. His sermons, while coherent and complete as compositions, were given with a warmth and intensity of expression with which scholarship and delicacy of thought are seldom united.

Mrs. Gore, of Boston, afterward known as Mrs. Joseph Russell, ornamented her parlors in Park Street with two fine Stuarts, painted by her order One of these portraits represented Cardinal Cheverus (or, as we Bostonians had rather call him, *Bishop* Cheverus), and the other Dr. John Sylvester John Gardiner, the rector of Trinity. Both these divines impressed themselves deeply upon the society of Boston, and many are the anecdotes that were once in circulation concerning them. Cheverus was greatly esteemed by my father, who was fond of relating the manner in which their acquaintance commenced. One day, near the beginning of the century, he was driving from Quincy to Boston in a pelting storm. When about five miles from his destination, he overtook a forlorn foot-passenger, who, drenched and draggled, was plodding along the miry road. My father drew up his horse, and called to the stranger to get in and ride with him. "That would be scarcely fair," was the man's reply. "My clothes are soaked with water and would spoil the cushions of your chaise, to say nothing of the wetting I could not avoid giving you." These objections were made light of, and with some difficulty the wayfarer was persuaded to take the offered seat. During the ride my father learned that his companion was a priest, named Cheverus, who was walking from Hingham, whither he had been to perform some offices connected with his profession; and thus commenced the acquaintance, which afterward ripened into friendship, between men whose beliefs and ways of life were outwardly so different. No person could have been better adapted to establish the Church of Rome in the city of the Puritans than the first bishop of Boston. The elevation of his character commanded the respect of the Protestant leaders of the place, and Channing confessed that no minister in the town would care to challenge a comparison between himself and this devoted priest. I have a distinct recollection of hearing Cheverus preach in the Franklin Street Cathedral. His style was very direct, and I remember how startling to my ears was the sentence with which he opened his discourse: "I am now addressing a congregation which has more thieves in it than any other assembled in this town." Owing to the social position and peculiar temptations of his people, the fact may have been as the Bishop stated it; but only a strong man would have ventured upon an opening so little conciliatory to his audience. But besides the great Christian virtues, Cheverus had those gifts of tact and humor which are not without value to an ecclesiastic. He had a sly way of reminding his Protestant friends that their forefathers had fled to this country, not to escape the persecution of Popery, but that of a Protestant Prelacy; and when theological topics were broached, he would treat our "invincible ignorance" with a kindly forbearance that was very winning. There was a story that he once entered into an argument with a Methodist minister, who, with more zeal than wisdom, sought to crush the Bishop with texts selected at random from all parts of the Bible and then dovetailed together to support his conclusions. Cheverus stood this sort of attack until the *argumentum ad absurdum*, or, rather, *ad hominem*, seemed to be a legitimate retaliation; and so, turning over the Bible, he said he would call his antagonist's attention to two texts which, when properly clinched together, would end all controversy between them. The first was to be found in the twenty-seventh chapter of Matthew, "*And Judas went and hanged himself;*" the second was from Luke x., "*Go and do thou likewise.*" I do not vouch for the truth of this anecdote, but only for its currency.

There is room for all temperaments among the clergy. The Church of Him who came eating and drinking, and whose chief apostle was willing to make himself all things to all men, touches this world as well as the heavens. It has uses not only for the meditative ascetic, but for the well-equipped scholar of genial presence and warm social tastes. Such a man was Dr. Gardiner, the rector of Trinity, a representative English Churchman; one who thought it no sin to enjoy a game of cards and a game supper afterward. At the time to which I refer I think he was the only Boston clergyman who was willing to be seen playing whist; and as for suppers, he possessed the noble British digestion which regards with scorn the weaker gastric fluids characteristic of Western civilization. "What is all this talk about stom-

achs?" I have heard him exclaim. "You don't give
them work enough. That's what the matter is. Eat
a hearty supper, as I do, keep a good conscience, and
don't *think* about them, and I'll be bound they'll give
you no trouble." And the good Doctor took his own
prescription with great success; and, with some modifications, it is not a bad one. In the pulpit Dr. Gardiner was interesting and gratified a refined taste; yet
he well knew the advantage of occasionally leaving
the graceful periods, of which he was master, to pass
to the direct language of every-day life. After making an urgent appeal in behalf of some charity, I once
heard him say, "Come now, you rich men, give liberally; and I'll answer for it that you shall have money
enough left to ruin all your children." Dr. Gardiner
was the best reader in the town, and it was rumored
that when among confidential friends he had been
known to interpret Shakespeare with great power. Of
this, however, I had no opportunity to judge, as public
sentiment would scarcely have permitted a minister
to entertain any general circle of hearers by rendering stage plays; but his reading of the liturgy, and
especially of the burial service, is never to be forgotten. In the latter office he introduced an effect
so dramatic and startling that it could only have
been inoffensive in the most judicious hands; but, as
Dr. Gardiner used it, it added to the solemnity of that
wonderful fifteenth chapter of Corinthians, which
has so often strengthened the afflicted children of
men. The apostle, after testifying how the faith of
the resurrection had sustained him in his trials, gives

in one terse sentence a philosophy of life which might seem plausible to those who rejected the gospel he taught: "Let us eat and drink, for to-morrow we die." Dr. Gardiner's whole manner changed when he reached this passage, and he gave the words with the full force of dramatic personation. I have heard them ring through the church almost as *Falstaff* might have uttered them in the tavern at Eastcheap. It was as if the Doctor determined that Satan should not complain that his sentiments had been marred in the delivery. And then this bold treatment gave the reader the right to assume also the personality of the inspired teacher in the solemn sentences which followed: "Awake to righteousness and sin not; for some have not the knowledge of God. *I speak this to your shame.*" I would that I could clothe these words with the sublimity with which the voice of the rector of Trinity still invests them to my ears. Singularly enough, Dr. Gardiner is remembered for one of the least of his many contributions to our literature. This was an adaptation of Milton's "Hymn on the Morning of Christ's Nativity" to the exigencies of public worship. The necessary alterations are made with good judgment, and I do not see why it should not always remain, what it is to-day, a beautiful and an appropriate opening for a Christmas service. I have heard people quote the added lines, and innocently attribute them to the Puritan poet, instead of to the amending Churchman. It is something to have mingled one's words with those of John Milton for the use of English-speaking Christians.

SOME PILLARS OF THE STATE.

NOT many years ago I was standing in the vestibule of the Mechanics' Charitable Society of Boston, gazing upon a full-length portrait which was there displayed. An intelligent citizen, near middle life, stopped beside me and asked if I could tell him the name of the subject of the picture. I started at the inquiry, but, supposing that the eyesight of the visitor might be defective, replied, "Why, Harrison Gray Otis, of course." "Ah! and who is Harrison Gray Otis?" was the rejoinder. Well, I really felt as strangely as if asked a similar question about George Washington or John Adams; for in the good old town of Boston, where I had grown up, inquiries concerning these latter personalities would have seemed no whit less preposterous. Mr. Otis was once the figure-head of our community. Graceful, handsome, eloquent, wearing worthily the mantle of his uncle, James Otis, the great orator of the Revolution, he easily took the first place in Boston, when there was a decidedly first place to take. Mr. Otis had represented Massachusetts in the United States Senate, and ardently desired to be governor of his State; but, with all his appreciation of the felicities of office, there was one thing he loved still better, and that was the Federal Party. It was well understood that Otis could have had political promotion by joining the Democrats, as John Quincy Adams and others had done; but he had been a delegate to the Hartford Convention and stood stanchly by the conquered cause. The notice in my journal which especially recalls Mr. Otis is found in an account of a great cattle-show at Worcester, held on the 6th of October, 1829. "I wish it were in my power," so I then wrote, "to preserve for posterity some traces of the wit, brilliancy, eloquence, and urbanity of Harrison Gray Otis; for when he is gone there is no man who can make good his place in society." A festival of rare enjoyment we had. The show and the dinner were of the best. A bovine procession (I think there were some hundred and fifty yoke of noble oxen) passed along the streets; the speeches by Otis and Everett were in the happiest vein; and a grand ball concluded the day. No, it did not conclude it, after all; for near midnight some gentlemen from Providence, who had arrived by the newly opened Blackstone Canal, invited a few of us to adjourn to a room they had engaged and taste some of "Roger Williams Spring," which they had brought all the way from the settlement he founded. Now this same spring, as it turned out, ran some remarkably choice Madeira, and this beverage, served with an excellent supper, furnished the material basis for brilliant displays of wit, flashing out upon the background of hearty and genial humor. Mr. Otis fairly surpassed himself.

He was simply wonderful in repartee, and his old-fashioned stories were full of rollicking fun. I well remember the account he gave of the first appearance of champagne in Boston. It was produced at a party given by the French consul, and was mistaken by his guests for some especially mild cider of foreign growth. The scene was beneath the dignity of history, to be sure; but, taken as a sort of side-show, it was very enjoyable. Deacons, as well as civil functionaries, figured among the actors; but I decline to tax my memory further. If it is not necessary to refrain when Heaven sends a cheerful hour, as John Milton's sonnet teaches us, it is surely well to refrain from reporting it. Mere words without the manner and the charm of the speaker are like the libretto of an opera without the music. Take this for a specimen. I remember saying to Mr. Otis, apropos to something which I forget, "I think, sir, your wish must have been father to the thought." He turned suddenly upon me, and exclaimed, "Why don't you give the full quotation, —

'Thy wish was father, *Harry*, to that thought.'"

"Well, sir," I said, "I did not think it would be polite to address you as Harry."

"Pooh! pooh! Never, while you live, mutilate a good quotation upon such a punctilio as that."

The fun is faint enough as here written; but as "Harry Otis" — for so his contemporaries called him — flashed it in the face of a young fellow brought up to regard him as one of the pillars of the State, it glowed with the perfection of social humor.

I may illustrate the intensity of Mr. Otis's Federalism by mentioning that he could never forgive Judge Story for his early attachment to the Democratic party. On the death of Chief Justice Marshall, the lawyers celebrated his services by a eulogy, which was succeeded by a bar dinner at East Boston. The friends of Joseph Story were very anxious that he should be appointed to the vacant place, and one of them, being called upon for a toast, recited the passage where Pharaoh says to Joseph: "There is none so discreet and wise as thou art. Thou shalt be ruler over my house, and according unto thy word shall my people be ruled." The hope was then expressed that the American executive might find occasion to use similar language. The toast-giver (and he who now tells the story was the guilty person) felt satisfied with the aptness of his quotation and the compliment it implied. "Joseph, indeed!" muttered Mr. Otis, when the sentiment was repeated to him. "Why, yes, an excellent comparison. *Pray, was anything said about his coat of many colors?*"

Turning backward the leaves of my journal, I come, in 1827, upon entries made the 22d of November and the day following. Mr. Otis was arguing in the Supreme Court, and I have noted my admiration of the graceful *finesse* with which he held our attention to a case of the very dryest description. The matter related to the ownership of certain lands adjoining the Mill Pond, which then occupied a large cove on the northern side of the peninsula. The property had formerly been owned by a Mr. Gee, a skip-builder, who held large estates at the North End. I remember a joke introducing the words περὶ τὴν γῆν which Mr. Otis made upon the name of this land-loving citizen; but the pronunciation of Greek at present in vogue at Harvard College has destroyed the pun. Some question arising as to the ownership of the sluiceway which emptied the pond, Mr. Otis took occasion to introduce an account of the feats of swimming he had performed there when a boy, and then, in the most humorous manner, asserted his own title to the property on the ground of occupancy. "At least," he added, "I think the Court will acknowledge that my own title to this watercourse is quite as valid as that which I am here to contest."

Mr. Otis lived for many years after his active life closed. He moved with difficulty, being sorely afflicted with the gout and other infirmities. The leader of his time was no longer recognized, but the courtly and genial gentleman survived to the end. I remember that he owned the first low-hung carriage which was seen in Boston, the old aristocratic coaches having formidable flights of steps, which must be let down before the passenger could climb up into them. One day the old gentleman appeared upon 'Change driven in his new vehicle. "What will you take for your carriage, Mr. Otis?" asked a friend, by way of expressing his admiration for this unusual turnout. "*The worst pair of legs in State Street!*" was the characteristic reply.

The last time I dined with Mr. Otis I sat with him for some time at his window, which looked upon the

Common. The trees had just put on their perfect foliage, and I remarked upon the beauty of an elm before the house. "When I came to this place," said the old gentleman, "that fine tree was a sapling. I have seen it grow, and it has seen me decline. It will be beautiful and stretch its branches over thousands long after I am forgotten." At the table that day his mind seemed to be running upon the past. He gave sketches of men once of note and consequence, whose names even had scarcely reached his younger guests. Those names were empty shells to us, — as empty of any rich and vigorous personality as will be the name of Harrison Gray Otis to the mass of readers who find it upon this page.

It is a great pity that the pew of the royal governors in the King's Chapel was removed, in order that two plebeian pews might be constructed upon its ample site. I used greatly to value this interesting relic, which was just opposite the pew that I occupied. It stood handsomely out, with ornamented pillars at the corners, and lifted its occupants two feet above that herd of miscellaneous sinners who confessed their miserable estate upon the level of undiscriminating democracy. I came too late into the world to see a royal governor enter this august pew, though the ghosts of some of them would occasionally seem to steal up the aisle and creep into it during the drowsier passages of the afternoon sermon; but the flesh-and-blood personage who occupied the pew in my day was, so to speak, as good a governor as the best of them. He was the son of a Massachu-

entertainment was far more prominent than the devices of the cook. There were no flowers and but small variety in meats and wines; but the conversation was always general and generally of the best. A tacit understanding assigned the prominent parts to those able to discharge them. My notes preserve some of the talk of these old Boston dinners; but I hesitate to quote them, because they are too meagre and scattered to do any justice to the subject. Both Sullivan and Otis were largely given to this pleasant form of hospitality, the former occasionally adding his gifts as a singer to his many graces as a host. I can hear even now the fine English songs he used to give us; but something better than these was the exquisitely courteous manner in which he would ask his wife's permission to exercise this talent. "Sally, may I sing?" was the simple formula, but the words seemed to carry all the tender chivalry of a natural gentleman.

I will conclude this paper with recollections of a statesman who vigorously impressed himself upon his contemporaries. This was Timothy Pickering, or *Colonel* Pickering, as he was always called, though I think he had held a higher military rank in the army. He had been Secretary of War and Secretary of State under Washington, and looked "a soldier fit to stand by Cæsar and give direction." Indeed, the title "Old Roman," which has been absurdly applied to General Jackson and divers later personages, fitted Pickering like a glove. More than six feet high, with a frame nobly set and a nose with the true Julian hook in it, he seemed to personify the martial spirit of the Revolution. He was worthy to have supported Washington at the battle of Brandywine. Colonel Pickering frequently visited my father, both in Boston and Quincy, and my journal gives an account of his dining with us in the latter place on the 13th of August, 1821. As a preliminary ceremony to the dinner, my father, who was an enthusiast in agriculture, insisted upon taking his guest to view his crops and barnyard. "So you've been over the farm, Colonel Pickering," said my mother, upon his return to the house. "Why, yes, madame," was the reply. "I have been all over the farm, *and a weary tramp I've had of it.*" Pickering was himself an agriculturalist of no small repute; but he found his own crops more interesting than those of other people, and was honest enough or blunt enough not to disguise his feelings with conventional civilities. I have sometimes thought that this speech explains all that needs explaining of his difficulties with John Adams. Both were plain-spoken men, and probably exposed their minds when a diplomatic reserve would have been politic, if not praiseworthy.

The Colonel was a masterly talker, and entertained us at dinner that day with an account of his best-beloved friend, Judge Peters, of Pennsylvania. To his substantial qualities he declared that Peters added a wealth of the lighter social graces that was unsurpassable. Jefferson had asserted that if all the good things Peters had said could be collected, they would make a mass of wit greater than had come from any other human being; and this his friend thought was no more than the truth. My journal preserves several specimens of the jests of this magistrate; but they lie flat beneath the pressure of threescore years, and lack the vivid acting and gestures of Colonel Pickering to re-excite the "peals of laughter" with which I mention that they were received. One will do for a specimen. Peters was known to be troubled with a vertigo, which seized him at unexpected moments and caused most unpleasant dizziness. At a certain dinner, where his voice rose clearly above the clash of crockery and buzz of conversation, a gentleman called out, "Well, Judge, I see you manage to keep your head above water!" Back flashed the reply, "Yes, sir; it has always been famous for swimming." But it is not in the power of ink and paper to preserve the flavor of old jokes. They should be allowed to die, and be newly created whenever posterity may require them. Of all the lost books of the ancient world that "Liber Jocularis" which recorded the puns of Cicero is least to be lamented.

Colonel Pickering's way of using "plain words stript of their shirts" gave his narrations a sharp impression of reality. The story of his abduction from Wyoming and of his sufferings in chains and captivity must be found somewhere in those four bulky volumes of his biography; but to hear him tell it was like sharing the experience in his company. Life has become too crowded to admit those exciting postprandial histories with which the survivors of the Revolution were wont to favor the younger generations. They abounded in illustrations and perhaps in snap judgments; but they furnished aliment for thought not to be got out of books. No rust of old age had touched Colonel Pickering. He was vigorous to the last, as his stormy controversy with President Adams remains to testify. "Exeunt fighting" is a common direction in Shakespeare's plays, and indeed, if the adversary be well chosen, there are many worse ways in which brave men might leave the stage of life. But it is pleasant to mention that these venerable heroes, to whom our country is so much indebted, put aside their differences when they met, unexpectedly, beneath my father's roof. "I hope to meet Colonel Pickering in heaven," said John Adams; "and the next best place to meet him is in this house." The scene has been so well described by my brother, Edmund Quincy, in his biography of my father, that I do not enlarge upon it here.

TWO NOTABLE WOMEN.

AT some hours of the day the visitor who enters the Boston Athenæum will find more women than men who are availing themselves of its privileges. Most of them, I suppose, would stare were they told that within the memory of a living person it required a certain sort of heroism for one of their sex to appear in the library. When the Athenæum was in Tremont Street, occupying the stuccoed building of two stories which stood on part of the land now occupied by the Probate Office, one solitary female ventured to claim the freedom of its alcoves and to endure the raising of the masculine eyebrows, provoked by the unaccustomed sight. And this "woman who dared" was the famous American authoress, Miss Hannah Adams. It was years before any sister authoress came to follow her example; but, nothing daunted, the little lady browsed among the books, content to look as singular and as much out of place as a woman of to-day would look who frequented a fashionable club designed for the exclusive accommodation of males. "My first idea of heaven," said Miss Adams, "was that of a place where my thirst for knowledge should be gratified."

And when, upon her arrival in Boston, William Smith Shaw introduced the lady to the library he had founded, it seemed as if the celestial gates could scarcely open upon greater privileges.

I was well acquainted with Miss Hannah Adams, who was as intimate in my father's family as a person so modest and retiring could be anywhere. She often stayed with us at Quincy, where she was held in awe by the servants, from her habit of talking to herself. This seemed to them a very weird and uncanny proceeding; but our guest had penetrated a world where they could not follow her, and her lips unconsciously uttered the thoughts that it suggested. There was a story illustrative of this habit of hers when confined to a sphere of wholly mundane considerations. A divinity student, who was going from Andover to Boston, thought himself in great luck in securing a seat in the stage next that to be occupied by Miss Adams. A *tête-à-tête* journey with the great authoress was a delightful prospect; and the young gentleman was determined to turn his opportunity to the best advantage and to get fresh instalments of the wisdom which had instructed him in her books. Alas! the fates were against him. It chanced that the lady was travelling with an unwonted amount of baggage, and the fear of forgetting any of its component parts continually haunted her mind. In vain the divinity student tempted conversation with well-framed questions. The answers were short and mechanical; but as soon as they were given were heard the words, "Great box, little box, bandbox!" This certainly not a sensational ending to a ghost story; but it is a conclusion so sensible that it deserves preservation.

When I call Miss Adams a famous authoress, I speak in the language of a time when she had absolutely no competitors. Her "Dictionary of Religions" went through four editions in this country, and was republished in England, — a high honor in the days when British scorn was poured on all American books. Upon her "History of New England" she lost money, and, what was still worse, the use of her eyes for a period of two years. Hoping to mend her fortunes from an abridgment of this latter book, she was greatly injured by the action of a person of some literary ability, who made a contemporaneous publication of a similar character. A controversy arose, and pamphlets overgrown into volumes were placed before the public. It is sufficient here to say that Miss Adams's friends were very indignant at the treatment she received. She herself, however, bore the injury in the sweetest spirit of Christian charity; and if the conversation strayed to this painful subject, she would turn it at once with a kind remark about the person who (as she and her friends conceived) had so grievously wronged her. An annual pension was settled upon Miss Adams, to which most of the leading men of Boston contributed, and it was my duty to collect the amount from the subscribers and pay it into her hands. An oil painting of this brave American lady, who had studied Latin and Greek and had written books, seemed to be among the rights of posterity. The artist Harding was, accordingly, employed to furnish a portrait, which was given to the Boston Athenæum; and there it should ever have remained, as a memorial of the first woman who valued the privileges of that fine library and laboriously used them for the public good. In the Art Museum, where it now hangs, the likeness of this modest lady is lost in a crowd of painted celebrities, and the significance of its original position is wholly gone. It is to be hoped that the literary women of Boston will use their influence to bring back this portrait of Miss Adams to the institution which should never have parted with it. There are enough busts of men in the beautiful book-hall of the Athenæum to run a nominating caucus, or, at any rate, the more important pre-caucus, which really does the business. I feel sure they would all agree that the women of old days are entitled to at least one representative in that hall; and that Hannah Adams, the pioneer of feminine culture in America, should there smile upon her sisters who have beaten a broad path where her solitary footsteps once trod.

There are persons among us, not very far past middle life, who remember Daniel Webster in his old age, and who will readily admit that in the third decade of the century, when he was in vigorous maturity, no nobler specimen of a man could have been found on this planet; but these same persons may say that the doctrine of chances wellnigh negatives the supposition that during that third decade Boston possessed a woman who as completely filled the ideal of the lovely and the feminine as did Webster the ideal of the intellectual and the masculine. Yet, notwithstanding such pardonable incredulity, there are a few old people still living who will justify me in saying that this was indeed the fact, and that centuries are likely to come and go before society will again gaze spell-bound upon a woman so richly endowed with beauty as was Miss Emily Marshall. I well know the peril which lies in superlatives,— they were made for the use of very young persons; but in speaking of this gracious lady even the cooling influences of more than half a century do not enable me to avoid them. She was simply perfect in face and figure, and perfectly charming in manners.

In the year 1821 the fashionable walk of the town was upon Dover Street Bridge, then known in popular parlance (out of compliment to the lovers who were to be met there) as the Bridge of Sighs. It stretched from South Boston to Washington Street, and traversed a fine sheet of water, much of which has long been made land. One afternoon in the year just mentioned I was taking my customary walk upon the bridge, and had reached a spot near where Harrison Avenue now crosses Dover Street, when I descried approaching a well-known gentleman, who was universally designated as Beau Watson. He was walking with a lady whose wonderful beauty riveted my attention. That was the first time I saw Miss Marshall, and the time, the place, the emotion of astonishment, are fixed indelibly in my memory. After this the lady's name has frequent appearance in my journals. On Friday, May 24, 1822 (it is well to be accurate about dates), I met her walking in the street with her friend, Miss Dana, and prose was not good enough to express my sense of her loveliness. And again, on the 7th of February, in the following year, in my description of Mrs. Blake's party, come the words: "Miss Marshall stood unrivalled. She is the most beautiful creature I ever saw." And then I relieve my feelings in a wretched epigram. The rhymes shall be mercifully suppressed. Their conceit is that the goddess of beauty, out of compliment to her lover, Mars, has herself appeared in a form which is *martial*. Can any of the aged and decayed punsters, for whom Dr. Holmes has generously endowed an asylum, show better claim to participate in his charity? But Miss Marshall has been celebrated, and in print, too, by a real poet, — at least, we thought Mr. Percival a poet in those simple days, — and his verses beginning

"Maid of the laughing lip and frolic eye!"

testify to the enthusiasm she enkindled in his breast. I could copy further notices of this lady from my journals, were it worth while to do so. Here she is at Mathews's last appearance before a Boston audience (January 28, 1823), "making the theatre beautiful by her presence." Again (it is the night of February 13th, the year following), a house in Franklin Street, just by the theatre, is lighted for company, and Miss Marshall receives her guests with such infinite grace of manner that one of them, at least, does not rest before he sets down his admiration in black and white. And this perfect personation of loveliness was beloved by women no less than she was admired by men. "What more shall I say of Miss Marshall?" I asked a lady who well remembers her. And this was the reply: "Say that no envious thought could have been possible in her presence; that her sunny ways were fascinating to all alike; that she was as kind and attentive to the stupid and tedious as if they were talented and of social prominence." I suppose that not many readers of the present day know much about the poet Mason, or have ever heard of his lines on the death of Lady Coventry, the famous Miss Gunning of Horace Walpole's letters; and so I will quote two of his stanzas, which, applied to Miss Marshall, give some of her characteristics with absolute accuracy and just as they live in my memory.

> "Whene'er with soft serenity she smiled,
> Or caught the Orient blush of quick surprise,
> How sweetly mutable, how brightly mild,
> The liquid lustre darted from her eyes.
>
> "Each look, each motion, waked a new-born grace
> That o'er her form its transient glory cast;
> Some lovelier wonder soon usurped the place,
> Chased by a charm still lovelier than the last."

The beauties of society have no longer the national fame which they once enjoyed. During the decade of 1820 who had not heard of the three great belles of the country, — Miss Cora Livingston, of New Orleans; Miss Julia Dickenson, of Troy; and Miss Emily

Marshall, of Boston? Two of these ladies had the large wealth and conspicuous position of their parents to aid them in attaining the sovereignty they exercised; but Miss Marshall took the supreme place without these aids. With her no struggle for social recognition was necessary. She simply stood before us a reversion to that faultless type of structure which artists have imagined in the past, and to that ideal loveliness of feminine disposition which poets have placed in the mythical golden age.

SOME RAILROAD INCIDENTS.

I SHALL merely glance at a great subject. The story of the inside management of our earlier railroads is aside from the purpose of the present papers. Students of finance would be interested in the perplexities which were surmounted, the expedients that were tried, the bitter opposition that was worked down; but for the general reader it is sufficient to say that the Massachusetts railroads were built by patriotic men for the public benefit. Few believed in them as investments, and the State, when her franchise was asked, burdened it with a condition most creditable to the foresight of her legislators. I quote the protective clause, which permits the people to foreclose on any one of the old railroads whenever they choose to do so: —

"The Commonwealth may at any time during the continuance of a charter of any railroad corporation, after the expiration of twenty years from the opening of said railroad for use, purchase of the corporation the said railroad and all the franchise, property, rights, and privileges of the corporation, by paying them therefor such a sum as will reimburse them the amount of capital paid in, with a net profit thereon of ten per cent per annum from the time of the payment thereof by the stockholders to the time of such purchase."

There is statesmanship looking out for to-morrow, as well as for to-day! Let us remember this when we are disposed to rail at the lack of intelligence in our democratic legislation. Proceeding upon the same line, Massachusetts, before giving her last instalment of assistance to the road connecting her capital with Albany and the West, reserved the right to purchase the same by paying the par value of the shares, with seven per cent thereon. It would take many millions of dollars to measure the value of these morsels of legislation to the Bay State. It might be worth dollars to be reckoned by the hundred million had all our States similar writings upon their statute books. It is not the actual use of such reserved rights, but their existence *in terrorem*, which protects the interests of society against the greed of some small minority of its members. In 1867 I petitioned the legislature of Massachusetts to exercise its power of purchase in the interest of the people, and to assume the ownership of the railroads connecting us with the West. The mighty corporations took the field like regular armies, well officered, well disciplined, and with a full commissariat. The people, so far as they could be heard from, were full of spirit; but they were an unorganized militia, without available funds to provide leaders and fee lawyers. The corporations managed to prevent a purchase, which would have doubled the business of Boston, and, by its influence upon other roads, would have gone far to settle the question of cheap transportation. But the popular feeling was so strong that the legislature was compelled to give much that was wanted, though not all that was asked. The railroads were compelled to do something to earn the ten per cent which they exacted from the public; some of it, too, representing no legitimate outlay in stock. On the 19th of April, 1880, my journal records a chance meeting with the late Judge Colt, one of the able counsel who were retained for the railroads. He spoke of the revival of commercial interests and of the increase of general prosperity which had resulted from the compulsory union of the Western and Worcester roads, together with the fiat of the legislature, which obliged the tracks to be carried to deep water. "You would never have brought this about," he said, "had it not been for that power of purchase which the State had reserved. That was the fulcrum upon which the lever rested by which inert masses were moved aside for the benefit of the public." It was even so.

There was one question which could not be avoided after the establishment of railroads: "What are the rights of negroes in respect to this new mode of locomotion?" And the general voice of the community replied in the usual chorus, "Neither here nor elsewhere have they any rights which a white man is bound to respect." The prejudice against persons of color can be but faintly realized at the present time. No public conveyance would carry them; no hotel would receive them, except as servants to a white master. The day in May when our State government was organized was universally called "Nigger 'Lection," because on that day negroes were accorded the privilege of appearing on the Common; whereas, if one of this class of citizens presumed to enter the Common on Artillery Election (which took place about a month later), he was liable to be pursued and stoned by a crowd of roughs and boys. After the Providence Railroad opened the shortest route to New York, it was found that an appreciable number of the despised race demanded transportation. Scenes of riot and violence took place, and in the then existing state of opinion, it seemed to me that the difficulty could best be met by assigning a special car to our colored citizens. Some of our cars were then arranged like the old stage-coaches, — there being three compartments upon a truck. These coaches communicated only by a small window at the top, and one of the compartments I assigned for the exclusive use of colored persons. One morning at Providence I entered the middle carriage, and was presently attracted by voices in the next division, — that allotted to travellers of the black race. I arose and looked through the little window just mentioned, and saw that a Southern gentleman (if by a stretch of courtesy he may be so called) had entered the compartment, which was occupied by a well-dressed negro, who wore spectacles. The Southerner was evidently much excited at finding a negro taking his ease in a first-class carriage. There had been some words between them, which I did not perfectly hear.

rise have always been interesting to explorers. They find some petty rivulet, which oozes out of the mud, and marvel that its feeble current should swell till it bears the commerce of a nation. The beginnings of great departments of human enterprise have something of the same interest, and I have just found an old letter, addressed to me on the 27th of October, 1838, which led to results quite overpowering in their magnitude. The writer is William F. Harnden. He tells me that he has applied for a post of conductor upon the Western Railroad, and solicits my influence, as treasurer of the road, "should you think me worthy of the office." Harnden had been selling tickets at the Worcester Railroad depot, but found this occupation much too sedentary for his active nature. He was a man who wanted to be moving. For some reason, which I do not recall, Harnden did not get the conductorship; but his application brought me in contact with this lithe, intelligent young fellow, who wished to be on the go, and I suggested to him a new sort of business, which in the hands of a bright man I thought might be pushed to success. As director and president of the Providence Railroad, I was compelled to make weekly journeys to New York, where the bulk of our stock was held. The days of my departure were well known, and I was always met at the depot by a bevy of merchants' clerks, who wished to intrust packages of business papers, samples of goods, and other light matters to my care. The mail establishment was at that time insufficient to meet the wants of the public.

The postage was seventeen cents upon every separate bit of paper, and this was a burdensome tax upon the daily checks, drafts, and receipts incident to mercantile transactions. I was ready to be of service to my friends, though some of them thought my good nature was imposed upon when they found that I was obliged to carry a large travelling-bag to receive their contributions. I kept this bag constantly in sight on my journey, and, upon arriving in New York, delivered it to a man whom the merchants employed to meet me and distribute its contents. Now, it occurred to me that here was an opportunity for somebody to do, for an adequate compensation, just what I was doing for nothing. I pointed out to Mr. Harnden that the collection and delivery of parcels, as well as their transportation, might be undertaken by one responsible person, for whose services the merchants would be glad to pay. The suggestion fell upon fruitful soil. Harnden asked me for special facilities upon the Boston and Providence road, which I gladly gave him, and with the opening year he commenced regular trips (twice a week, I think he made them), bearing in his hand a small valise; and that valise contained in germ the immense express business, — contained it as the acorn contains the forest of oaks that may come from it; but many generations are required to see the magnificence of the forests, while the growths of human enterprise expand to their wonderful maturity in one short life. Harnden's fate was that too common with pioneers and inventors. He built up a great business by steady industry, saw all its splendid possibilities, tried to realize them before the time was ripe, and died a poor man, at the age of thirty-three. In attempting to extend the express business to Europe, he assumed risks that were ruinous, and the stalwart Vermonter, Alvin Adams, took his place as chief in the great industry which had arisen under his hands.

"When you speak of the opposition that our early railroads encountered," said a young man to me the other day, "you refer, of course, to the difficulty of inducing people to take stock in them. Nobody could have objected to the increase of facilities for transportation, provided he was not asked to pay the bills." But it happened that I did mean just what I said; and perhaps the most singular phenomenon in the history of early railroads was the bitter opposition they encountered from leading men, whose convenience and pecuniary interests they were directly to promote. The believer in railroads was not only obliged to do the work and pay the bills for the advantage of his short-sighted neighbor, but, as Shakespeare happily phrases it, "cringe and sue for

[1] It may be worth while to mention that after the publication of this paper the author received a newspaper cutting which challenged his title to the first suggestion of Harnden's Express. His remark was that, as the business was clearly called for, a similar suggestion might have come from twenty others, and that the question of priority would be as difficult to settle as it was unimportant. He found nothing to alter in his printed statement. He believed himself to have been the first expressman after the manner narrated in the text, and was sure that he had advised Mr. Harnden to succeed him as the second.

leave to do him good." Can I furnish proof of this incredible statement? Yes, I have it before me at this moment, and it is worth giving with some detail.

The old town of Dorchester, which some years ago was annexed to Boston, has within its ancient limits nine railroad stations, and at those most frequented about fifty trains stop daily. The main road, known as the Old Colony, passes over a route which I caused to be surveyed at my own expense, with the view of providing cheap transportation for the towns of Dorchester and Quincy and others to the south of them. I need not say that the land made accessible by this railroad has become very valuable, and that the business and population of the old town of Dorchester cluster about the stations. If any tyrant could tear up those tracks and prevent them from being relaid, his action would paralyze a prosperous community, and might well be called a *calamity* by those most careful in weighing their words. Now, can the reader believe that the very word I have Italicized was chosen so late as 1842 by the inhabitants of the town of Dorchester, in regular town-meeting, assembled to express their sense of the injury that would result to them and their possessions by laying a railroad track through any portion of their territory? No, there can be no mistake about it. Here is the report of their meeting, authentic in contemporaneous type, and duly attested by Mr. Thomas J. Tolman, town clerk. A leading business man was chosen moderator, and a committee of six prominent citizens was appointed to oppose the passage of a railroad through the town. The resolutions are worth reporting with some fulness. The first declares it to be the opinion of the inhabitants of the town of Dorchester that a railroad upon either of the lines designated by those asking for a charter "will be of incalculable evil to the town generally, in addition to the immense sacrifice of private property which will also be involved. A great portion of the road will lead through thickly settled and populous parts of the town, crossing and running contiguous to public highways, and thereby making a permanent obstruction to a free intercourse of our citizens, and creating great and enduring danger and hazard to all travel upon the common roads." The second resolution declares that if, in spite of the protest of the inhabitants of Dorchester, their town must be blighted by a railroad, "it should be located upon the marshes and over creeks," and by thus avoiding all human habitations and business resorts "a less sacrifice will be made of private property and a much less injury inflicted upon the town and public generally." The concluding resolution is one of those jewels (rather more than five words long) that must suffer by any curtailment: —

"*Resolved*, That our representatives be instructed to use their utmost endeavors to prevent, if possible, *so great a calamity to our town as must be the location of any railroad through it;* and, if that cannot be prevented, *to diminish this calamity as far as possible* by confining the location to the route herein designated."

The Italics are, of course, mine. They are quite

irresistible. But when "calamities" threaten, the good man does not do his whole duty by protesting in town-meeting. There is the powerful agency of the press, throughout which oppressors may be rebuked and their horrible projects brought to naught. Let me quote a few extracts from a newspaper article. It was written by a citizen of Dorchester and appeared shortly after the meeting. The writer has been speaking of existing facilities for water transportation, which he thinks should content certain inhabitants of the town of Quincy who are petitioning for a railroad.

"What better or more durable communication can be had than the Neponset River or the wide Atlantic? By using these, no thriving village will be destroyed, no enterprising mechanics ruined, no beautiful gardens and farms made desolate, and no public or private interests most seriously affected. Look at the rapid growth of Neponset village, through which this contemplated road is to run (the citizens of which are as enterprising and active as can be found, many of whom have invested their *all* either in trade, mechanics, manufactures, or real estate), and all — all are to be sacrificed under a car ten thousand times worse for the public than the car of Juggernaut! Look at the interests, for instance, of the public house in this place, kept by a most estimable citizen, who has ever—"

But I have no heart to copy further. In the wreck of an entire community we can spare no tears for the woes of a single tavern-keeper. The ruins of that once prosperous village of Neponset are, even to this day, visited by reflective tourists. I think I mentioned that the Old Colony Company has a way of stopping some fifty trains there, in order to accommodate moralists, who take a melancholy satisfaction in musing among them.

Yes, of all the difficulties that were met in establishing locomotion by steam, the obstruction offered by blind, stolid, unreasoning conservatism was not the least. It required not only men of foresight, but those of strong enthusiasm, like my old friend, Mr. P. P. F. Degrand, to tunnel through these craggy prejudices. There is a certain vital energy which thrills in French nerves in greater plenitude than in those of other nationalities, and this Boston broker had enough of it to run a Napoleon. I used to enrich an old lecture, entitled "Our Obligations to France," with a sketch of Degrand, — a man not famous as the world goes, but one to whom the public is far more indebted than to many of the politicians who get their column in the biographical dictionaries.

To the older railroad men of Massachusetts her iron thoroughfares are consecrated ground, — consecrated by the labor, the anxieties, the sacrifices which they cost. They are monuments to the public spirit of the dead, not vulgar instruments for extorting a maximum of money for a minimum of service. There is probably no short and precise solution to the difficult problem which the private control of these arteries of the body politic presents to thoughtful men. The railroads have come to hold a power which should only be committed to the State, unless, indeed, some way can be devised of holding their managers to strict accountability. I have said elsewhere what I have had to say upon this subject, and will avoid the temptation of mingling prophecies and suggestions with the uncontroversial matter which belongs to reminiscences.

JACKSON IN MASSACHUSETTS.

I.

I WAS fairly startled, a few days ago, at the remark of a young friend who is something of a student of American history. "Of course," said he, "General Jackson was not what you would call a gentleman!" Now, although I had only a holiday acquaintance with the General, and although a man certainly puts on his best manners when undergoing a public reception, the fact was borne in upon me that the seventh President was, in essence, a knightly personage, — prejudiced, narrow, mistaken upon many points, it might be, but vigorously a gentleman in his high sense of honor and in the natural straightforward courtesies which are easily to be distinguished from the veneer of policy; and I was not prepared to be favorably impressed with a man who was simply intolerable to the Brahmin caste of my native State. Had not the Jackson organs teemed with abuse of my venerated friend, John Adams? Had not the legislature of New Hampshire actually changed the name of a town from Adams to Jackson; thereby performing a contemptible act of flattery, which, to the excited imaginations of the period, seemed sufficient to discredit republican government forever after? Had not this man driven from their places the most faithful officers of government, to satisfy a spirit of persecution relentless and bitter beyond precedent?

I did not forget these things when I received Governor Lincoln's order to act as special *aide-de-camp* to the President during his visit to Massachusetts; and I felt somewhat out of place when I found myself advancing from one side of Pawtucket Bridge (on the morning of June 20, 1833) to meet a slender, military-looking person, who had just left the Rhode Island side of that structure. Lawyers are credited with the capacity of being equally fluent upon all sides of a question; and if I had suddenly received orders to express to General Jackson my detestation of his presidential policy, I think I should have been equal to the occasion. My business, however, was to deliver an address of welcome, and here was Jackson himself, advancing in solitary state to hear it. Well in the rear of the chief walked the Vice-President and heir-apparent, Martin Van Buren; and slowly following came the Secretaries of War and the Navy, Cass and Woodbury. It is awkward to make a formal speech to one man, and I missed the crowd which the military upon both sides of the bridge were keeping upon *terra firma*. I seemed to be the mouthpiece of nobody but myself. The address somehow got itself delivered, the distinguished guest made his suitable reply, and then we walked together to the fine barouche and four which was to take us through the State. The President and Vice-President were waved to the back of the carriage, Colonel Washburn and myself occupied the front seat, the Cabinet were accommodated with chariots somewhat less triumphal behind us, the artillery fired (breaking many windows in Pawtucket, for which the State paid a goodly bill), and we were off.

Our first stop was for breakfast, at Attleborough, after which meal we visited the manufactories of jewelry for which the town is famous. "You have been interfering with our business, Mr. President," said the manager of one of these establishments, "and should feel bound in honor to take these buttons off our hands." So saying, he produced numerous cards of buttons stamped with the palmetto tree. These, he said, had been ordered by the Southern nullifiers as distinguishing badges; but they had been rendered quite worthless by the President's proclamation. Jackson made some reply, that I did not catch, and seemed greatly amused at the discovery that treason in South Carolina had its commercial value in Massachusetts. And here let me say that it was that famous proclamation at the close of 1832 which gave its author the hearty reception he received among us. Indeed, the reception might have been called enthusiastic by one who had not witnessed the great wave of popular emotion which bore Lafayette through Massachusetts, eight years before. Such an uprising as that is not likely to be seen again in the world's history; but Jackson had come to us at a period when his bitterest opponents, if not quite ready to forget their grievances in view of the sturdy stand he had taken in behalf of the Union, were prepared to remain in the background and make no protest to mar the popular cordiality.

As we rode through divers small towns, receiving salutes and cheers at their centres, the President talked constantly and expressed himself with great freedom about persons. His conversation was interesting from its sincerity, decision, and point. It was easy to see that he was not a man to accept a difference of opinion with equanimity; but that was clearly because, he being honest and earnest, Heaven would not suffer his opinions to be other than *right*. Mr. Van Buren, on the other hand, might have posed for a statue of Diplomacy. He had the softest way of uttering his cautious observations, and evidently considered the impression every word would make.

At Roxbury, which we reached about four o'clock in the afternoon, we found a triumphal arch, and Mr. Jonathan Dorr to speak for the assembled citizens. The orator was, mercifully, very brief; indeed, his speech consisted of little more than an original couplet, which, if not quite so melodious as some of Pope's, had doubtless the sincerity which the Twickenham poet often failed to put into his compositions.

"And may his powerful arm long remain nerved
Who said: *The Union, it must be preserved!*"

"Sir," exclaimed Jackson, in reply, "it shall be preserved as long as there is a nerve in this arm!" Both of which speeches are concentrated enough to keep. Those who want rhetoric can add it for themselves, as we do water to the Brunswick soups. I was determined that General Jackson should enter Boston in the saddle, as I knew he greatly preferred this mode of locomotion. Horses had been ordered to be in readiness at the Norfolk House, and the President rejoiced in spirit as he threw his leg over the fine animal which had been provided for him. My neighbor, Mr. Thomas J. Claflin (the veteran conductor of the Old Colony Railroad), tells me that, as a boy in the crowd, he saw Jackson mount his horse that day. He remembers how the General fell forward upon the neck of the animal, as an old and tired man might do; then recovering himself he shot upwards, as if impelled by a spring, to the stiff soldierly position: it was a sight not to be forgotten. But, alas! the dismounting was soon to follow; for at the city line we came upon the mayor, seated in a barouche, and this functionary would by no means consent to have the President enter his dominions otherwise than at his side. We timidly pleaded that the President had been driven through a long day, and found himself much refreshed by a change of position. It was of no use. Civic etiquette was paramount, and the poor man was made to descend from the elevation to which he had risen with such buoyancy. The staff, however, might do as they pleased. So Colonel Washburn and I rode on either side of the august party in the carriage, to our great contentment.

I have no idea of providing my readers with free passes to the banquets, collations, military manœuvres, and ceremonial visits which followed the President's arrival. There is, however, one little matter about which I was blamed most unjustly, which the muse of history may now be requested to put right. On the afternoon of the 21st there was a review of the Boston Brigade, then under the command of General Tyler and in admirable condition. I had engaged trained parade horses for the Cabinet and suite, as I supposed they would all follow the President to the field; but in the course of the morning Mr. Van Buren told me that he had consulted the other gentlemen, and that they had decided unanimously not to appear at the review. As there was a great demand for horses, I sent word to the livery stable that those I had engaged would not be required, and they were, of course, instantly taken by officers of the Brigade. After dinner, however, the Vice-President sent for me, and said that he and his friends had reversed their decision, and now wanted horses to go to the review. I frankly told him that I had given up the animals that had been engaged, and that the party must now take such leavings as might be had. Remembering that, from a militia standpoint, the trappings are about seven eighths of the horse, I at once ordered the finest military saddles, with the best quadrupeds under them that were procurable. They appeared in due time, and we mounted and proceeded to the field in good order; but the moment we reached the Common the tremendous discharge of artillery which saluted the President scattered the Cabinet in all directions. Van

Buren was a good horseman and kept his seat; but, having neither whip nor spur, found himself completely in the power of his terrified animal, who, commencing a series of retrograde movements of a most unmilitary character, finally brought up with his tail against the fence which then separated the Mall from the Common, and refused to budge another inch. In the mean time the President and his staff had galloped cheerfully round the troops and taken up their position on the rising ground near the foot of Joy Street, to receive the marching salute. "Why, where's the Vice-President?" suddenly exclaimed Jackson, turning to me for an explanation. "About as nearly on the fence as a gentleman of his positive political convictions is likely to get," said I, pointing him out. I felt well enough acquainted with Jackson by this time to venture upon a little pleasantry. "That's very true," said the old soldier, laughing heartily; "and you've matched him with a horse who is even more non-committal than his rider." Now, the Democrats were very sensitive about Mr. Van Buren, and among them started a report that I had provided their prince imperial with this preposterous horse in order to put him in a ridiculous position. I was much annoyed by this story, and, although it may be thought a little late to give it a formal contradiction through the press, I feel constrained to do so. It was the Vice-President's own fault, and no neglect on the part of the managing *aide-de-camp*, that placed him in a position to which his party so reasonably objected.

On Monday the President was confined to his room and, indeed, to his bed by indisposition. He asked me to read the newspapers to him, and took great delight in the narratives of Jack Downing (the Mark Twain of the period), who purported to accompany the presidential party and to chronicle its doings. "The Vice-President must have written that," said Jackson, after some specially happy hit. "Depend upon it, Jack Downing is only Van Buren in masquerade." If it were permitted to doubt the infallibility of the medical faculty, I should have questioned whether phlebotomy was the best prescription in the world for the thin elderly gentleman upon the bed; but when my valued family physician, Dr. Warren, twice guided the lancet, a layman's dissent would have been preposterous. I remember, upon another occasion, standing over the bedside of a friend prostrated by a not uncommon disorder and instinctively protesting when three of the most eminent physicians of Boston declared that there was no safety but in a thorough blood-letting. I mentioned the disorder in question to a distinguished doctor of the present day, and asked him whether bleeding would be resorted to in its treatment. "Never!" was the prompt reply. "Not under any circumstances?" "Under no circumstances whatever!" was the answer. Now, no sensible person would speak otherwise than respectfully of the faculties of theology, law, medicine, or science; and yet it does not require the teachings of history, but only the observation of a single lifetime, to suggest that the instincts of intelligent laymen, when opposed to the dicta of these august bodies, are — well, I will say, worth considering.

General Jackson's illness kept him closely confined for two days, and prevented his witnessing the entrance of the frigate "Constitution" to the new dry dock at the Charlestown Navy Yard. I attended Mr. Van Buren to this spectacle, and saw Commodore Isaac Hull, with a huge silver trumpet in his hand, giving commands from the same quarter-deck upon which he had stood during the memorable battle with the "Guerrière." I well remember the visit which this gallant commander paid to my father, at Quincy, only a day or two after this famous sea-fight. I was a boy then, and had among my possessions the hull of a toy vessel. This my mother asked me to show her guest, who would tell me if it was a good model. I produced it with some reluctance, saying that it was not much of a ship, for it had no masts. "*Well it has as many masts as the 'Guerrière'!*" was the reply which the bluff sailor stamped for life upon my memory.

The morning of Wednesday, the 25th, was chilly and overcast, not at all the sort of day for an invalid to encounter the fatigues of travel and reception. At ten o'clock, nevertheless, the President appeared, and took his seat in the barouche, and was greeted with the acclamations which will always be forthcoming when democratic sovereignty is seen embodied in flesh and blood. Very little flesh in this case, however, and only such trifle of blood as the doctors had thought not worth appropriating. But the spirit in

Jackson was resolute to conquer physical infirmity. His eye seemed brighter than ever, and all aglow with the mighty will which can compel the body to execute its behests. He was full of conversation, as we drove to Cambridge, to get that doctorate whose bestowal occasioned many qualms to the high-toned friends of Harvard. College degrees were then supposed to have a meaning which has long ago gone out of them; and to many excellent persons it seemed a degrading mummery to dub a man Doctor of Laws who was credited with caring for no laws whatever which conflicted with his personal will. John Quincy Adams, I remember, was especially disturbed at this academic recognition of Jackson, and actually asked my father, who was then president of the College, whether there was no way of avoiding it. "Why, no," was the reply. "As the people have twice decided that this man knows law enough to be their ruler, it is not for Harvard College to maintain that they are mistaken." But Mr. Adams was not satisfied, and the bitter generalization of his diary that "time-serving and sycophancy are the qualities of all learned and scientific institutions" was certainly not to be modified by his successor's visit to Cambridge. It did not require Jack Downing's fun to show the delicious absurdity of giving Jackson a literary degree; but the principle that wandering magistrates, whether of state or nation, might claim this distinction had been firmly established, and there were difficulties in limiting its application.

II.

There is a familiar expression by which newspaper reporters denote the strong current of feeling which sometimes runs through an assembly, and yet reaches no audible sound of applause or censure. It has been decided that the word [*sensation*], put in brackets as it is here printed, shall convey those tremors of apprehension or criticism which cannot be exhibited with definiteness. Nobody who knows anything about Harvard College can doubt that there will be *sensation* whenever the people decide that Governor B. F. Butler shall appear upon the stage of Sanders Theatre to receive the compliment of the highest degree which can there be offered; but I will venture to say that an emotion much stronger than this was felt by the throng which filled the College Chapel when Andrew Jackson, leaning upon the arm of my father, entered the building from which he was to depart a Doctor of Laws. Fifty years have taught sensible men to estimate college training at its true worth. It is now clear that it does not furnish the exclusive entrance to paths of the highest honor. The career of Abraham Lincoln has made impossible a certain academic priggishness which belonged to an earlier period of our national existence. Jackson's ignorance of books was perhaps exaggerated, and his more useful knowledge of things and human relations was not apparent to his political opponents, to whom the man was but a dangerous bundle of chimeras and prejudices; but I do not need the testimony of a diary now before me to confirm the statement that his appearance before that Cambridge audience instantly produced a toleration which quickly merged into something like admiration and respect. The name of Andrew Jackson was, indeed, one to frighten naughty children with; but the person who went by it wrought a mysterious charm upon old and young. Beacon Street had been undemonstrative as we passed down that Brahmin thoroughfare, on our way to Cambridge; but a few days later I heard an incident characteristic enough to be worth telling. Mr. Daniel P. Parker, a well-known Boston merchant, had come to his window to catch a glimpse of the guest of the State, regarding him very much as he might have done some dangerous monster which was being led captive past his house. But the sight of the dignified figure of Jackson challenged a respect which the good merchant felt he must pay by proxy, if not in person. "Do some one come here and salute the old man!" he suddenly exclaimed. And a little daughter of Mr. Parker was thrust forward to wave her handkerchief to the terrible personage whose doings had been so offensive to her elders.

The exercises in the Chapel were for the most part in Latin. My father addressed the President in that language, repeating a composition upon which he somewhat prided himself, for Dr. Beck, after making two verbal corrections in his manuscript, had declared it to be as good Latin as a man need write. Then we had some more Latin from young Mr. Francis

Bowen, of the senior class, a gentleman whose name has since been associated with so much fine and weighty English. There were also a few modest words, presumably in the vernacular, though scarcely audible, from the recipient of the doctorate.

But it has already been intimated that there were two Jacksons who were at that time making the tour of New England. One was the person whom I have endeavored to describe; the other may be called the Jackson of comic myth, whose adventures were minutely set forth by Mr. Jack Downing and his brother humorists. The Harvard degree, as bestowed upon this latter personage, offered a situation which the chroniclers of the grotesque could in no wise resist. A hint of Downing was seized upon and expanded as it flew from mouth to mouth, until, at last, it has actually been met skulking near the back door of history in a form something like this. General Jackson, upon being harangued in Latin, found himself in a position of immense perplexity. It was simply decent for him to reply in the learned language in which he was addressed; but, alas! the Shakespearian modicum of "small Latin" was all that Old Hickory possessed, and what he must do was clearly to rise to the situation and make the most of it. There were those college fellows, chuckling over his supposed humiliation; but they were to meet a man who was not to be caught in the classical trap they had set for him. Rising to his feet just at the proper moment, the new Doctor of Laws astonished the assembly with a Latin address, in which Dr. Beck himself was

unable to discover a single error. A brief quotation
from this eloquent production will be sufficient to
exhibit its character: "Caveat emptor: corpus delicti:
ex post facto: dies iræ: e pluribus unum: usque ad
nauseam: Ursa Major: sic semper tyrannis: quid
pro quo: requiescat in pace." Now this foolery was
immensely taking in the day of it; and mimics were
accustomed to throw social assemblies into paroxysms
of delight by imitating Jackson in the delivery of his
Latin speech. The story was, on the whole, so good,
as showing how the man of the people could triumph
over the crafts and subtleties of classical pundits,
that all Philistia wanted to believe it. And so it
came to pass that, as time went on, part of Philistia
did believe it, for I have heard it mentioned as an
actual occurrence by persons who may not shrink
from a competitive examination in history whenever
government offices are to be entered through that
portal. Human annals get muddied by the wits, as
well as by the sentimentalists. Some taking rhap-
sody, be it of humor or fancy, is flung in the direction of an innocent mortal, and the best historian
cannot wash him quite clean of it. Vainly, I fear,
does Mr. Samuel Roads, Jr., prove to the readers of
his book that the "horrd horrt" of Skipper Ireson
may have been quite as tender as Mr. Whittier's, and
that "the women of Marblehead" were presumably
in bed when that unlucky mariner took his dismal
ride through their town. Ah! Mr. Phillips, let us
not altogether despise the poor "fribbles" who keep
journals. They do manage to keep a few myths out

of history, after all. For in spite of the matchless oration we listened to the other day,[1] I venture to advise my younger readers to make some record of what they see and learn. It improves the observing powers, strengthens the memory, and impresses life's lessons upon the mind. "You can count on the fingers of your two hands all the robust minds that have kept journals," says my eminent friend. Well, perhaps you can; but I think it might require all the hands of Briareus to number the robust minds that have lamented that they took no written note of the scenes and persons among which they passed. Most pathetic in its regret was the language I have heard from Judge Story and other first-class men respecting this omission. It has rung in my ears when, tired and full of business, I was disposed to shirk the task. So let us possess our souls in patience even if our "sixpenny neighbor" is keeping a journal. "Respectable mediocrity" though he be, he may prove a check upon some future orator as charming as Mr. Phillips, — but, alas, far less scrupulous, — whose instinct for rhetorical effect might tempt him to turn some wholesome human biography into a panegyric or a satire. Surely any competent historian may discern whether a given diary reflects the unchangeable heavens, or only the fogs which shut in the writer of it. Whoever mistook Boswell's judgments for the judgments of anybody but Boswell; yet who would give up the scenes and characters which

[1] See the Phi Beta Kappa oration by Wendell Phillips, June 30, 1881.

that note-book of his so exquisitely photographs? It is Arthur Helps who says that poor "sixpenny" Pepys has given us "the truest book that ever was written;" — no slight praise this, as it seems to me. But let not the reader fear that any chronicles of mine shall be catalogued among the diaries and journals from which Mr. Phillips would deliver us. I have taken stringent measures to secure him and his posterity from so great a calamity.

To return to the real Jackson, who held what Dickens says Americans call a lĕ-vēe, after the exercises in the chapel. He stood at one end of the low parlor of the President's house, and bowed to the students as they passed him. "I am most happy to see you, gentlemen," he said; "I wish you all much happiness;" "Gentlemen, I heartily wish you success in life;" and so on, constantly varying the phrase, which was always full of feeling. The President had begun his reception by offering his hand to all who approached; but he found that this would soon drain the small strength which must carry him through the day. He afterward made an exception in favor of two pretty children, daughters of Dr. Palfrey. He took the hands of these little maidens, and then lifted them up and kissed them. It was a pleasant sight, — one not to be omitted when the events of the day were put upon paper. This rough soldier, exposed all his life to those temptations which have conquered public men whom we still call good, could kiss little children with lips as pure as their own.

waiting our appearance, to trail its colors and trappings about the streets of the town. We did not think of telegraphing the President's condition from Charlestown, or even of sending a messenger by the railroad to tell the Salem people to postpone their celebration. Do not judge us harshly, you young people, who have been born into a world which is run by steam, electricity, and newspaper extras. If Hamlet is to be left out of the play, the little omission is well advertised beforehand, and those who take no interest in the rest of the characters have the option of staying at home. But we were living before the days when everybody knows everything which is going on in the world, and for us there was nothing to be done but to go through a grand Jackson reception, without any Jackson. After some delay the Presidential barouche, Mr. Van Buren and myself now occupying the back seat thereof, was got into its place in the order of march. It was now verging toward dark, and a clamorous welcome was accorded to that barouche, as it followed the band about the streets. Indeed, the immense interest we excited soon forced upon me the very unpleasant conviction that the *aide-de-camp* of the Governor of Massachusetts was passing for the President of the United States. And naturally enough, too; for there was really no way of informing the crowd that Jackson was necessarily absent from his ovation, and it seemed clear to them that the person in the cocked hat, with gold lace trimmings, who was riding by the side of the Vice-President could be no other than their favorite general. The situation was awkward enough. I could only ride bolt upright, gazing stolidly at vacancy, and urge Mr. Van Buren to accept the applause as his personal dues and to bow graciously right and left; but this the modest gentleman was very loath to do, for it was obvious that the bursts of enthusiasm were never intended for *him*. We were both glad enough to get out of a preposterous scrape, which a few clicks of the modern telegraph would have enabled us to avoid.

No person who had seen the collapsed condition in which the President was deposited at the hotel would have imagined that he could resume his travels the next day; and it was, undoubtedly, by an exertion of the will of which only the exceptional man is capable that he was able to do so. But the art of mastering the physical nature was familiar to Jackson, who had gone through the fatigues of generalship in the field when supported only by a few grains of rice. An immaterial something flashed through his eye as he greeted us in the breakfast-room, and it was evident that the faltering body was again held in subjection. After a brief visit to the East India Museum, we set off for Andover. The weather was perfect. The President was brighter than I had yet seen him, and well disposed to talk. "And now, General," said Mr. Van Buren, when we were fairly on our way, " tell us all about the battle of New Orleans, whereof, like Desdemona, by parcels I have something heard, but not intentively." And the hero of that wonderful fight, occasionally stimulated by a few questions, gave us the story as he remembered it. It was, undoubtedly, the most interesting narrative I ever heard, and my journal preserves — not one word of it. Upon one point only my memory is distinct. Jackson certainly asserted that the watchword "Booty and Beauty" had been given by General Packenham, — asserted it as if it were a fact within his personal knowledge; yet we know he was mistaken, as his admirable biographer, Mr. Parton, has conclusively shown.

How inexplicable are the freaks of memory! It relaxes its hold upon things we would gladly recall, and then offers us some wretched trifle, as if it were a golden proverb into which the world's wisdom had been distilled. While I cannot give a sentence from Jackson's thrilling story of the battle, I can quote *verbatim* a scrap of after-dinner talk which occurred after we had partaken of the Andover collation and were driving toward Lowell. The day was growing sultry and the Vice-President began to nod. "*Jackson* (slapping his neighbor on the knee). Why, sir, are you going to sleep? *Van Buren.* Well, yes. On a warm day, after dinner, it is my habit to catch a nap. *Jackson.* That argues that you possess a more peaceful conscience than your political adversaries give you credit for. *Van Buren.* You are right, sir. It argues not only a quiet conscience, but an unambitious mind." How is it that I can repeat that poor bit of chaff, word for word, giving the reader (if a telephone only connected us) the very intonations of the interlocutors, while I can furnish no fragment of most interesting matter, which he would be as glad to hear as I should to recall? "Accept a miracle in place of wit," says the most perfect epigram in the English language. In place of Jackson's account of the battle of New Orleans I must ask the reader to accept a puzzle in mnemonics.

General Jackson, the unscrupulous, did have a few scruples after all. "Constitutional scruples" was the name he gave them, and they had something to do with a protective tariff. Now the manufacturing town of Lowell, or rather the wealthy men who conducted it, had one ineradicable prejudice, and held in abhorrence a certain detestable heresy known as Free Trade. The meeting of mighty opposites is not always so dangerous to baser natures as Hamlet considered it. On the contrary, the aforesaid opposites will sometimes try to capture one another by elegant blandishments, which are not without delight to the baser natures who are looking on. Lowell did her very best to captivate the President, and prepared such a show in his honor as nobody but the Queen of the Amazons ever saw before. Passing beneath triumphal arches of evergreen, the President was summoned to review an army of nice, intelligent American young women. Some said there were three thousand, some declared there were five thousand, of these fresh, good-looking girls. I was much too dazed to think of counting them. All or most of them were employed in the mills, and all wore snow-white dresses, with sashes of bright color. Happily, too, they were bareheaded; for the bonnet of the period was a hideous monstrosity, a proper companion for that masculine section-of-stove-pipe hat, which even to this day demonstrates the great doctrine of the survival of the unfittest. The fair army bore parasols, instead of muskets, and most of these were green parasols; but the costumers of the pageant came to the President lamenting that all the parasols were not green. They had done their best, they said. Boston had been ransacked in vain, and New York was in those days far too distant to be drawn upon. But when these same parasols were waved in graceful salute, as the bearers passed before their Chief Magistrate, Jackson's enthusiasm mounted high, and he was pleased to say that this distressing variation in color did not mar his satisfaction with the scene. And well might Old Hickory be delighted with the sight of those bright, self-respecting daughters of American yeomanry, who wrought so cheerfully with the machinery of the mills. Alas! it was a sight not soon to be repeated among men. Not until wise forms of co-operation shall solve the labor problem which now perplexes the world can any successor of Jackson be received by such operatives in a manufacturing town.

Lowell certainly treated our party very handsomely. One of the mills was set going for our benefit, and we were generously dined in the evening. Jackson was evidently much impressed with what he had seen, and, indeed, talked of little else till we reached the State line, about noon the next day. He took leave of me with hearty cordiality. "Come and see me at the White House; or, better still, at the Hermitage, if I live to return to it." I left him feeling that he had moderated his views, and would be a wiser President than he had been. The astounding measure known as the Removal of the Deposits soon dissipated these hopeful fancies. The transferrence of the national money to the "Pet Banks" produced temporary inflation, to be followed by years of utter business stagnation. Never again could President Jackson have been warmly welcomed to Massachusetts.

One more incident shall conclude this paper. At the New Hampshire line I met a young gentleman, who was acting as aid to the Governor of that State, and had come to escort the President through his dominions. There was time for quite a little talk between us, and he was curious to know all the particulars of our progress through the Bay State. I told him what I could remember, not forgetting that very awkward ride through Salem, when I was mistaken for the Head of the Nation. I did not add: "Now, if *you* happen to pass for the President of the United States, there will be no embarrassment whatever. It will anticipate history a little; that is all!" I did *not* say this, for who does say the right thing just at the right moment? I wonder what Mr. Franklin Pierce would have thought of the remark, had it occurred to me to make it!

JOSEPH SMITH AT NAUVOO.

I.

IT is by no means improbable that some future text-book, for the use of generations yet unborn, will contain a question something like this: What historical American of the nineteenth century has exerted the most powerful influence upon the destinies of his countrymen? And it is by no means impossible that the answer to that interrogatory may be thus written: *Joseph Smith, the Mormon prophet.* And the reply, absurd as it doubtless seems to most men now living, may be an obvious commonplace to their descendants. History deals in surprises and paradoxes quite as startling as this. The man who established a religion in this age of free debate, who was and is to-day accepted by hundreds of thousands as a direct emissary from the Most High, — such a rare human being is not to be disposed of by pelting his memory with unsavory epithets. Fanatic, impostor, charlatan, he may have been; but these hard names furnish no solution to the problem he presents to us. Fanatics and impostors are living and dying every day, and their memory is buried with them; but the wonderful influence which this founder of a religion exerted and still exerts throws him into relief before us, not as a rogue to be criminated, but as a phenomenon to be explained. The most vital questions Americans are asking each other to-day have to do with this man and what he has left us. Is there any remedy heroic enough to meet the case, yet in accordance with our national doctrines of liberty and toleration, which can be applied to the demoralizing doctrines now advanced by the sect which he created? The possibilities of the Mormon system are unfathomable. Polygamy may be followed by still darker "revelations." Here is a society resting upon foundations which may at any moment be made subversive of every duty which we claim from the citizen. Must it be reached by that last argument which quenched the evil fanaticisms of Mülhausen and Münster? A generation other than mine must deal with these questions. Burning questions they are, which must give a prominent place in the history of the country to that sturdy self-asserter whom I visited at Nauvoo. Joseph Smith, claiming to be an inspired teacher, faced adversity such as few men have been called to meet, enjoyed a brief season of prosperity such as few men have ever attained, and, finally, forty-three days after I saw him, went cheerfully to a martyr's death. When he surrendered his person to Governor Ford, in order to prevent the shedding of blood, the prophet had a presentiment of what was before him. "I am going like a lamb to the slaughter," he is reported to have said; "but I am as calm as a summer's morning. I have a conscience void of offence and shall die innocent." I have no theory to advance respecting this extraordinary man. I shall simply give the facts of my intercourse with him. At some future time they may be found to have some bearing upon the theories of others who are more competent to make them. Ten closely written pages of my journal describe my impressions of Nauvoo, and of its prophet, mayor, general, and judge; but details, necessarily omitted in the diary, went into letters addressed to friends at home, and I shall use both these sources to make my narrative as complete as possible. I happened to visit Joseph Smith in company with a distinguished gentleman, who, if rumor may be trusted, has been as conscientious a journal-writer as was his father. It is not impossible that my record may one day be supplemented by that of my fellow-traveller, the Hon. Charles Francis Adams.

It was on the 25th of April, 1844, that Mr. Adams and myself left Boston for the journey to the West which we had had for some time in contemplation. I omit all account of our adventures — and a very full account of them is before me — until the 14th of May, when we are ascending the clear, sparkling waters of the Upper Mississippi in the little steamboat "Amaranth." With one exception we find our fellow-passengers uninteresting. The exception is Dr. Goforth. A chivalric, yet simple personage is this same doctor, who has served under General Jackson at the battle of New Orleans and is now going to Nauvoo, to promote the election of the just nominated Henry Clay. It is to this gentleman we owe our sight of the City of the Saints, which, strangely enough, we had not intended to visit. Though far from being a Mormon himself, Dr. Goforth told us much that was good and interesting about this strange people. He urged us to see for ourselves the result of the singular political system which had been fastened upon Christianity, and to make the acquaintance of his friend, General Smith, the religious and civil autocrat of the community. "We agreed to stop at Nauvoo," says my journal, "provided some conveyance should be found at the landing which would take us up to General Smith's tavern, and prepared our baggage for this contingency. Owing to various delays, we did not reach the landing till nearly midnight, when our friend, who had jumped on shore the moment the boat stopped, returned with the intelligence that no carriage was to be had, and so we bade him adieu, to go on our way. But, as we still lingered upon the hurricane deck, he shouted that there was a house on the landing, where we could get a good bed. This changed our destiny, and just at the last moment we hurried on shore. Here we found that the 'good bed' our friend had promised us was in an old mill, which had been converted into an Irish shanty. However, we made the best of it, and, having dispossessed a cat and a small army of cockroaches of their quarters on the coverlet, we lay down in our dressing-gowns and were soon asleep."

We left our lowly bed in the gray light of the morning, to find the rain descending in torrents and the roads knee-deep in mud. Intelligence of our arrival had in some mysterious manner reached General Smith, and the prophet's own chariot, a comfortable carryall, drawn by two horses, soon made its appearance. It is probable that we owed the alacrity with which we were served to an odd blunder which had combined our names and personalities and set forth that no less a man than ex-President John Quincy Adams had arrived to visit Mr. Joseph Smith. Happily, however, Dr. Goforth, who had got upon the road before us, divided our persons and reduced them to their proper proportions, so that no trace of disappointment was visible in the group of rough-looking Mormons who awaited our descent at the door of the tavern. It was a three-story frame house, set back from the street and surrounded by a white fence, that we had reached after about two miles of the muddiest driving. Pre-eminent among the stragglers by the door stood a man of commanding appearance, clad in the costume of a journeyman carpenter when about his work. He was a hearty, athletic fellow, with blue eyes standing prominently out upon his light complexion, a long nose, and a retreating forehead. He wore striped pantaloons, a linen jacket, which had not lately seen the washtub, and a beard of some three days' growth. This was the founder of the religion which had been preached in every quarter of the earth. As Dr. Goforth introduced us to the prophet, he mentioned the parentage of my companion. "God bless *you*, to begin with!" said Joseph Smith, raising his hands in the air and letting them descend upon the shoulders of Mr. Adams. The benediction, though evidently sincere, had an odd savor of what may be called official familiarity, such as a crowned head might adopt on receiving the heir presumptive of a friendly court. The greeting to me was cordial — with that sort of cordiality with which the president of a college might welcome a deserving janitor — and a blessing formed no part of it. "And now come, both of you, into the house!" said our host, as, suiting the action to the word, he ushered us across the threshold of his tavern.

A fine-looking man is what the passer-by would instinctively have murmured upon meeting the remarkable individual who had fashioned the mould which was to shape the feelings of so many thousands of his fellow-mortals. But Smith was more than this, and one could not resist the impression that capacity and resource were natural to his stalwart person. I have already mentioned the resemblance he bore to Elisha R. Potter, of Rhode Island, whom I met in Washington in 1826. The likeness was not such as would be recognized in a picture, but rather one that would be felt in a grave emergency. Of all men I have met, these two seemed best endowed with that kingly faculty which directs, as by intrinsic right, the feeble or confused souls who are looking for guidance. This it is just to say with emphasis; for the reader will find so much that is puerile and even shocking in my report of the prophet's conversation that he might never suspect the impression of rugged power that was given by the man.

On the right hand, as we entered the house, was a small and very comfortless-looking bar-room; all the more comfortless, perchance, from its being a dry bar-room, as no spirituous liquors were permitted at Nauvoo. In apparent search for more private quarters, the prophet opened the door of a room on the left. He instantly shut it again, but not before I perceived that the obstacle to our entrance was its prior occupancy by a woman, in bed. He then ran up-stairs, calling upon us to follow him, and, throwing open a door in the second story, disclosed three Mormons in three beds. This was not satisfactory; neither was the next chamber, which was found, on inspection, to contain two sleeping disciples. The third attempt was somewhat more fortunate, for we had found a room which held but a single bed and a single sleeper. Into this apartment we were invited to enter. Our host immediately proceeded to the bed, and drew the clothes well over the head of its occupant. He then called a man to make a fire, and begged us to sit down. Smith then began to talk about himself and his people, as, of course, we encouraged him to do. He addressed his words to Mr. Adams oftener than to me, evidently thinking that this gentleman had or was likely to have political influence, which it was desirable to conciliate. Whether by subtle tact or happy accident, he introduced us to Mormonism as a secular institution before stating its monstrous claims as a religious system. Polygamy, it must be remembered, formed no part of the alleged revelations upon which the social life at Nauvoo was based; indeed, the recorded precepts of its prophet were utterly opposed to such a practice, and it is, at least, doubtful whether this barbarism was in any way sanctioned by Smith. Let a man who has so much to answer for be allowed the full benefit of the doubt; and Mormonism, minus the spiritual wife system, had, as it has to-day, much that was interesting in its secular aspects. Its founder told us what he had accomplished and the terrible persecutions through which he had brought his people. He spoke with bitterness of outrages to which they had been subjected in Missouri, and implied that the wanton barbarities of his lawless enemies must one day be atoned for. He spoke of the industrial results of his autocracy in the holy city we were visiting, and of the extraordinary powers of its charter, obtained through his friend, Governor Ford. The past had shown him that a military organization was necessary. He was now at the head of three thousand men, equipped by the State of Illinois and belonging to its militia, and the Saints were prepared to fight as well as to work. "I decided," said Smith, "that the commander of my troops ought to be a lieutenant-general, and I was, of course, chosen to that position. I sent my certificate of election to Governor Ford, and received in return a commission of lieutenant-general of the Nauvoo Legion and of the militia of the State of Illinois. Now, on examining the Constitution of the United States, I find that an officer must be tried by a court-martial composed of his equals in rank; and as I am the only lieutenant-general in the country, I think they will find it pretty hard to try me."

At this point breakfast was announced, and a substantial meal was served in a long back kitchen. We sat down with about thirty persons, some of them being in their shirt-sleeves, as if just come from work. There was no going out, as the rain still fell in torrents; and so, when we had finished breakfast, the prophet (who had exchanged his working dress for a broadcloth suit while we lingered at the table) proposed to return to the chamber we had quitted, where he would give us his views of theology. The bed had been made during our absence and the fire plentifully replenished. Our party was now increased by the presence of the patriarch, Hiram Smith; Dr. Richards, of Philadelphia, who seemed to be a very modest and respectable Mormon; Dr. Goforth; and a Methodist minister, whose name I have not preserved. No sooner were we seated than there entered some half-dozen leaders of the sect, among whom, I think, were Rigdon and Young; but of their presence I cannot be positive. These men constituted a sort of silent chorus during the expositions of their chief. They fixed a searching, yet furtive gaze upon Mr. Adams and myself, as if eager to discover how we were impressed by what we heard. Of the wild talk that we listened to I have preserved but a few fragments. Smith was well versed in the letter of the Scriptures, though he had little comprehension of their spirit. He began by denying the doctrine of the Trinity, and supported his views by the glib recitation of a number of texts. From this he passed to his own claims to special inspiration, quoting with great emphasis the eleventh and twelfth verses of the fourth chapter of Ephesians, which, in his eyes, adumbrated the whole Mormon hierarchy. The degrees and orders of ecclesiastical dignitaries he set forth with great precision, being careful to mention the interesting revelation which placed Joseph Smith supreme above them all. This information was plentifully besprinkled with cant phrases or homely proverbs. "There, I have proved that point as straight as a loon's leg." "The curses of my enemies run off from me like water from a duck's back." Such are the specimens which my journal happens to preserve, but the exposition was constantly garnished with forcible vulgarisms of a similar sort. The prophet referred to his miraculous gift of understanding all languages, and took down a Bible in various tongues, for the purpose of exhibiting his accomplishments in this particular. Our position as guests prevented our testing his powers by a rigid examination, and the rendering of a few familiar texts seemed to be accepted by his followers as a triumphant demonstration of his abilities. It may have been an accident, but I observed that the bulk of his translations were from the Hebrew, which, presumably, his visitors did not understand, rather than from the classical languages, in which they might more easily have caught him tripping.

"And now come with me," said the prophet, "and I will show you the curiosities." So saying, he led the way to a lower room, where sat a venerable and respectable-looking lady. "This is my mother, gentlemen. The curiosities we shall see belong to her. They were purchased with her own money, at a cost of six thousand dollars;" and then, with deep feeling, were added the words, "And that woman was turned out upon the prairie in the dead of night by a mob." There were some pine presses fixed against the wall of the room. These receptacles Smith opened, and disclosed four human bodies, shrunken and black with age. "These are mummies," said the exhibitor. "I want you to look at that little runt of a fellow over there. He was a great man in his day. Why, that was Pharaoh Necho, King of Egypt!" Some parchments inscribed with hieroglyphics were then offered us. They were preserved under glass and handled with great respect. "That is the handwriting of Abraham, the Father of the Faithful," said the prophet. "This is the autograph of Moses, and these lines were written by his brother Aaron. Here we have the earliest account of the Creation, from which Moses composed the First Book of Genesis." The parchment last referred to showed a rude drawing of a man and woman, and a serpent walking upon a pair of legs. I ventured to doubt the propriety of providing the reptile in question with this unusual means of locomotion.

"Why, that's as plain as a pikestaff," was the rejoinder. "Before the Fall snakes always went about on legs, just like chickens. They were deprived of them, in punishment for their agency in the ruin of man." We were further assured that the prophet was the only mortal who could translate these mysterious writings, and that his power was given by direct inspiration.

It is well known that Joseph Smith was accustomed to make his revelations point to those sturdy business habits which lead to prosperity in this present life. He had little enough of that unmixed spiritual power which flashed out from the spare, neurasthenic body of Andrew Jackson. The prophet's hold upon you seemed to come from the balance and harmony of temperament which reposes upon a large physical basis. No association with the sacred phrases of Scripture could keep the inspirations of this man from getting down upon the hard pan of practical affairs. "Verily I say unto you, let my servant, Sidney Gilbert, plant himself in this place and establish a store." So had run one of his revelations, in which no holier spirit than that of commerce is discernible. The exhibition of these august relics concluded with a similar descent into the hard modern world of fact. Monarchs, patriarchs, and parchments were very well in their way; but this was clearly the nineteenth century, when prophets must get a living and provide for their relations. "*Gentlemen,*" said this *bourgeois* Mohammed, as he closed the cabinets, "*those who see these curiosities generally pay my mother a quarter of a dollar.*"

II.

THE clouds had parted when we emerged from the chamber of curiosities, and there was time to see the Temple before dinner. General Smith ordered a capacious carriage, and we drove to that beautiful eminence, bounded on three sides by the Mississippi, which was covered by the holy city of Nauvoo. The curve in the river enclosed a position lovely enough to furnish a site for the Utopian communities of Plato or Sir Thomas More; and here was an orderly city, magnificently laid out, and teeming with activity and enterprise. And all the diligent workers, who had reared these handsome stores and comfortable dwellings, bowed in subjection to the man to whose unexampled absurdities we had listened that morning. Not quite unexampled either. For many years I held a trusteeship which required me to be a frequent visitor at the McLean Asylum for the Insane. I had talked with some of its unhappy inmates, victims of the sad but not uncommon delusion that each had received the appointment of vicegerent of the Deity upon earth. It is well known that such unfortunates, if asked to explain their confinement, have a ready reply: "I am sane. The rest of the world is mad, and the majority is against me." It was like a dream to find one's self moving through a prosperous community, where the repulsive claim of one of these pretenders was respectfully acknowledged. It was said that Prince Hamlet had no need to recover his wits when he was despatched to England, for the demented denizens of that island would never detect his infirmity. If the blasphemous assumptions of Smith seemed like the ravings of a lunatic, he had, at least, brought them to a market where "all the people were as mad as he." Near the entrance to the Temple we passed a workman who was laboring upon a huge sun, which he had chiselled from the solid rock. The countenance was of the negro type, and it was surrounded by the conventional rays.

"General Smith," said the man, looking up from his task, "is this like the face you saw in vision?"

"Very near it," answered the prophet, "except" (this was added with an air of careful connoisseurship that was quite overpowering) — "except that the nose is just a thought too broad."

The Mormon Temple was not fully completed. It was a wonderful structure, altogether indescribable by me. Being, presumably, like something Smith had seen in vision, it certainly cannot be compared to any ecclesiastical building which may be discerned by the natural eyesight. It was built of limestone, and was partially supported by huge monolithic pillars, each costing, said the prophet, three thousand dollars. Then in the basement was the baptistery, which centred in a mighty tank, surrounded by twelve wooden oxen of colossal size. These animals, we were assured, were temporary. They were to be replaced by stone oxen as fast as they could be made. The Temple, odd and striking as it was, produced no effect that was commensurate with its cost. Perhaps it would have required a genius to have designed anything worthy of that noble site. The city of Nauvoo, with its wide streets sloping gracefully to the farms enclosed on the prairie, seemed to be a better temple to Him who prospers the work of industrious hands than the grotesque structure on the hill, with all its queer carvings of moons and suns. This, however, was by no means the opinion of the man whose fiat had reared the building. In a tone half-way between jest and earnest, and which might have been taken for either at the option of the hearer, the prophet put this inquiry : " Is not here one greater than Solomon, who built a Temple with the treasures of his father David and with the assistance of Huram, King of Tyre ? Joseph Smith has built his Temple with no one to aid him in the work."

On returning to the tavern, dinner was served in the kitchen where we had breakfasted. The prophet carved at one end of the board, while some twenty persons, Mormons or travellers (the former mostly coatless), were scattered along its sides. At the close of a substantial meal a message was brought to the effect that the United States marshal had arrived and wished to speak to Mr. Adams. This officer, as it turned out, wanted my companion's advice about the capture of some criminal, for whom he had a warrant. The matter was one of some difficulty, for, the prophet being absolute in Nauvoo, no man could be arrested or held without his permission. I do not remember what was the outcome of this interview, which was so protracted that it caused Mr.

Adams to miss one of the most notable exhibitions of the day.

"General Smith," said Dr. Goforth, when we had adjourned to the green in front of the tavern, "I think Mr. Quincy would like to hear you preach." "Then I shall be happy to do so," was the obliging reply; and, mounting the broad step which led from the house, the prophet promptly addressed a sermon to the little group about him. Our numbers were constantly increased from the passers in the street, and a most attentive audience of more than a hundred persons soon hung upon every word of the speaker. The text was Mark xvi. 15, and the comments, though rambling and disconnected, were delivered with the fluency and fervor of a camp-meeting orator. The discourse was interrupted several times by the Methodist minister before referred to, who thought it incumbent upon him to question the soundness of certain theological positions maintained by the speaker. One specimen of the sparring which ensued I thought worth setting down. The prophet is asserting that baptism for the remission of sins is essential for salvation. *Minister.* Stop! What do you say to the case of the penitent thief? *Prophet.* What do you mean by that? *Minister.* You know our Saviour said to the thief, "This day shalt thou be with me in Paradise," which shows he could not have been baptized before his admission. *Prophet.* How do you know he was n't baptized before he became a thief? At this retort the sort of laugh that is provoked by an unexpected hit ran through the audience;

but this demonstration of sympathy was rebuked by a severe look from Smith, who went on to say: "But that is not the true answer. In the original Greek, as this gentleman [turning to me] will inform you, the word that has been translated paradise means simply a place of departed spirits. To that place the penitent thief was conveyed, and there, doubtless, he received the baptism necessary for his admission to the heavenly kingdom." The other objections of his antagonist were parried with a similar adroitness, and in about fifteen minutes the prophet concluded a sermon which it was evident that his disciples had heard with the heartiest satisfaction.

In the afternoon we drove to visit the farms upon the prairie which this enterprising people had enclosed and were cultivating with every appearance of success. On returning, we stopped in a beautiful grove, where there were seats and a platform for speaking. "When the weather permits," said Smith, "we hold our services in this place; but shall cease to do so when the Temple is finished." "I suppose none but Mormon preachers are allowed in Nauvoo," said the Methodist minister, who had accompanied our expedition. "On the contrary," replied the prophet, "I shall be very happy to have you address my people next Sunday, and I will insure you a most attentive congregation." "What! do you mean that I may say anything I please and that you will make no reply?" "You may certainly say anything you please; but I must reserve the right of adding a word or two, if I judge best. I promise to speak of you in the most respectful manner." As we rode back, there was more dispute between the minister and Smith. "Come," said the latter, suddenly slapping his antagonist on the knee, to emphasize the production of a triumphant text, "if you can't argue better than that, you shall say all you want to say to my people, and I will promise to hold my tongue, for there's not a Mormon among them who would need my assistance to answer you." Some back-thrust was evidently required to pay for this; and the minister, soon after, having occasion to allude to some erroneous doctrine which I forget, suddenly exclaimed, "Why, I told my congregation the other Sunday that they might as well believe Joe Smith as such theology as that." "Did you say Joe Smith in a sermon?" inquired the person to whom the title had been applied. "Of course I did. Why not?" The prophet's reply was given with a quiet superiority that was overwhelming: "Considering only the day and the place, it would have been more respectful to have said Lieutenant-General Joseph Smith." Clearly, the worthy minister was no match for the head of the Mormon church.

I have before me some relics of my visit to Nauvoo. Here is the Book of Mormon, bearing the autograph which its alleged discoverer and translator wrote, at my request; and here are some letters addressed to the same personage, which I came by strangely enough. I took them from a public basket of wastepaper, which was placed for the service of the inmates of the tavern. Three of these abandoned epistles I asked leave to keep as memorials of my visit, and no objection was made to my doing so. The most interesting of these letters is dated "Manchester, August 29, 1842," and comes from an English convert to Mormonism. The man writes four pages of gilt-edged paper to his "beloved brother in the Lord," and sends him by the favor of Elder Snider the following presents: "A hat, a black satin stock with front, and a brooch." He would fain join the prophet in Nauvoo; but the way is blocked by that not-unheard-of obstacle, a mother-in-law, and until this excellent lady "falls asleep" the disciple must deny his eyes the sight of the master's face. The account of himself given by this correspondent shows with what pathetic sincerity the divine commission of Smith was accepted by a class of men which would seem to be intellectually superior to so miserable a delusion. Suppressing the name of the writer, I shall give a portion of this letter, as it furnishes food for reflection, and shows that the secret of the Mormon prophet is not to be fathomed at a glance: —

"I take the liberty of writing a few lines, being assured that you are a man of God and a prophet of the Most High, not only from testimony given by the brethren, but the Spirit itself beareth witness. It is true that mine eyes have not seen and mine ears heard you; but the testimony I have received shows plainly that God does reveal by his Spirit things that the natural man has not seen by his natural eyes. You may perhaps wonder who the individual is that has written this letter. I will tell you, in a few words: My father died about twenty-four years since,

leaving my mother a widow with seven children. . . .
I remember her teachings well, which were these:
Fear God, be strictly honest, and speak the truth. I
remember, when about three or four years old, being
with her in a shop. I saw a pin on the floor. I
picked it up and gave it to her. She told me to
give it to the shopman, with a sharp reprimand, showing me that it was a sin to take even a pin. The
remembrance of this slight circumstance has followed
me from that time to the present. [An account of
the writer's conversion to Mormonism follows, after
which he goes on thus.] Previously to joining this
Church, I was a singer in the Church of England,
had eight pounds a year, and a good situation in the
week-time at a retail hat shop. My wife's brother
told me I was robbing my children of their bread in
giving up the eight pounds. I told him I was not
dependent on that for bread, and said unto him the
Lord could make up the difference. He laughed at
me; but, beloved brother, in about one month from
the time I left the Church of England my master
raised my wages four shillings a week (which was
about one shilling per week more than that just sacrificed), and this has continued on ever since, which
is now two years this month, for which I thank the
Lord, together with many other mercies."

I have quoted enough to show what really good
material Smith managed to draw into his net. Were
such fish to be caught with Spaulding's tedious romance and a puerile fable of undecipherable gold
plates and gigantic spectacles? Not these cheap and

wretched properties, but some mastering force of the man who handled them, inspired the devoted missionaries who worked such wonders. The remaining letters, both written a year previous to my visit, came from a certain Chicago attorney, who seems to have been the personal friend as well as the legal adviser of the prophet. With the legal advice come warnings of plots which enemies are preparing, and of the probability that a seizure of his person by secret ambush is contemplated. "They hate you," writes this friendly lawyer, "because they have done evil unto you. . . . My advice to you is not to sleep in your own house, but to have some place to sleep strongly guarded by your own friends, so that you can resist any sudden attempt that might be made to kidnap you in the night. When the Missourians come on this side and burn houses, depend upon it they will not hesitate to make the attempt to carry you away by force. Let me again caution you to be every moment upon your guard." The man to whom this letter was addressed had long been familiar with perils. For fourteen years he was surrounded by vindictive enemies, who lost no opportunity to harass him. He was in danger even when we saw him at the summit of his prosperity, and he was soon to seal his testimony — or, if you will, to expiate his imposture — by death at the hands of dastardly assassins. If these letters go little way toward interpreting the man, they suggest that any hasty interpretation of him is inadequate.

I should not say quite all that struck me about

Smith if I did not mention that he seemed to have a keen sense of the humorous aspects of his position. "It seems to me, General," I said, as he was driving us to the river, about sunset, "that you have too much power to be safely trusted to one man." "In your hands or that of any other person," was the reply, "so much power would, no doubt, be dangerous. I am the only man in the world whom it would be safe to trust with it. Remember, I am a prophet!" The last five words were spoken in a rich, comical aside, as if in hearty recognition of the ridiculous sound they might have in the ears of a Gentile. I asked him to test his powers by naming the successful candidate in the approaching presidential election. "Well, I will prophesy that John Tyler will not be the next President, for some things are possible and some things are probable; but Tyler's election is neither the one nor the other." We then went on to talk of politics. Smith recognized the curse and iniquity of slavery, though he opposed the methods of the Abolitionists. His plan was for the nation to pay for the slaves from the sale of the public lands. "Congress," he said, "should be compelled to take this course, by petitions from all parts of the country; but the petitioners must disclaim all alliance with those who would disturb the rights of property recognized by the Constitution and foment insurrection." It may be worth while to remark that Smith's plan was publicly advocated, eleven years later, by one who has mixed so much practical shrewdness with his lofty philosophy. In

1855, when men's minds had been moved to their depths on the question of slavery, Mr. Ralph Waldo Emerson declared that it should be met in accordance "with the interest of the South and with the settled conscience of the North. It is not really a great task, a great fight for this country to accomplish, to buy that property of the planter, as the British nation bought the West Indian slaves." He further says that the "United States will be brought to give every inch of their public lands for a purpose like this." We, who can look back upon the terrible cost of the fratricidal war which put an end to slavery, now say that such a solution of the difficulty would have been worthy a Christian statesman. But if the retired scholar was in advance of his time when he advocated this disposition of the public property in 1855, what shall I say of the political and religious leader who had committed himself, in print, as well as in conversation, to the same course in 1844? If the atmosphere of men's opinions was stirred by such a proposition when war-clouds were discernible in the sky, was it not a statesmanlike word eleven years earlier, when the heavens looked tranquil and beneficent?

General Smith proceeded to unfold still further his views upon politics. He denounced the Missouri Compromise as an unjustifiable concession for the benefit of slavery. It was Henry Clay's bid for the presidency. Dr. Goforth might have spared himself the trouble of coming to Nauvoo to electioneer for a duellist who would fire at John Randolph, but was not brave enough to protect the Saints in their rights as American citizens. Clay had told his people to go to the wilds of Oregon and set up a government of their own. Oh yes, the Saints might go into the wilderness and obtain justice of the Indians, which imbecile, time-serving politicians would not give them in the land of freedom and equality. The prophet then talked of the details of government. He thought that the number of members admitted to the Lower House of the National Legislature should be reduced. A crowd only darkened counsel and impeded business. A member to every half million of population would be ample. The powers of the President should be increased. He should have authority to put down rebellion in a state, without waiting for the request of any governor; for it might happen that the governor himself would be the leader of the rebels. It is needless to remark how later events showed the executive weakness that Smith pointed out, — a weakness which cost thousands of valuable lives and millions of treasure; but the man mingled Utopian fallacies with his shrewd suggestions. He talked as from a strong mind utterly unenlightened by the teachings of history. Finally, he told us what he would do, were he President of the United States, and went on to mention that he might one day so hold the balance between parties as to render his election to that office by no means unlikely.

Who can wonder that the chair of the National Executive had its place among the visions of this

Dorr, Jonathan, 355.
"Downing, Jack," 359.
Dummer, Mrs. A. C., 197.

E.

Eliot, W. H., 112.
Emerson, R. W., 16–18, 50, 398.
Emmett, Thomas Addis, 250, 251.
Everett, Edward, 23, 107–109, 164, 166, 167.
Everett, William, 95.

F.

Farrar, John, 28.
Finn, Henry J., 145.
Folger, William C., 185.
Ford, Governor, 383.

G.

Gaillard, John, 216, 217.
Gallatin, Albert, 260.
Garcia, 301.
Gardiner, J. S. J., 313–315.
Gilbert, Sidney, 387.
Gillespie, Miss Anna, 201.
Goforth, Dr., 379, 391.

H.

Hall, David P., 97.
Hamilton, Alexander, 81.
Hancock, John, 94.
Harnden, William F., 344, 345.
Hayne, Robert Young, 226.
Hedge, Miss Abby, 176.
Helen, Miss Mary, 68, 284.
Helps, Arthur, 367.
Henry, Patrick, 66.
Henry, Mrs., 145.
Henry, Miss, 145.
Hill, Aaron, 185, 186.
Hillhouse, James A., 141.

Hoffman, Mrs. David, 268.
Holley, Mrs. Hamilton, 201.
Huger, Francis K., 113–126, passim.
Hughes, Christopher, 299.
Hull, Isaac, 360.

I.

Incledon, 28.

J.

Jackson, Andrew, 352–375, passim.
Jay, John, 81.
Jefferson, Joseph, 204.
Jefferson, Thomas, 242.
Johnson, Miss, 297.
Johnston, Josiah Stoddard, 220.

K.

Kean, Edmund, 30.
Kent, Edward, 19.
King, Charles, 260.
Kirkland, John Thornton, 21.
Knapp, John, 192, 193.

L.

Lafayette, Gen. G. M., 55–57, 101–156, passim.
Lafayette, G. W., 111.
Lincoln, Levi, 127, 128, 174–187, passim.
Livingston, Miss Cora, 269–273.

M.

Macduffie, George, 283–285.
Maffitt, J. N., 305, 306.
Marshall, Miss Emily, 334–337.
Marshall, Judge, 242–244.

INDEX OF NAMES.

Mason, John Y., 155.
McCobb, Mr., 182.
Mitchell, Aaron, 182.
Mitchell, S. L., 140.
Moniac, 92.

N.

Norton, Rev. Mr., 304.

O.

Oliver, Robert, 293.
Otis, George, 42.
Otis, H. G., 47, 316-321.

P.

Palfrey, J. G., 110.
Parker, Daniel P., 363.
Percival, J. G., 335.
Person, William, 3-5.
Peter, Mrs., 275, 276.
Peters, Judge, 325, 326.
Phillips, Judge, 2.
Phillips, Wendell, 366.
Pickering, Timothy, 324-327.
Pierce, Franklin, 375.
Popkin, John S., 33, 34.
Potter, Elisha R., 276, 279, 381.
Powell, Mrs., 145.
Prescott, James, 46.
Purdy, Mr., 97, 98.
Putnam, Colonel, 142.

Q.

Quincy, Judge Edmund, 81.
Quincy, Josiah, [H. U. 1728], 82.
Quincy, Josiah [H.U. 1790], 245, 361, 363.

R.

Randolph, John, 98-100, 209-229.

Randolph, Tudor, 210.
Reed, James, 24.
Reed, William G., 4, 5.
Richards, Dr., 384.
Ryk, Admiral, 157-173, passim.

S.

Saxe-Weimar, Duke of, 157-173, passim.
Sergeant, John, 203.
Smith, B., 93.
Smith, Hiram, 384.
Smith, Joseph, 376-400.
Snider, Elder, 394.
Stetson, Caleb, 44.
Stockton, Robert F., 230-239.
Storer, Ebenezer, 64.
Storer, Mrs., 53, 64, 65.
Storrs, Henry R., 286, 287.
Story, Joseph, 188-206, 366.
Stuart, General, 293.
Stuart, Gilbert, 82-85.
Sullivan, William, 322, 323.

T.

Thaxter, Joseph, 132.
Thorndike, Colonel, 139.
Tichenor, Governor, 70.
Ticknor, George, 22, 116, 117.
Troup, Governor, 208.
Tyler, John, 397.

U.

Upham, Charles W, 16, 293.

V.

Van Buren, Martin, 353, 357, 358, 371.
Van Rensselaer, Catherine, Miss, 270.
Van Tromp, 107, 159.

W.

Wadsworth, Daniel, 134.
Wallenstein, 117.
Walsh, Robert, 300.
Ware, Henry, 107, 159.
Warren, Charles H., 176.
Warren, J. C., 359.
Washington, Bushrod, 244, 245.
Webster, Daniel, 46-48, 132, 136-139, 249, 250, 254-259, 265, 266, 267, 281, 282.

Wells, E. M. P., 5, 6.
Wheaton, Henry, 203.
White, Mrs. J. M., 268.
Whitney, George, 69.
Whitney, Peter, 61.
Williamson, Mrs., 145.
Wirt, Mrs. William, 268.
Wirt, Miss, 268.
Withington, William, 54.
Worth, William J., 69.